Automotive Heating, Ventilation, and Air Conditioning Systems

Shop Manual

Third Edition

Chek-Chart

Warren Farnell, Revision Author

James D. Halderman, Series Advisor

PEARSON
Prentice Hall

Upper Saddle River, New Jersey
Columbus, Ohio

Library of Congress Cataloging-in-Publication Data

Automotive heating, ventilation, and air conditioning systems / Chek-Chart.—3rd ed.
  p. cm.
Includes index.
Contents: [1] Classroom manual—[2] Shop manual.
ISBN 0-13-048286-2 (pbk.)—ISBN 0-13-064780-2 (spiral)
  1. Automobiles—Heating and ventilation. 2. Automobiles—Air conditioning.
3. Automobiles—Heating and ventilation—Maintenance and repair. 4. Automobiles—Air
conditioning—Maintenance and repair. I. Chek-Chart Publications (Firm)

TL271 .A87 2004
629.2'772'0288—dc21   2002193060

TEXT
629.2
FAR
2004

Editor in Chief: Stephen Helba
Executive Editor: Ed Francis
Editorial Assistant: Jennifer Day
Production Editor: Stephen C. Robb
Production Supervision: Marilee Aschenbrenner, Carlisle Publishers Services
Design Coordinator: Diane Y. Ernsberger
Cover Designer: Jeff Vanik
Cover photo: Transtock, Inc.
Production Manager: Brian Fox
Marketing Manager: Mark Marsden

This book was set in Times by Carlisle Communications, Ltd. It was printed and bound by Courier Kendallville, Inc. The cover was printed by Phoenix Color Corp.

Pearson Education Ltd.   Pearson Education Australia Pty. Limited
Pearson Education Singapore Pte. Ltd.   Pearson Education North Asia Ltd.
Pearson Education Canada, Ltd.   Pearson Educación de Mexico, S.A. de C.V.
Pearson Education—Japan   Pearson Education Malaysia Pte. Ltd.

10 9 8 7 6 5 4 3 2 1
ISBN 0-13-064780-2

Preface

Automotive Heating, Ventilation, and Air Conditioning Systems is part of the Chek-Chart automotive series. The entire series is job-oriented and is designed especially for students who intend to work in the automotive service profession. The package for each course consists of two volumes, a *Classroom Manual* and a *Shop Manual*.

This third edition of *Automotive Heating, Ventilation, and Air Conditioning Systems* has been completely revised to include in-depth coverage of the latest developments in automotive heating and refrigeration systems. Students will be able to use the knowledge gained from these books and from the instructor to diagnose and repair automotive heating and ventilation systems used on today's automobiles.

This package retains the traditional thoroughness and readability of the Chek-Chart series. Furthermore, both the *Classroom Manual* and the *Shop Manual,* as well as the *Instructor's Manual,* have been greatly enhanced.

CLASSROOM MANUAL

New features in the *Classroom Manual* include:

- A chapter devoted to retrofitting R-12 systems to R-134a
- More than 120 new illustrations
- Objectives in each chapter that alert the students to important themes and learning goals
- An Appendix—described by a reviewer as "the best that I have ever seen in a textbook"—that includes conversion tables, compressor lubricants for each manufacturer's compressors, manufacturer retrofit bulletin numbers, AC Websites, EPA-certified reclaimers, and identification numbers for SAE documents related to air conditioning

SHOP MANUAL

Each chapter of the completely revised *Shop Manual* correlates with the *Classroom Manual*. Like the *Classroom Manual,* the *Shop Manual* features an overhauled illustration program. It includes more than 250 new or revised figures and extensive photo sequences showing step-by-step repair procedures.

INSTRUCTOR'S MANUAL

The *Instructor's Manual* includes task sheets that cover the entire NATEF task list for Heating and Air Conditioning. Instructors may reproduce these task sheets for use by the students in the lab or during an internship. The *Instructor's Manual* also includes a test bank and answers to end-of-chapter questions in the *Classroom Manual*.

The *Instructor's Resource CD* that accompanies the *Instructor's Manual* includes Microsoft® PowerPoint® presentations and photographs that appear in the *Classroom Manual* and the *Shop Manual*. Each photograph included on the *Instructor's Resource CD* cross-references the figure number in either the *Classroom Manual* or the *Shop Manual*. These high-resolution photographs are suitable for projection or reproduction.

Because of the comprehensive material, hundreds of high-quality illustrations, and inclusion of the latest automotive technology, these books will keep their value over the years. In fact, *Automotive Heating, Ventilation, and Air Conditioning Systems* will form the core of the master technician's professional library.

How to Use This Book

WHY ARE THERE TWO MANUALS?

Unless you are familiar with the other books in this series, *Automotive Heating, Ventilation, and Air Conditioning Systems* will not be like any other textbook you've ever used before. It is actually two books, the *Classroom Manual* and the *Shop Manual*. They have different purposes, but they should be used together.

The *Classroom Manual* teaches you what you need to know about automotive HVAC systems: how they are designed, how they work, and what the different kinds are. The *Classroom Manual* will be valuable in class and at home, for study and for reference. You can use the text and illustrations for years to refresh your memory about the basics of automotive heating, ventilation, and air conditioning systems.

In the *Shop Manual*, you will learn test procedures, troubleshooting, and how to overhaul the systems and parts you read about in the *Classroom Manual*. The *Shop Manual* provides the practical hands-on information you need to work on automotive HVAC systems. Use the two manuals together to fully understand how HVAC systems work and how to fix them when they don't work.

WHAT'S IN THESE MANUALS?

These key features of the *Classroom Manual* make it easier for you to learn and to remember what you learn:

- Each chapter is divided into self-contained sections for easier understanding and review. The organization shows you clearly which parts make up which systems and how various parts or systems that perform the same task differ or are the same.
- Most parts and processes are fully illustrated with drawings or photographs. Important topics appear in several different ways, to make sure you can see other aspects of them.
- Important words in the *Classroom Manual* text are printed in **boldface type** and are defined in a glossary at the end of the manual. Use these words to build the vocabulary you need to understand the text.
- Review questions are included for each chapter. Use them to test your knowledge.
- Every chapter has a brief summary at the end to help you to review for exams.

The *Shop Manual* has detailed instructions on overhaul, test, and service procedures for modern components and current HVAC systems. These are easy to understand and often have step-by-step explanations to guide you through the procedures. The *Shop Manual* contains:

- Helpful information that tells you how to use and maintain shop tools and test equipment
- A thorough coverage of the metric system units needed to work on modern HVAC systems
- Safety precautions
- System diagrams to help you locate trouble spots while you learn to read diagrams
- Test procedures and troubleshooting hints that will help you work better and faster
- Tips the professionals use that are presented clearly and accurately

There is a sample test at the back of the *Classroom Manual*, similar to those given for Automotive Service Excellence (ASE) certification. Use it to help you study and prepare yourself when you are ready to be certified as an expert in one of several areas of automobile technology.

WHERE SHOULD I BEGIN?

If you already know something about HVAC systems and know how to repair them, you will find that this book is a helpful review. If you are just starting in the automotive industry, then the book will give you a solid foundation on which to develop professional-level skills.

Your instructor will design a course to take advantage of what you already know and what facilities and equipment are available to work with. You may be asked to read certain chapters of these manuals out of order. That's fine. The important thing is to really understand each subject before you move on to the next.

Study the vocabulary words in boldface type. Use the review questions to help you understand the material. When you read the *Classroom Manual,* be sure to refer to your *Shop Manual* to relate the descriptive text to the service procedures. And when you are working on actual vehicle systems and components, look back to the *Classroom Manual* to keep the basic information fresh in your mind. Working on such a complicated piece of equipment as a modern vehicle isn't always easy. Use the information in the *Classroom Manual,* the procedures in the *Shop Manual,* and the knowledge of your instructor to help you.

The *Shop Manual* is a good book for work, not just a good workbook. Keep it on hand while you're working on equipment. It lies flat on the workbench and under the car, and can stand quite a bit of rough handling.

When you perform test procedures and overhaul equipment, you will need a complete and accurate source of manufacturers' specifications, and the techniques for pulling computer trouble codes. Most auto shops have either the vehicle manufacturers' annual shop service manuals, which list these specifications, or an independent guide, such as the Chek-Chart *Car Care Guide.* This unique book, with 10-year coverage, is updated each year to give you service instructions, capacities, and troubleshooting tips that you need to work on specific vehicles.

Acknowledgments

The publisher sincerely thanks the following vehicle manufacturers, industry suppliers, and individuals for supplying information and illustrations used in the Chek-Chart Series in Automotive Technology.

AIRSEPT®, INC.
Bright Solutions, INC.
CIMAT
CLIPLIGHT MANUFACTURING
DaimlerChrysler
Everco
Ford Motor Company
General Motors Corporation
    ACDelco Division
    Buick Motor Division
    Cadillac Motor Division
    Chevrolet Motor Division
    Harrison Radiator Division
    Oldsmobile Division
    Pontiac Motor Division
Honda Motor Co., Ltd.
INFICON
International Mobile Air Conditioning Association (IMACA)

MAC Tools, Inc.
Mazda Motor Corporation
Mobile Air Conditioning Society Worldwide (MACS)
Nartron Corporation
Nissan Motor Corporation
Prestone, Union Carbide Corporation
Raytek Corporation
Snap-on Tools Corporation
SPX Corporation
Kent-Moore Tool Group
Robinair Automotive Division
Toyota Motor Corporation
Volkswagen of America
Weiss Environmental

The publisher gratefully acknowledges the reviewers of this edition: Ron Chappell, Santa Fe Community College; Roger Donovan, Illinois Central College; Robert C. Dunion, DaimlerChrysler Technical Training, Inc.; Paul Rossiter, Central Florida Community College; Donald Schinker, Madison Area Technical College; and Mitchell Walker, St. Louis Community College.

The publisher also thanks Series Advisor James D. Halderman.

Contents

PART ONE

Introduction

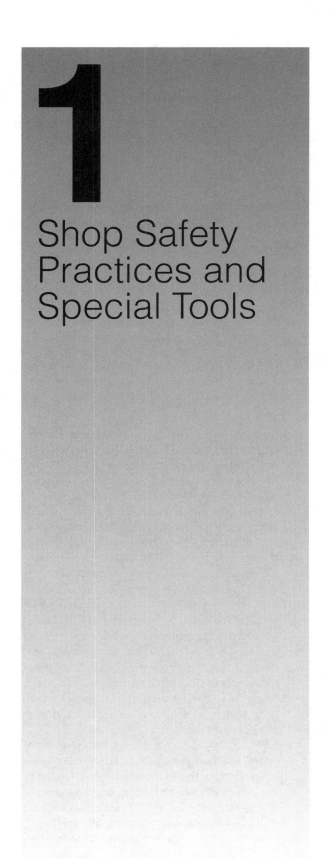

1

Shop Safety Practices and Special Tools

This chapter covers important shop practices that allow you to work safely and efficiently in any workplace. This chapter also overviews some of the special tools that you will need to perform air conditioning work.

SAFE WORK PRACTICES

Safety is important to you and to the people who work around you. No job is worth an injury, or the lost time and income resulting from a preventable accident. Yet many technicians constantly practice poor shop safety techniques. Taking a little extra time to be sure that safety is properly practiced will mean far fewer accidents happen to you, your coworkers, your equipment, and your customer's vehicle. Too often safety practices are not enforced until after an accident happens. *Remember, safety is your responsibility.*

Shop Clothing

It is important to wear the appropriate shop attire in order to prevent accidents and to protect yourself.

- Make certain you always wear eye protection. This may be the most important safety rule of all, figure 1-1.
- Tie back long hair or contain it under a cap. This prevents it from getting caught in moving parts, obstructing your view, and becoming soiled.
- Tuck in any loose clothing. Loose shirts can easily become caught in moving parts.
- Wear the appropriate shop uniform shirt or shop coat. This provides safety outerwear and provides additional protection to your own clothing.

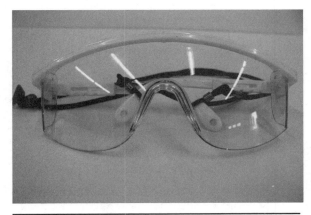

Figure 1-1. Eye protection is a must when performing AC work. If refrigerant gets into your eyes, serious damage can occur.

- Make certain that you wear protective work boots with oil-resistant soles to prevent foot injury and slippage.
- If wearing long-sleeve shirts, make sure they are buttoned or rolled up out of your way.
- Avoid wearing rings, watches, bracelets, necklaces, or other jewelry that could become caught in moving parts, caught in equipment, or become a conductor for electric current. Note that a ring can weld itself to a battery terminal and become red-hot in a second. A necklace or long hair can easily be caught and pull you into moving engine parts.

The Work Area

Familiarize yourself with the area in which you'll be working. Look around and know the locations of doors, aisles, lighting, shop equipment, and safety equipment. Make certain that your work area is clean and safe at all times.

- Keep all floors, aisles, tools, workbenches, and work materials clean and neatly organized. This will prevent injuries, contamination of new parts, and will save you time in finding parts and equipment, figure 1-2.
- Always make certain that all loose objects are picked up and all spills are cleaned up quickly.
- Know the location of the fire extinguishers in your shop and how to use them; this includes knowing how to put out chemical fires versus electrical fires.
- Know the location and operation of your shop's fire alarm and emergency exits.
- Know the location of all specific emergency equipment, including eyewashes, emergency showers, and first aid kits, figure 1-3.

Figure 1-2. A clean and well-organized shop provides a safe working environment.

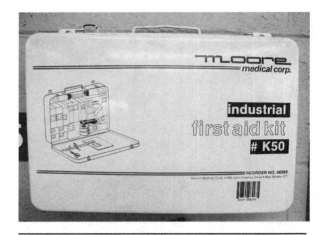

Figure 1-3. Every shop should have a well-stocked, and easily accessible, first aid kit.

Tool Safety Maintenance and Use

There are many types of hand tools and shop equipment. Knowing how to keep them maintained and organized will be a big step in practicing proper shop safety.

- Make certain to keep your personal toolbox clean, well organized, and properly outfitted for the jobs you will be doing.
- Never work with broken, worn, or loose tools.
- Always clean your tools as soon as possible after completing a job. Practice cleaning your tools as you work and when you are finished using the tool, so there is less cleaning to do at the end of the job.
- If you put your tools away after each job, it is easier to keep track of your tools. You will know if you have left any tools under the hood or in the vehicle. Tools are expensive, so you will want to avoid replacing tools that you have lost.
- Be sure you know the location and function of all shop-provided equipment, including compressors, impact tools, electrical tools, and analyzers. If you are not totally comfortable, always ask the shop leader or instructor before attempting to use an unfamiliar tool.
- Keep all shop equipment clean and well maintained. If a tool appears damaged, worn, or questionable, bring this to the immediate attention of the shop leader before using such equipment.
- Always know the location of emergency shut-off switches before you begin a job, figure 1-4.
- Make certain to keep any cutting or sharp edges facing away from you when you carry tools.
- Never carry sharp or oversized tools in your pockets.

Figure 1-4. An emergency shut-off switch should be clearly marked and located in a location that is quickly accessible.

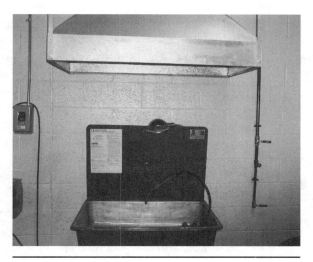

Figure 1-5. A fume hood will remove unwanted vapors.

Hazardous Materials

Hazardous and toxic materials are a part of shop operations. Hazardous waste includes both solids and liquids. Hazardous waste materials are categorized in four ways:

1. *How ignitable a substance is.* The liquid flash point (the temperature at which liquid will ignite) of a hazardous material is below 140°F (45.8°C). A solid material is classified as hazardous if it will spontaneously ignite due to heat generated by a reaction of materials.
2. *How corrosive a substance is.* Will the substance burn skin or dissolve metals?
3. *How a substance reacts.* The substance may react violently with water or other substances, release dangerous gases when exposed to low-acid solutions, or generate toxic fumes, vapors, mist, or flammable gas.
4. *How toxic a substance is.* The substance may prove harmful to human health or the environment. Most shops contain cleaning solvents, thinners, lubricants, paints, and other materials. These are often flammable and poisonous. Make sure you understand how to keep them properly stored and handled in order to prevent accidents and personal injury.
    - Keep all flammable and toxic materials properly stored and out of the way. Do not expose any flammable materials to open flame, sparks, or lit cigarettes. Do not smoke in or around the workshop at any time.

- Keep all spray cans and refrigerants away from heat sources. Heated containers may explode.
- Air conditioning refrigerants are hazardous if improperly handled. Refrigerants mixed with open flame create a very toxic gas. Refrigerants can also displace oxygen, creating breathing difficulties in enclosed, unventilated spaces.
- Make sure the shop has adequate ventilation whether the shop doors are open or closed. If you have fume hoods, be sure they operate properly and know how to use them, figure 1-5.
- Always use protective gloves and eyewear when handling any chemical that is toxic or flammable.
- Always read packaging instructions before using any new cleaning material. Some cleaners do not mix with other chemicals and can become caustic, explosive, or corrosive.
- Use only the recommended solvents in parts washers. Using the wrong fluids can increase fire risk, expose you to toxic chemicals, and can even destroy the parts you want to clean.
- Do not splash cleaning solvents when putting parts into or taking them out of the parts washer.
- If air drying any cleaned parts with compressed air, make certain to point the air stream away from you, from others, and from any other automotive part or finish.
- Clean up any spills right away. Do not let spilled chemicals sit in contact with any parts, clothing, or your skin.
- Thoroughly wash any chemicals off your skin with soap and water or other appropriate

cleaner. Do not use gasoline, cleaning solvent, or paint thinner to clean your hands, as these chemicals will be absorbed into your skin and create harmful effects.

- Always wash your hands after working with chemicals, especially before eating, drinking, smoking, or using the toilet.
- All used chemicals must be disposed of properly. Do not dump any chemicals down the drains either inside or outside the shop.

Electrical Hazards

Many heating, ventilation, and air conditioning systems use electric or electronic components or controls. These, plus the vehicle's starting and charging system, are sources of possible damage or injury if not treated with appropriate caution.

- Keep flames and sparks away from the vehicle and chemicals at all times. Batteries give off explosive hydrogen gas. Batteries being charged are especially dangerous.
- Refrigerants and flame mix to cause toxic gases.
- Make sure your hands, the floor, and your entire workspace are dry before touching electrical switches or plugs, or before using any electrical equipment.
- Always disconnect the battery when working on or near electrical components. Remove the negative (ground) battery cable and be sure it is isolated. However, use your best judgment before you disconnect the battery for basic service. Once the battery has been disconnected, it may take the computer quite awhile to relearn all of its settings.
- Nonconductors can develop a static charge that can ignite chemicals or vapors. These electrostatic discharges can also damage sensitive electronic components. Make certain to follow precautions when handling sensitive electronic components, figure 1-6.
- Never use the battery top as a tool tray. A tool that accidentally touches both battery terminals will melt and cause an electric spark or explosion, figure 1-7.

Fire Hazards

There are four classes of fire extinguishers. Each class should be used on specific types of fires only:

1. Class A extinguishes general combustibles, such as cloth, paper, and wood.
2. Class B extinguishes flammable liquids and grease, including gasoline, oil, thinners, and solvents.

Figure 1-6. This is the symbol used to identify a component that is sensitive to Electrostatic Discharge (ESD). Follow precautions when handling or working on components identified with this symbol.

Figure 1-7. *Do not* use the battery as a storage tray for your tools. If a tool accidentally touches both terminals a spark and possible explosion could occur.

3. Class C extinguishes electrical fires only.
4. Class D extinguishes combustible metals, such as aluminum, sodium, and magnesium.

Avoiding fire hazards is absolutely critical in the confined space of the repair shop. There are too many additional hazards in the shop that can create explosions and toxic gases when fires break out.

- Make certain that there is always a fully charged chemical fire extinguisher in a marked location in the work area, figure 1-8. Make sure you know how to use the extinguisher correctly.

Figure 1-8. Make sure fire extinguishers are well marked, easy to access, and tested annually.

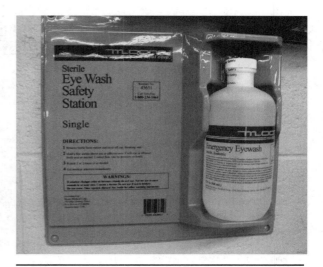

Figure 1-9. An eye wash station or kit should be available in a location close to the work area in case of accidental eye contamination.

- Know the different types of fire extinguishers.
- Never use water on electrical or chemical fires. Water will only spread these types of fires and will not extinguish them.
- Remember that the vehicle's fuel tank contains explosive vapors. Keep open flame away from the fuel tank and the rest of the vehicle fuel system at all times.
- Before using an acetylene torch around the vehicle, carefully inspect for any fuel or oil leaks in the engine compartment and under the vehicle.
- Do not smoke inside the shop or while you are working around any chemical cleaners or refrigerant.
- Make certain to avoid any sparks, the use of open flame, or welding equipment around any flammable materials.

When Accidents Occur

When an accident occurs in the shop, you must be prepared to respond immediately. This can prevent further damage or injury and might even save lives.

- Know the location and use of the first-aid equipment. This includes bandages, ointments, wound cleaners, and latex gloves.
- If caustic materials are splashed into the eyes or the skin, the area must be washed and treated immediately. Soap and water are used to clean any skin and hair, while an eye wash station is used

to wash any foreign materials or objects out of the eyes, figure 1-9.
- Know what to do in case any toxic material is accidentally swallowed. Review the basic first-aid procedures with your instructor.
- Following emergency treatment for any accident, always contact medical personnel for follow-up treatment immediately.

SHOP SAFETY PROGRAMS AND LEGAL REQUIREMENTS

Every well-managed shop will have a safety program in place, including training, information posters, booklets, and other information to ensure that all shop workers are trained in safety techniques and know what to do. The Occupational Safety and Health Administration (OSHA) has established certain safety guidelines and federal laws so that all workers are aware of their individual rights and responsibilities. This is covered under the Employee Right to Know regulations. Review the hazardous Materials Safety Data Sheet, figure 1-10. These sheets specifically cover how hazardous materials are to be properly handled, stored, labeled, recorded, and disposed of. All shops should have a booklet containing these sheets for all of the hazardous chemicals that are used in the shop.

The Employee Right to Know program provides you with training and information specific to your work environment and what you should know about any hazardous materials and potential dangers that might exist in your workplace. OSHA rules provide guidelines to ensure your workplace is properly run

---

	General Motors Corporation	
September, 1999	**Material Safety Data Sheet**	Page 200

SECTION 01: CHEMICAL PRODUCT & COMPANY ID

TRADENAME: REFRIGERANT 12
 1051053
SAFE USE CATEGORY AND DESCRIPTION: 01 -HALOGENATED SOLVENTS
MSDS CREATE DATE: 1985-01-01
LAST UPDATED DATE: 1991-05-01
MANUFACTURER'S ID (MID): 000550203
MANUFACTURER'S NAME: GLIDDEN CO./ICI PAINTS / FORM. ICI AMERI
MANUFACTURER'S EMERGENCY PHONE NUMBER/TEXT:
US 302-886-3000 EMERGENCY
US 800-327-8633 MEDICAL
MANUFACTURER'S MAILING ADDRESS:
 ALSO SEE GMBA #552787
 CONCORD PIKE & MURPHY RD
 WILMINGTON DE 19897
 US
CHEMICAL FAMILY NAME: COMPRESSED GAS

SECTION 02: COMPOSITION & INGREDIENT INFO

CAS#	FORMULATION	W/V	CHEMICAL NAME
000075718=100.0000/0.0000%		N	METHANE, DICHLORODIFLUORO-

THRESHOLD LIMIT VALUE: 1000 PPM, 8-HOUR TWA
PERMISSIBLE EXPOSURE LIMIT: 1000 PPM, 8-HOUR TWA.
CERCLA (SUPERFUND) REPORTABLE QUANTITY (LBS): THIS PRODUCT DOES NOT CONTAIN ANY CHEMICALS SUBJECT TO THE REPORTING REQUIREMENTS OF SARA

SECTION 313.

SECTION 03: HAZARDS IDENTIFICATION

PRIMARY ENTRY ROUTE INDICATORS:
SKIN PRIMARY ENTRY ROUTE INDICATOR = Y
EYE PRIMARY ENTRY ROUTE INDICATOR = Y
INHALATION PRIMARY ENTRY ROUTE INDICATOR = Y
INGESTION PRIMARY ENTRY ROUTE INDICATOR = N
PRIMARY ROUTES OF ENTRY TEXT: SKIN AND EYE CONTACT, INHALATION
EFFECTS OF OVEREXPOSURE: HEALTH HAZARDS: INHALATION (TLV), HARMFUL (CARDIAC SENSITIZATION). GENERAL: LIMITED TOXICITY DATA ARE AVAILABLE ON THIS SPECIFIC PRODUCT; THIS HEALTH HAZARD ASSESSMENT IS BASED ON THE INFORMATION FROM THE LITERATURE. INGESTION: THIS MATERIAL IS A GAS AT ROOM TEMPERATURE; THEREFORE, INGESTION IS NOT LIKELY TO OCCUR. EYE CONTACT: THE LIQUID FORM OF THIS MATERIAL CAN INDUCE A CHILLING SENSATION AND/OR FREEZE BURNS OF THE EYES. SKIN CONTACT: A FREEZE BURN CAN POSSIBLY RESULT AFTER CONTACT WITH RAPIDLY EVAPORATING LIQUID. SKIN ABSORPTION: THIS PRODUCT IS NOT LIKELY TO BE ABSORBED THROUGH UMAN SKIN. INHALATION: THIS MATERIAL MAY CAUSE SIMPLE ASPHYXIA, CENTRAL NERVOUS SYSTEM DEPRESSION AND/OR CARDIAC SENSITIZATION. OTHER: EXPOSURES TO HIGH VAPOR CONCENTRATIONS INDUCES TOXICITY PROGRESSING FROM GIDDINESS, SLURRED SPEECH, APPREHENSION, HEADACHE, RINGING IN EARS, WEAKNESS, DIZZINESS, IMPAIRED COORDINATION AND NAUSEA TO UNCONSCIOUSNESS. IN SUSCEPTIBLE INDIVIDUALS, CARDIAC SENSITIZATION TO CIRCULATING EPINEPHRINE-LIKE COMPOUNDS CAN RESULT IN SUDDEN, FATAL HEART ARRHYTHMIAS. CONTACT WITH THE LIQUID MATERIAL REMOVES NATURAL SKIN OILS, INDUCES SKIN FREEZE BURNS, CRACKING AND IRRIT TION.
ADDITIONAL HEALTH HAZARD DATA: TSCA REGULATIONS, 40 CFR 710: ALL INGREDIENTS ARE ON THE TSCA SECTION 8(B) INVENTORY. HEALTH HAZARDS: INHALATION (TLV), HARMFUL (CARDIAC SENSITIZATION).

SECTION 04: FIRST AID MEASURES

EMERGENCY FIRST AID PROCEDURES - GENERAL: SKIN: WASH MATERIAL OFF THE SKIN WITH PLENTY OF WATER. IF REDNESS, ITCHING OR A BURNING SENSATION DEVELOPS, GET MEDICAL ATTENTION. EYES: IMMEDIATELY FLUSH WITH PLENTY OF WATER FOR AT LEAST 15 MINUTES. IF REDNESS, ITCHING OR A BURNING SENSATION DEVELOPS, HAVE EYES EXAMINED AND TREATED BY MEDICAL ERSONNEL. INHALATION: REMOVE VICTIM TO FRESH AIR. IF COUGH OR OTHER RESPIRATORY SYMPTOMS DEVELOP, CONSULT MEDICAL PERSONNEL. IF NOT BREATHING, GIVE ARTIFICIAL RESPIRATION, PREFERABLY MOUTH TO MOUTH. IF BREATHING IS DIFFICULT, GIVE OXYGEN. CONSULT MEDICAL PERSONNEL. NOTE TO PHYSICIAN: PRODUCT IS AN ASPHYXIANT AND CAN INDUCE CARDIAC MUSCLE SENSITI-

ZATION TO CIRCULATING EPINEPHRINE-LIKE COMPOUNDS, RESULTING IN POTENTIALLY FATAL HEART ARRHYTHMIAS. DO NOT GIVE ADRENALINE OR SIMILAR SYMPATHOMIMETIC DRUGS OR ALLOW VICTIM TO EXERCISE VIGOROUSLY UNTIL 24 HOURS FOLLOWING A POTENTIALLY TOXIC EXPO URE. FREEZE BURNS OF TISSUES CAN DEVELOP FOLLOWING CONTACT WITH THE LIQUID FORM OF THIS MATERIAL.

SECTION 05: FIRE-FIGHTING MEASURES

EXTINGUISHING MEDIA: N/A; USE WATER TO COOL FIRE-EXPOSED CYLINDERS OR OTHER CONTAINERS.
SPECIAL FIRE FIGHTING PROCEDURES: SELF-CONTAINED BREATHING APPARATUS WITH FULL FACEPIECE AND PROTECTIVE CLOTHING IF INVOLVED IN A FIRE OF OTHER MATERIALS.
UNUSUAL FIRE AND EXPLOSION HAZARDS: HEAVY VAPORS CAN SUFFOCATE. HIGHLY TOXIC DECOMPOSITION PRODUCTS.
FLASH POINT TEXT: DOES NOT FLASH
FLASH POINT METHOD: DNF

SECTION 06: ACCIDENTAL RELEASE MEASURES

SPILL OR LEAK PROCEDURES: AVOID RELEASE TO THE ATMOSPHERE BECAUSE OF POSSIBLE OZONE DEPLETION IN THE STRATOSPHERE. RECOVER ANY LIQUID AND VENTILATE SPILL AREA. USE SELF-CONTAINED BREATHING APPARATUS TO AVOID SUFFOCATION. PROTECT AGAINST FROSTBITE FROM EVAPORATING LIQUID.

SECTION 07: HANDLING AND STORAGE

PRECAUTIONS TO BE TAKEN IN HANDLING AND STORAGE: STORE IN A COOL AREA WITH GOOD VENTILATION. KEEP VAPORS AWAY FROM HIGH TEMPERATURE SURFACES TO AVOID TOXIC AND CORROSIVE DECOMPOSITION PRODUCTS. ENFORCE NO SMOKING RULES IN AREAS OF USE.

SECTION 7 - OTHER INFORMATION:
AUTOIGNITION TEMP: NONE.

SECTION 08: EXPOSURE CONTROLS - PROTECTION

EYE PROTECTION: CHEMICAL TIGHT GOGGLES; FULL FACESHIELD IN ADDITION IF SPLASHING IS POSSIBLE.
RESPIRATORY PROTECTION: IN HIGH CONCENTRATIONS OR IN OXYGEN-DEFICIENT ATMOSPHERES, USE MSHA/NIOSH APPROVED SELF-CONTAINED BREATHING APPARATUS (SCBA).
PERSONAL PROTECTIVE EQUIPMENT: IMPERVIOUS APRON. ADDITIONAL PROTECTION MAY BE REQUIRED SUCH AS ARM COVERS OR A FULL BODY SUIT UNDER SEVERE CONDITIONS. EYEWASH STATION AND SAFETY SHOWER IN WORK AREA.
PROTECTIVE GLOVES (SPECIFY TYPE): IMPERVIOUS GLOVES

SECTION 09: PHYSICAL & CHEMICAL PROPERTIES

BOILING POINT TEMPS: 21.00F TO 29.00F
BOILING POINT TEXT: -21.6F/-29.8C
SPECIFIC GRAVITY VALUES: = 1.4640
SPECIFIC GRAVITY TEXT: =1.464 @30C
VAPOR DENSITY VALUES: 4.7000
VAPOR DENSITY TEXT: 4.7
VAPOR PRESSURE TEXT: NO DATA
PERCENT VOLATILE BY VOLUME: 100.0000
PERCENT VOLATILE BY VOLUME TEXT: 100
SOLUBILITY IN WATER TEXT: SLIGHT
PH OF PRODUCT IN SOLUTION WITH WATER/TEXT: NO DATA
APPEARANCE: COLORLESS GAS WITH SLIGHT ODOR. READILY LIQUEFIED UNDER PRESSURE AND/OR COOLING.
PHYSICAL STATE: GAS
PHYSICAL STATE TEXT: GAS

SECTION 10: STABILITY & REACTIVITY

STABILITY INDICATOR: Y
STABILITY - CONDITIONS TO AVOID: STABLE UNDER NORMAL CONDITIONS.
STABILITY - TEXT: YES
INCOMPATIBLE MATERIALS: REACTS VIOLENTLY WITH SODIUM, POTASSIUM, AND BARIUM METAL. REACTS WITH FINELY DIVIDED ALUMINUM, ZINC, AND MAGNESIUM, ESPECIALLY AT HIGH TEMPERATURES.

Figure 1-10. A Material Data Safety Sheet provides important information for every chemical used in the shop. (Reprinted with permission of General Motors Corporation.)

and equipped to provide you and the customers adequate safety. Always immediately report any unsafe working conditions, damaged equipment, or accident to your shop supervisor or instructor.

Safety for Heating and Air Conditioning Systems

Since the heating system is part of the engine cooling system, always allow the engine to cool so there is no pressure in the system before you service it. The air conditioning (AC) system involves extremely high and low pressures and temperatures. Protect yourself against burns, freezing, and other damage that the AC system components can cause.

- Never open the engine cooling system when the coolant is hot and under pressure. The coolant may boil rapidly when the pressure is released, causing severe burns. Do not touch the radiator cap, heater hoses, radiator hoses, or the coolant drain plugs when the system is pressurized.
- The radiator contains toxic coolant. Always drain and capture coolant in an approved container for storage, recycling, or disposal, figure 1-11. Coolant is poisonous to humans and animals. *Do not dispose of coolant in any sink or sewer drains.*
- R-12 is a chlorofluorocarbon (CFC) material that has been proven to contribute to ozone depletion. Therefore, R-12 must always be recovered, recycled, stored, and recharged to an air conditioning system only with approved types of equipment and storage containers. Never purposely release R-12 to the atmosphere.
- R-134a, the only vehicle manufacturer approved alternate to R-12, is a non-chlorofluorocarbon material (non-CFC). It is a hydrofluorocarbon (HFC) and does not readily contribute to atmospheric ozone depletion. However, by law, R-134a must be handled using only approved recovery and recycling equipment and approved storage containers.
- Refrigerant is stored as a liquid under pressure. Cans or drums of refrigerant should not be exposed to direct sunlight or stored in areas where they are exposed to other heat sources.
- If a refrigerant can is punctured, the refrigerant sprays out at such a high pressure that it can penetrate your skin. At the very least, the high-pressure liquid will instantly vaporize and freeze any skin that it contacts. If this happens, immediately splash large amounts of cool water on the affected area. If the eyes are involved, use an eyewash, then seek immediate medical help.

Figure 1-11. Coolant should be disposed of properly. Many shops collect the coolant and send it to a waste hauler to be recycled.

- Never randomly disconnect AC hoses or components. The refrigerant must be recovered first, using approved equipment. This prevents the accidental loss of refrigerant, captures refrigerant to be recycled and reused, and lowers the pressure in the system so that it may safely be opened.
- Never perform an air conditioning system recovery or recharge with an open flame in the area.

Common Sense and Thinking Ahead

While your shop is equipped with proper safety equipment and you will be taught how to use the equipment and materials, it is still up to you to be prepared and practice safety first. *Remember that safety is your responsibility.*

- Plan your workspace, tools, and materials to achieve maximum safety and efficiency.
- If in doubt about a procedure or practice, refer to the shop manual or ask someone. Never assume that everything will be safe.
- Before starting a job that involves possibly dangerous equipment or materials, review your safety regulations and plan ahead in case of an accident.
- Never use equipment that has safety features bypassed or equipment that is unsafe.

SPECIAL TOOLS

Proper work practices also involve obtaining, understanding, and using the correct tools. The majority of HVAC services will require normal tools found in a typical, well-equipped toolbox, yet some tasks require specialized tools and equipment. It is important that you understand the special kinds of tools you need and how they function in order to make your service and diagnostic job easier and more accurate.

There are a number of tools that could be required during any heating or air conditioning service. Generally, these systems require checking the heating capabilities, coolant hoses and connections, vacuum hoses, functions of the controls, and operation of the blower fan.

Hand-Operated Vacuum Pump

Many components in the HVAC system are operated by vacuum motors and have a number of vacuum hoses connecting the respective parts. The lines connecting the vacuum motors may contain check valves, figure 1-12, which prevent the reverse flow of vacuum and/or function to release vacuum when needed. Vacuum reservoirs, figure 1-13, are also used with some of these vacuum-operated systems.

A hand-operated vacuum pump, figure 1-14, allows you to create either vacuum or pressure, and take the appropriate reading on the attached gauge. This tool allows you to locate leaks and check for proper operation of diaphragms, vacuum motors, doors, check valves, and other such devices in the system.

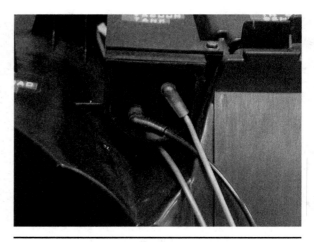

Figure 1-13. Some systems use a vacuum reservoir to store vacuum that can be used under conditions of low engine vacuum.

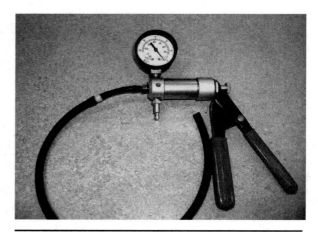

Figure 1-14. A hand-held vacuum pump is useful for testing vacuum check valves and vacuum-operated mode doors.

Belt Tensioners and Tension Gauges

Installing drive belts to drive water pumps, engine fans, and air conditioning compressors can sometimes be difficult without assistance. You may need to hold idler pulleys or tensioners away from the belt during positioning. You may also need to hold the component in a nontensioned position in order to get the belt into place on the pulley.

There are special belt tensioning tools available to assist you. These tools are designed to give you leverage, relieve tension, and/or help with adding tension during component tightening, figure 1-15. Once a belt is installed, it must be tensioned to allow optimal performance of the components that it drives. Over-tightening belts can cause damaged pulley

Figure 1-12. Vacuum check valves are used to prevent vacuum from bleeding off from the system.

Figure 1-15. This tool is used to assist in releasing the tension on the belt tensioner.

Figure 1-17. Most engines equipped with serpentine belts use a belt tensioner to automatically keep the correct tension on the belt.

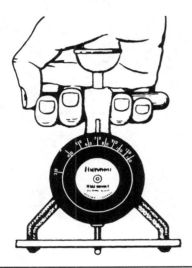

Figure 1-16. Correct belt tension is important for efficient component operation. Tension can be easily checked with a drive belt tensioning gauge.

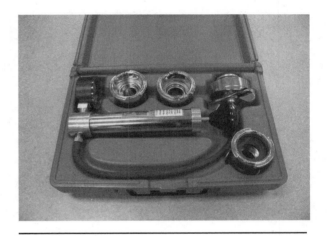

Figure 1-18. A coolant pressure tester is used to pressurize the cooling system to test for leaks.

bearings or internal component parts, and will shorten the belt life. If there is not enough tension on the belt, slippage, squealing, and improper operation can occur.

The tension gauge will help you properly install the belt to the correct tension. A typical belt tension gauge, figure 1-16, will measure the force necessary to deflect the belt to the specified settings. This deflection ensures there is enough tension, but not too much.

Some belts, especially serpentine style belts, have built-in tensioning wheels or levers to automatically set the tension, so a measurement or adjustment is not needed once the belt is properly installed, figure 1-17. Vehicle service information specifies when tension needs to be measured. Always follow the manufacturer's specifications exactly.

Coolant System Pressure Tester

The coolant system pressure tester, figure 1-18, is used to test the vehicle's coolant system for leaks. It is installed in place of the radiator cap, or the coolant expansion tank cap and allows the technician to

pressurize the coolant system to the operating pressure for the vehicle. The technician can then check for leaks at the various hose connections, radiator, heater core, or other fittings.

Never exceed the manufacturer's recommended pressure when using the pressure tester as damage may occur.

Coolant Combustion Tester

A coolant combustion tester is used to test for the presence of combustion gases in the coolant system, figure 1-19. Combustion gases leaking into the coolant system can be caused by blown cylinder head gaskets, cracked cylinder heads, or a cracked block. The combustion tester contains a liquid that changes color under the presence of combustion gases. It is relatively inexpensive and easy to use. Another way to detect

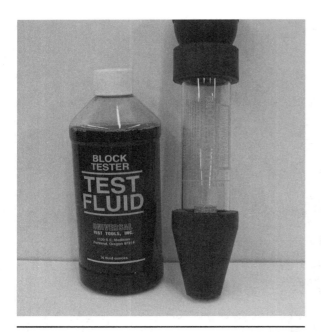

Figure 1-19. A coolant combustion tester is used to check for the presence of combustion gases in the cooling system.

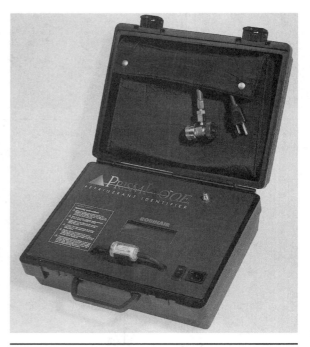

Figure 1-20. Use your electronic refrigerant identifier to confirm the refrigerant type before you open the system for any type of service. Identifiers are also used to confirm the type of refrigerant stored in containers.

combustion gases is by the use of an emission analyzer to detect the presence of hydrocarbons in the coolant system. When using this method, care must be taken not to draw any coolant into the emission analyzer, or damage to the unit can result.

Electronic Refrigerant Identifier

One of the most important tools an air conditioning technician uses is the electronic refrigerant identifier, figure 1-20. You must know what type of refrigerant is in the system before you begin any type of service. This includes recovering refrigerant from storage containers as well. A container labeled R-134a is not a guarantee that the container is filled with pure R-134a. You must confirm it. Do not risk the chance of damaging your shop service equipment because you did not confirm the refrigerant type or composition. Do not guess or assume the refrigerant type based on the pressure, fittings, or label. There is no room for error in this determination. You must use an electronic refrigerant identifier to be certain. Some states now require that all shops performing AC work have a refrigerant identifier.

Although the general procedure is the same, electronic refrigerant identifiers vary slightly. Some identifiers are more advanced and supply more information than others. If a basic identifier is all you can afford when you first start out, buy it. Your identifier is a wise investment. You can upgrade your identifier as your career advances. The most basic identifiers sample the

refrigerant in a system and identify whether it is R-12 or R-134a. Other identifiers alert you if a refrigerant blend is detected. Some identifiers are capable of identifying and measuring air contamination (highly recommended). Other refrigerant identifiers can measure the purity of the refrigerant. The general procedure for identifying refrigerant is as follows:

1. When you first turn on the machine, allow the tool to warm up as required, figure 1-21.
2. Connect the refrigerant identifier hose to the vehicle's low-side service port, or the storage tank being tested, figure 1-22.
3. The display reads "Testing" for approximately 20 seconds as the tool samples the refrigerant.
4. The display reads "R-12, R-134a, or Other," figure 1-23 (depending on its capabilities).
5. The display also may show the percentage of air contamination and the purity, if capable, figure 1-24.

Refrigerant Leak Detectors

It is normal for a small amount of an air conditioning system's refrigerant to seep out over an extended period of time. This is due to the porous material of AC hoses, fittings that become loose, or normal wear on the system connections and seals.

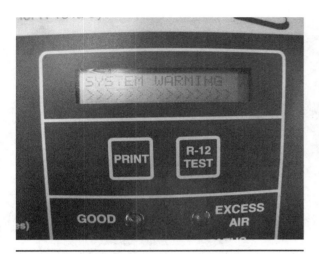

Figure 1-21. The refrigerant identifier must first warm up before testing refrigerant.

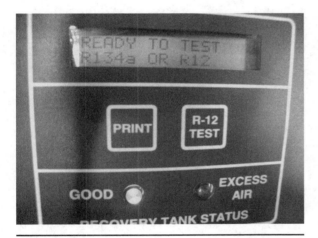

Figure 1-22. After warm up the tester will indicate that it is ready to test the refrigerant.

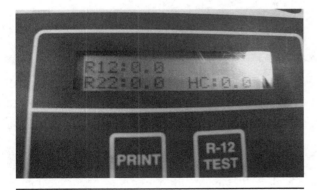

Figure 1-23. Some identifiers will show the percentage of different refrigerants.

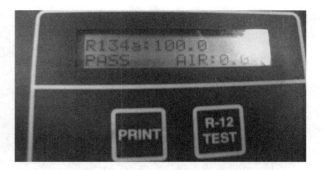

Figure 1-24. Some identifiers will show the percentage of air in the refrigerant.

Refrigerant loss affects cooling and can eventually cause system failures. If the refrigerant is low, always inspect the system for leaks and repair them immediately. Leaks allow moisture and air to enter the system components and cause damage.

"Cold leaks" occur due to seepage when the system is off. These are caused by a seal that does not effectively hold refrigerant in the system, or by a hose that has deteriorated and allows refrigerant to escape.

"High pressure leaks" occur when the system is operating and pressurized. System pressure is enough to force significant amounts of refrigerant through fittings, seals, hoses, or other areas that might not leak when the system is not under pressure.

To find refrigerant leaks, you will need the help of a leak detector. Since refrigerant is heavier than air, it will seep downward. Since it is odorless, you will not be able to smell if a leak is present. Generally, there are two ways to locate a refrigerant leak:

- Leak detection with dye
- Electronic leak detector

NOTE: Other methods have been used in the past such as the halide leak detector and soap solutions. While at one time these methods were effective they are no longer appropriate methods to use on late model HVAC systems.

Electronic Leak Detector

This type of leak detector has gained popularity due to its sensitivity and reliability. An electronic detector, figure 1-25, draws a small sample of air through a probe tip and examines it electronically. If refrigerant is present in the air sample, a tone or beeper will sound. As the probe is moved around the system, the sound will increase in volume and speed as the probe gets closer to the leak. You need to be aware of what type of equipment your shop uses. Older models will only

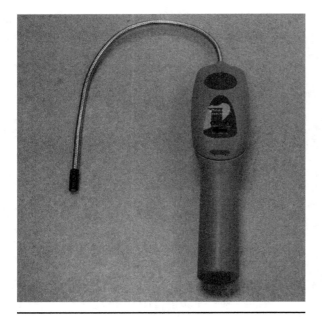

Figure 1-25. When choosing a leak detector, make sure that it meets SAE Standard J1627 for leak test performance such as this model shown from INFICON. (Courtesy of INFICON.)

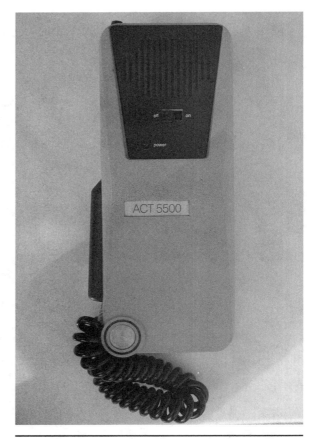

Figure 1-26. This electronic detector can only be used to detect R-12 and R-22 refrigerant.

test R-12 refrigerant, figure 1-26, while newer models will be able to test both R-12 and R-134a refrigerants. Make sure that the leak detector meets SAE standards J1627 (Performance Criteria for Electronic Refrigerant Leak Detectors). These standards ensure that the detector meets guidelines for the maximum allowable leak rates. The detector:

- Must be capable of detecting a 0.5 oz. per year leak.
- Must be able to detect the leak when the probe is held 0.25 inches from the leak source.
- Must be able to detect the leak when being moved at a rate of two inches per second.
- Must clearly indicate the leak in 9 out of 10 passes.
- Must clearly alert the operator of the leak detection.

Dye Leak Detectors

Colored dyes that are compatible with refrigerant can aid in finding a leak, figure 1-27. The dye is injected into the AC system through the manifold gauge set or by using special equipment provided with the dye. Some dyes can be seen in plain daylight, while others require an ultraviolet light to be seen. Once the fluorescent dye is in the system, it may take a few days for the dye to circulate and ap-

Figure 1-27. This dye leak detector uses a fluorescent dye, which becomes visible using a ultraviolet light.

pear with the leaking refrigerant. A black light is then run along the air conditioning components to look for the dye, figure 1-28. Many vehicles now come

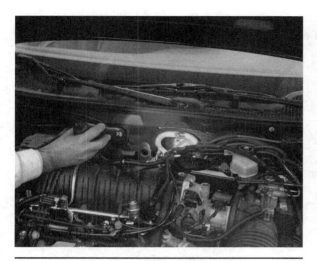

Figure 1-28. An ultraviolet lamp is used to check for leaks after injecting the fluorescent dye.

Figure 1-29. This rotary thermometer is inexpensive and easy to read without removing it from the duct.

from the manufacturer with a dye already added to the refrigerant.

Thermometers

Temperature measurement is essential in AC service. Aside from ordinary pocket thermometers, there are several types of temperature measuring devices used in AC service:

- Rotary-dial thermometer
- Electronic thermometer
- Infrared thermometer

Rotary-Dial Thermometer

The most widely used type of thermometer is the rotary-dial thermometer, figure 1-29. The rotary dial has a round face. The thermometer has a stem-measuring device. The stem fits into the dash panel outlets and the face can easily be read. This is much more convenient than the column type thermometer since the rotary dial does not have to be removed from the vent to read the temperature. It also can be used to measure the temperature of the coolant in the cooling system.

Electronic Thermometer

Electronic thermometers are accurate and convenient. These units can be add-on features to a standard digital multimeter (DMM) used in most service shops, figure 1-30. The electronic thermometer may have

Figure 1-30. The thermocouple attaches to a digital meter to display temperature readings.

readouts in digital or analog style. They can also be stand-alone units (not attached to a DMM) and used only for temperature measurements. Electronic thermometers are becoming the industry standard for performance testing and system diagnosis.

Figure 1-31. A noncontact infrared thermometer senses infrared radiation from an object and electronically calculates its temperature.

Figure 1-32. An electric vacuum pump can be used to draw vacuum for testing or to fully evacuate an air conditioning system of all air and moisture after the refrigerant has been removed. Recovery/recycling equipment may have a vacuum pump built into the station.

Infrared Thermometer

While still relatively expensive, noncontact infrared thermometers are becoming more popular, figure 1-31. These units emit an infrared light wave to measure the surface temperature of different components. They are very versatile and allow temperature measurements to be taken from various components without having to directly access the component. As an example, the condenser temperature can be taken at various locations to determine if the condenser is blocked. Inlet and outlet temperature of the evaporator can be measured much easier with this type of thermometer.

Vacuum Pump

When you disassemble an AC system to replace components, or if you have recovered refrigerant from the system to repair a leak, the AC system must be completely evacuated of all air and moisture before recharging with new or recycled refrigerant.

In order to do this, you must apply a vacuum of about 28 to 29 in-Hg to the system and hold it for a period of time. (*This time will vary according to the type of equipment used and altitude; however, a generally accepted industry standard is 20 to 30 minutes.*) The application of the vacuum lowers the effective "boiling" point of any moisture in the system, then easily draws it out as vapor. In addition, any air that may have entered the system is removed. Leaving moisture in the system is asking for trouble later due to damaged compressor seals, frozen expansion valves, and other kinds of problems.

Be sure that the vacuum pump you are using has enough capacity (at least three cubic feet per minute). A vacuum pump with a suitable gauge is used for this purpose, figure 1-32. If a manifold gauge set is used, the pump is attached to the center service line of the gauge set. In a recovery/recycling station, the vacuum pump may be internal and the function is provided electronically or through a switch setting.

One other reason for using the vacuum pump is that when vacuum is applied and held, you will see whether any further leaks exist in the system by watching the vacuum gauge. If the vacuum does not hold after the vacuum pump is shut off, it indicates that a leak still exists in the system.

Compressor Clutch and Component Service Tools

Service work on the compressor, compressor clutch, or other system components may require, or at least be made easier with special tools. This section describes some of these specialty tools.

Compressor Shaft and Bearing Service Tools

The most difficult seal to replace in the AC system is the seal between the compressor shaft and housing behind the clutch assembly. This seal must contain the pressure of the system as well as endure the constant rotation of the shaft. This seal often requires replacement.

A shaft seal and bearing service kit, figure 1-33, contains tools for various makes and models of compressors. The kit includes special pulley removal tools, bearing removal tools, seal removal tools, and a special drive plate tool.

Since there are many variations of clutch, seal, and bearing assemblies, many repair shops either send the compressor to specialty rebuild shops for repairs, or install a rebuilt compressor assembly with a new seal and bearing already in place. Many manufacturers no longer allow seal replacement on their compressors. Each shop performing AC work makes a decision as to whether they will try to service compressor shaft seals and bearings, or simply replace the compressor with a new or rebuilt unit.

Special Refrigerant Hose Adapters

Various special adapters are available to simplify service hose connections to the vehicle's AC system, figure 1-34. Right-angle adapters aid in connecting service hoses in cramped quarters. Other adapters are available for nonstandard size Schrader valves (valves with pressure release cores, somewhat like a tire valve stem). There are different fittings for different types of refrigerant systems. These differences prevent connecting the wrong equipment to the wrong refrigerant system.

Fin Straightener

Evaporator and condenser tubing, much like the structure of the radiator, are connected with delicate cooling fins. These fins increase the surface area to improve the transfer of heat. If these cooling fins become folded, bent, or otherwise damaged, airflow is restricted. This means the heat transfer and cooling capability of the AC system will be reduced. The fin straightener, figure 1-35, is useful in straightening the bent fins of the evaporator, condenser, or radiator.

Figure 1-34. A variety of AC line adapters are available to allow you to connect your service equipment to the air conditioning system.

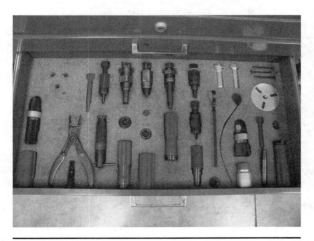

Figure 1-33. This is a universal compressor service toolbox. It contains most of the compressor service tools needed to service a wide variety of compressors.

Figure 1-35. A fin straightener can be used to straighten any bent fins on a condenser.

Scan Tools

On late model vehicles, many powertrain control modules (PCM) that manage engine systems also have sensors that monitor the AC system operation. This is especially true of electronically controlled automatic AC systems.

Computer-controlled engine systems use a series of diagnostic trouble codes (DTCs) to alert the driver and technician that a problem has occurred and where it might be located. The same is true of the monitoring functions affecting the AC system. These DTCs sometimes may be accessed through the AC control panel or may require a scan tool to access the codes. Some of the more typical problems that may be indicated by these DTCs are:

- System refrigerant low
- Malfunctioning compressor clutch
- Malfunctioning AC system delivery doors
- Improper or nonoperation of a particular sensor or circuit

If the vehicle is not equipped with a DTC readout on the control panel, a scan tool is needed to access, read, and clear codes, figure 1-36. A scan tool is a hand-held computer that, when properly connected, communicates with a vehicle's onboard computer. Some scan tools include definitions for each DTC and may even include some diagnostic information on how to proceed with troubleshooting to pinpoint the problem.

Test Meters

The two types of test meters you will see in automotive service are analog and digital. Before electronics became common in cars, most test meters were analog. Analog meters use a mechanism called a D'Arsonval movement to move a needle over a printed scale to indicate test values, figure 1-37. They are called analog meters because the meter can indicate a continuous range of values across its scale. Most analog meters have a low input impedance. Impedance is the opposition to current flow resulting from the combined effects of the resistance, inductance, and capacitance of the meter.

The low input impedance of analog meters can lower the resistance of the circuit being tested, which can cause the current flow to increase. These traits distort the accuracy of the measurement, sometimes considerably, and can cause serious problems with low current circuits. The input impedance of most analog meters is in the range of 5,000 to 20,000 ohms (Ω) per volt. Analog meters are not recommended for testing most automotive electronic systems.

Use a modern digital volt-ohmmeter (DVOM or DMM) to check electronic circuits and components,

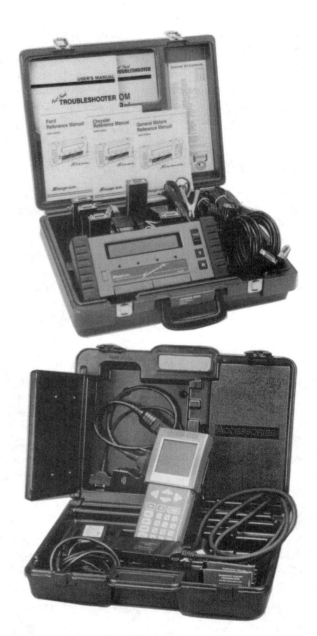

Figure 1-36. A hand-held scan tool is used to access diagnostic trouble codes (DTCs) and to help pinpoint problem circuits or components. Scan tools are available from a wide variety of sources and perform a wide range of functions.

figure 1-38. A DMM converts the analog signals it measures into a digital format, and displays them as digits, or numbers, on a light-emitting diode or liquid crystal display.

Digital meters have a very high input impedance, usually greater then 10 mega-ohms per volt. Many components and circuits that are solid state must be tested with a high impedance meter. The low imped-

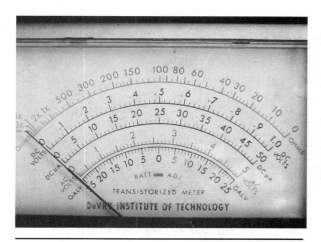

Figure 1-37. Most analog meters have too low of an input impedence to safely test solid-state circuits.

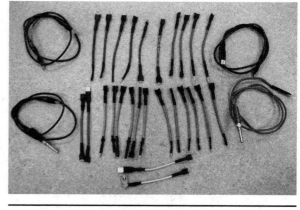

Figure 1-39. A selection of jumper wires is needed to perform electrical tests on circuits without damaging terminals.

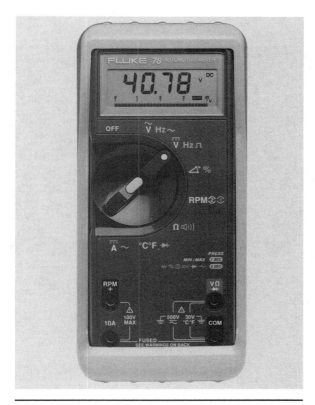

Figure 1-38. A digital volt ohmmeter (DVOM) is required to safely test electronic circuits and components. DVOMs have a wide range of settings for performing various testing.

ance of the analog meter could damage devices by allowing too much current to flow in the circuit. High impedance meters will not cause excessive current to flow, avoiding damage. They also allow more accurate measurements to be obtained.

Other Electronic Test Tools

Wiring probes, jumper connectors, and jumper leads are also necessary to aid you in making measurements on these circuits and devices, figure 1-39. These allow you to make voltage and resistance measurements without causing damage to wiring terminals. As with most electronic and electrical systems, AC system trouble spots often show up as poor or dirty electrical connections or improper ground connections. These interrupt electrical flow through circuits and components. Later in the *Shop Manual* you will learn diagnostic routines to help avoid misdiagnosing problems and replacing parts unnecessarily.

Electronic Air Conditioner Diagnostic Testers

Electronic air conditioner diagnostic testers have recently been developed to aid in the diagnosis of air conditioning systems, figure 1-40. These testers are designed to aid the technician in diagnosing air conditioning performance complaints. They usually consist of a hand-held unit that connects to the low-side and high-side fittings to record pressures, temperature probes, ambient air temperature measurement, relative humidity measurement, and electrical data from the pressure cycling switch. Depending on the unit, it may have the capability of printing the results of the diagnostic test, figure 1-41, or showing the results on a digital display, figures 1-42 and 1-43.

In addition to recording the operating conditions of the AC system, some of these diagnostic units provide a list of possible causes and suggested repair solutions, figure 1-44.

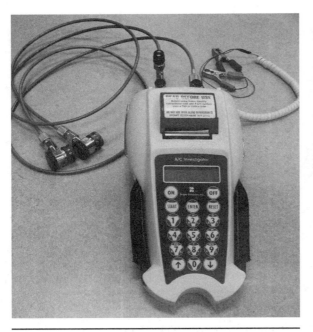

Figure 1-40. This electronic air conditioning system diagnostic tester by Bright Solutions, Inc. provides the technician with a comprehensive test and diagnosis of the refrigeration system. (Courtesy of Bright Solutions.)

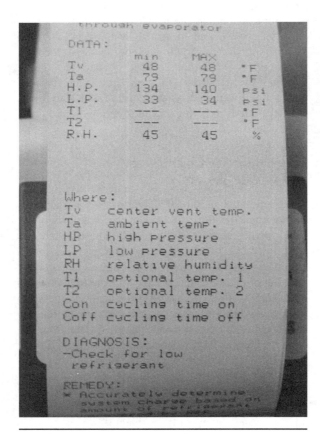

Figure 1-41. In addition to providing diagnostics for the technician, a printed copy is available for the customer. (Courtesy of Bright Solutions.)

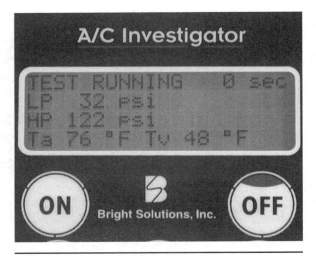

Figure 1-42. Comprehensive test results are available to the technician and can be printed out for the customer. (Courtesy of Bright Solutions.)

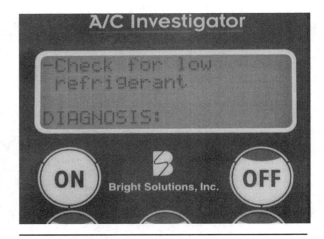

Figure 1-43. This electronic tester has the capability of providing diagnostics for the technician. (Courtesy of Bright Solutions.)

Other Special Air Conditioning Service Tools

There is a wide variety of specialty hand tools you will acquire and use as you progress through AC services. For example, on Ford and some other AC systems, you will find that the hoses are attached with quick-disconnect couplings. These couplings require a special tool, figure 1-45, for removal.

There are special tools for diagnostic operations, service operations, and repairs. Since there are many variations on the types of AC system components and features, based on the vehicle type, you will find it helpful to talk regularly with your tool supplier to keep up to date with what kinds of tools are available.

Bright Solutions
A/C INVESTIGATOR
Vers. 05.00.31
Date: 03-09-02 04:51

Tel.#:
Fax #:

User name:

Customer name:

Vehicle Make & Model:
2
C

Vehicle ID:
BOB11

Work order number:

Type of refrigerant:
        R134a

Type of A/C system:
-Orifice tube system
 const. running compr.
DIAGNOSIS:
-Check for low
 refrigerant
-Restricted liquid
 line or condenser
-Check orifice tube
-Low airflow
 through evaporator

DATA: min MAX

Tv   48   52   °F
Ta   73   73   °F
H.P.   105 112 psi
L.P.   31   32   psi
T1   66   66   °F
T2   62   63   °F
R.H.   29   29   %

Where:
Tv   center vent temp.
Ta   ambient temp.
HP   high pressure
LP   low pressure
RH   relative humidity
T1   optional temp. 1
T2   optional temp. 2
Con   cycling time on
Coff   cycling time off

DIAGNOSIS:
-Check for low
 refrigerant

REMEDY:
*Accurately determine
 system charge based on
 amount of refrigerant
 recovered by R&R
 machine. Add
 refrigerant to vehicle
 specification and
 inspect system for
 refrigerant leak(s)
*Inject dye for system
 leak detection
*Operate system for
 sufficient time for
 dye to appear at leak
 site and use UV lamp
*Recover the system
*Repair all system
 leaks
*Charge the system to
 specification
*Operate system and
 check the performance

DIAGNOSIS:
-Restricted liquid
 line or condenser

REMEDY:
*Check liquid line for
 restriction. Repair or
 replace if necessary
*Check condenser for
 restriction. Repair or
 replace if necessary
*Charge the system to
 specification
*Operate system and
 check the performance

DIAGNOSIS:
-Low airflow
 through evaporator

REMEDY:
*Check evaporator for
 dirt or obstruction,
 clean if required
*Check operation of the
 cooling fan. Repair if
 necessary
*Charge the system to
 specification

DIAGNOSIS:
-Check orifice tube

REMEDY:
*Check orifice tube.
 Replace if necessary
*Charge the system to
 specification
*Operate system and
 check the performance

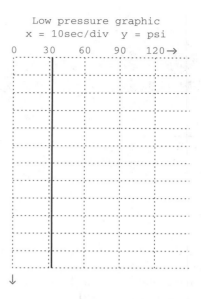

Low pressure graphic
x = 10sec/div   y = psi
0   30   60   90   120→

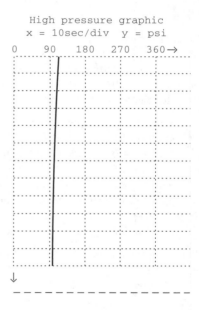

High pressure graphic
x = 10sec/div   y = psi
0   90   180 270 360→

Figure 1-44. A printout showing test results as well as a diagnosis and possible causes. (Courtesy of Bright Solutions.)

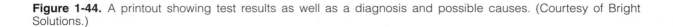

Figure 1-45. These quick-disconnect coupler tools are used to release quick-disconnect couplings used by some manufacturers on their lines.

Of course, the service information will indicate what specialty tools are required. You will find that many specialty tools are similar to other tools that you already have. Many air conditioning repair shops will keep the most-needed tools on hand so the individual technician does not need to buy all of these tools.

COMPLIANCE WITH THE CLEAN AIR ACT

All technicians who repair or service R-12 or R-134a air conditioning systems must be certified by an EPA-approved group. Certified technicians can handle any EPA-approved refrigerant blend on the market. The reasons for the required training include:

- Keeping up to date with changes in technology
- Demonstrating an understanding of the different types of refrigerants and their effects on the AC system
- Knowing how to service an AC system with an approved recovery/recycling station
- Understanding the hazardous effects of refrigerant to humans and the environment

This training and certification is different from the ASE certification. ASE (National Institute for Automotive Service Excellence) offers testing and certification in a wide range of automotive and truck repair areas. The ASE certification of Heating and Air Conditioning (A7 & T7) is to verify a technician's working knowledge of the operation, diagnosis, and repair of these systems.

MVAC (Motor Vehicle Air Conditioning) testing and certification is provided by a number of institutions around the country, including ASE. These programs must be EPA approved.

ENVIRONMENTAL FRIENDLINESS

Disposal of Hazardous Waste

Proper workshop safety demands appropriate handling and disposal of all hazardous waste. It is not legal to dump hazardous waste materials down sink or floor drains or to let them run out onto ground areas. You must be familiar with the proper handling, storage, and disposal of hazardous waste. This is for your personal safety as well as the safety of the environment.

The EPA, OSHA, and local regulations require that hazardous materials are labeled and properly stored. Service shops must keep accurate records of all hazardous materials kept on hand. Once you are done working with any hazardous material, you must dispose of it in the specified holding container.

Generally a shop has arrangements with a local waste handling service to pick up and properly dispose of all hazardous wastes. Your shop must have all waste material containers clearly identified, in accordance with hazardous materials handling regulations. This is necessary so the disposal service knows what materials they are handling and how to protect and dispose of each hazardous material. Such handling is necessary to protect our water and land from becoming contaminated with dangerous materials.

You are probably already aware of the contamination from lead (found in used engine coolant), mercury, and used motor oils. You need to know which materials are classified hazardous so you can take appropriate steps to ensure your safety and the safety of the environment.

Recycling

Recycling any toxic material is critical. It is also an important part of heating and air conditioning service. As already discussed, recovery of discharged refrigerant is a requirement under current laws. The same holds true for coolant being drained from the radiator—it is illegal to dump used coolant into sewers, drains, or let it run off into the ground.

There are two aspects to recycling. The first is to recover and collect used toxic materials, like coolant and refrigerants, so they can be disposed of properly. Often, used materials can be recycled by specialty waste treatment companies and remanufactured into the same or other usable materials.

The second aspect of recycling is on the spot reuse of the same material that has been properly drained and collected or recovered. In some service situations, it may be appropriate to reuse the same coolant or the recovered and recycled refrigerant. In these cases you will want to be sure the coolant is clean and not contaminated; then it can safely be reinstalled.

Recycling has a big impact on your community. Your recycling efforts are environmentally beneficial, help conserve resources, and provide a way to reuse the materials.

THE METRIC SYSTEM

As an automotive technician, you must be able to use the metric system in order to service modern automobiles. While the United States has not adopted the metric system as the official measurement of weights and measures, metric requirements are used throughout the automotive industry. Most vehicles use a majority of metric-sized fasteners, speedometers appear in both standard and metric, and many service specifications are given in metric measurements only. You must have the tools and the knowledge to service vehicles with metric specifications. You need to have some or all of the following types of metric tools:

- Wrenches
- Sockets
- Rulers
- Taps and Dies
- Hand-held testers
- Micrometers and other measuring devices
- Metric-to-standard conversion charts or formulas

In the past, service publications often gave specifications in both standard and metric units as a convenience to technicians. Today you may encounter times when measurements are given only in metric. Luckily, you only need to know five or six metric measures to work on almost any system. The measurements for heating and air conditioning service work are discussed below.

Metric Prefixes

The prefix is the first part of a unit of measurement. For instance, "milli" is the prefix of "millimeter." The prefix of a measurement informs you how large the unit is. All measurements change in units of 10.

The basic unit of length, or distance, in the metric system is the meter. Most of us think of a meter as being slightly longer than a yard. You can determine the size of the units that are smaller than the meter with the following prefixes:

- Centi = one-hundredth of a meter (centimeter)
- Milli = one-thousandth of a meter (millimeter)

A centimeter is equal to 10 mm. A millimeter is equal to about 0.040 inch.

Units of measure that are larger use prefixes to indicate the additional size. These prefixes are not limited to metric units only. The prefixes are used with any unit to indicate the size. The most commonly used terms in automotive applications are:

- Kilo = one thousand units (or times 1,000)
- Mega = one million units (or times 1,000,000)

The same prefixes, figure 1-46, are used to indicate the same basic division or multiples of all units, such as distance, weight, force, torque, volts, amps, pressure, and so forth.

The basic unit of volume is the liter (l). This is equal to the space occupied by a cube that is one-tenth of a meter on each side, and is slightly larger than a quart. The basic unit of weight is the gram (g). One thousand grams make up the most commonly used next largest unit, the kilogram (k), which is 2.2 pounds.

Refer to the appropriate conversion chart, figure 1-47, to determine any metric equivalents to U.S. standards that you need to compute. As you work with metric units, try to think in terms of these units. The biggest danger of conversion is computing an answer that is way off and not recognizing that it is wrong. Try to have a "ballpark" answer in your mind before you convert a measurement, so you will be able to check if your answer is not in the "ballpark."

STANDARD METRIC PREFIXES AND MULTIPLES			
Prefix			
Giga	1,000,000,000	or billion	G
Mega	1,000,000	or million	M
Kilo	1,000	or thousand	k
Hecto	100	or hundred	h
Deka	10	or ten	da
Deci	1/10	or one-tenth	d
Centi	1/100	or one one-hundredth	c
Milli	1/1,000	or one one-thousandth	m
Micro	1/1,000,000	or one one-millionth	μ
Nano	1/1,000,000,000	or one one-billionth	n

Figure 1-46. In the metric system, a prefix designates a specific multiple of 10, no matter what the unit of measure is.

CONVERSIONS BETWEEN DIFFERENT UNITS OF MEASUREMENT

To convert from left to right, multiply by the conversion number. To convert from right to left, divide by the conversion number.

	UNIT	CONVERSION	UNIT
LENGTH	inch	25.4	mm
	foot	0.305	meter
	mile	1.609	kilometer
VOLUME	gallon	3.785	liter
	fluid ounce	29.57	milliliter
	cubic in (in^3)	0.0164	liter
	liter	61	cubic in (in^3)
WEIGHT	pound	0.4538	kilogram
	pound	16	ounce
	ounce	28.35	gram
	ounce	0.02835	kilogram
	kilogram	35.27	ounce
	kilogram	2.2	pound
PRESSURE	psi	6.9	kPa
	psi	2	in-Hg
	BAR	14.5	psi
	kg/cm^2	14.2	psi
TORQUE	in-lb	0.113	Nm
	ft-lb	1.36	Nm
VACUUM	in-Hg	0.5	psi
	in-Hg	25.4	mm-Hg
TEMPERATURE	°C	Multiply by 1.8, then add 32	°F
	°F	Subtract 32, then divide by 1.8	°C

Conversion numbers have been rounded off.

Figure 1-47. Use this chart to convert metric units to or from the U.S. Customary equivalent.

Pressure and Vacuum

There are generally two units of pressure used in the metric system:

- Kilopascals (kPa)
- Kilograms per square centimeters (kg/cm^2)

Kilograms per square centimeter is an older metric measurement, while kilopascals is the newer International Standards Organization (ISO) measurement. The measurement of 1 kPa is 0.145 psi, and 1 kg/cm^2 equals 14.2 psi.

Air conditioning and fuel injection commonly use BAR, which equals 14.5 psi, or 100 kPa. The measurement of kg/cm^2 and BAR are almost the same; in most cases, the difference is not significant. Pressure always refers to any pressure that is higher than atmospheric pressure (positive pressure). When atmospheric pressure is used as the starting point of zero pressure, it is called "gauge" pressure.

When atmospheric pressure is also counted, it is called "absolute" pressure. An absolute pressure reading will start at atmospheric pressure (14.7 psi) at sea level. If you have a gauge reading of 14.7, and your gauge is not connected to a component, you have an absolute pressure reading.

Vacuum or negative pressure refers to the absence of positive pressure. Vacuum is any pressure that is less than atmospheric pressure. When measuring vacuum, both the metric system and the standard system use readings from a mercury barometer. Normal atmospheric pressure lifts a mercury column about 30 inches, or 762 millimeters. The scientific symbol for mercury is Hg. Therefore, these barometric readings are referred to as 30 inches of mercury (30 in-Hg) or 762 mm of mercury (762 mm-Hg). A vacuum reading on an absolute gauge will read less than atmospheric but will show a positive number. Remember that any amount of pressure that is lower than 14.7 psi is vacuum. *For the purpose of this manual, pressure will be "gauge" pressure, and vacuum will be given in in-Hg. Be aware that when using a scan tool, the pressure may be absolute.*

Torque

Torque is the measurement of the twisting force that is required to move an object, such as the specification that is commonly used for tightening bolts. The metric measurement of torque is the Newton-meter (Nm). This corresponds to the standard of the foot-pound (ft-lb). One Nm equals 0.7376 ft-lbs.

Torque wrenches, the special tools that you use to set fasteners to their torque settings, have adjustable settings to remove all the guesswork. Note whether you are using a standard or metric torque wrench. Also note that some torque wrenches measure inch-pounds instead of foot-pounds.

Temperature

In the United States, temperature is measured in degrees of Fahrenheit (°F). In most other countries (and in the metric conversions in your service information), temperature is measured in degrees of Celsius (°C).

- To convert from °F to °C, subtract 32 from the °F reading, and then divide by 1.8. The result will be °C.
- To convert from °C to °F, multiply the °C reading by 1.8, then add 32. The result will be °F.

SOME FINAL SAFETY REMINDERS

There are a lot of new and revised service rules and regulations governing heating and AC service. Be aware of these rules and follow them. They are designed for your safety, to help ensure proper service and repairs, and to meet environmental and federal regulations.

- When doing any service that may result in discharging refrigerant, it is required by law that you always use approved recovery/recycling equipment.
- If you find a leak during service and inspection, offer to make the proper repairs. This will provide optimal system operation for the customer. However, at this time, repairing AC system leaks is not required by law.
- Be sure that you understand which refrigerants are available and approved for use by the EPA. Check each system's requirements with accurate vehicle service information before proceeding. New alternative refrigerants may come onto the market in the next few years. Make sure you understand what kinds of special service procedures may be needed. Do not attempt to shortcut any repairs or use a questionable refrigerant alternative.
- Remember that R-12 and R-134a are the only vehicle manufacturer approved refrigerants. The use of any other refrigerant as an alternative to R-12 may cause system damage or inadequate performance.
- Remember that R-134a and R-12, or any other refrigerants, do not mix in any amounts. Use extreme caution to make sure contamination does not occur.
- Read and understand any bulletins, notices, or late-breaking industry information about changes in heating and air conditioning. Along with trade organizations and industry magazines, there are many automotive and government websites that offer valuable information for the modern technician.

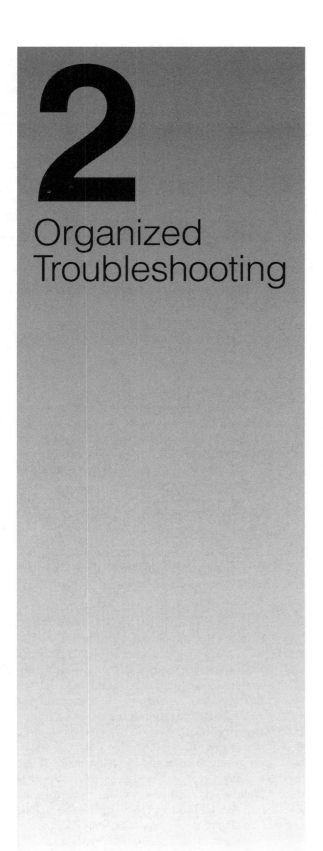

2

Organized
Troubleshooting

To effectively diagnose and repair heating, ventilation, and air conditioning (HVAC) problems, you must develop organized troubleshooting strategies. Diagnosing the source of the malfunction is a process of elimination that begins with general area checks and leads to specific circuit and component tests. Bypassing a test to take a shortcut often ends with inconclusive results that are more time-consuming in the long run.

An important part of any repair is finding the correct information to fix it. There are several sources available, which will be introduced in this chapter. After you obtain a manual, locating the exact information needed sometimes presents a challenge. Some manuals are laid out in a manner that is easy to understand, while others require a more detailed search to locate the information. This chapter details common information found in service manuals and other sources. Spend some time reading the various information sources to become familiar with the different ways that manufacturers organize their information.

ORGANIZED TROUBLESHOOTING

When repairing an HVAC system, always take the same approach in your diagnosis, so you can quickly and easily find the problem. Diagnosis and repair should follow a logical approach similar to the one outlined below.

1. Identify the complaint
2. Verify the complaint
3. Familiarize yourself with the system
4. Test systematically
5. Performance test
6. Verify the test results
7. Make the repairs
8. Verify the repairs

Identify the Complaint

Accurate diagnosis begins with understanding exactly what the problem is, and the only person who can provide this information is the customer, figure 2-1. Ask the customer, or make sure that the service writer asks specific questions, to determine if the problem is a result of other service, if it occurred suddenly, or if it appears intermittently. Typical customer questions include:

- Does the problem exist all the time or some of the time? Does it occur regularly or randomly? Is it happening now?
- When was the last time that the problem occurred? Was it while accelerating or climbing hills? Was the engine hot, had it been sitting overnight, or somewhere in-between?

Figure 2-1. Ask your customer to detail exactly what the problem is.

- What are the symptoms? Are there noises, vibrations, smells, or performance problems?

Find out if the problem is new or if it has occurred before. Have any repairs been performed to fix the problem? If so, what was done and when? When was the last time that the vehicle was serviced and what was done to it? It is important to understand what type of information you need to get from the customer in order to make an accurate diagnosis. It is also important to get all the information before you begin troubleshooting.

Verify the Complaint

Keep in mind that the way a customer describes a problem is probably very different from the way you would describe it. Therefore, it is important to verify the complaint. Do not attempt to make a repair unless you have actually experienced the symptoms of the problem. If your work order states "no heat," make sure that there is no heat coming from the vents. If the problem is "low heat," the source of the problem may be very different. A performance test of the system should be performed to verify correct operation of the entire system. Many times a customer may only notice one symptom when in fact there may be other symptoms present. The performance test will verify proper operation of the entire HVAC system.

Familiarize Yourself with the System

Familiarize yourself with the particular system being serviced. What type of air conditioning system does the vehicle have? Are the related systems, such as the electrical and cooling systems, functioning properly?

Even though all air conditioning systems operate in a similar manner, each system has unique features. These differences require accurate service information for the particular system and vehicle application. Begin troubleshooting by reviewing the vehicle service manual to get a general idea of what components and circuits are involved. Also review technical service bulletins that apply to the model being serviced to determine if the symptoms fit any of the identified pattern failures. Technical service bulletins are available from the vehicle manufacturers, aftermarket suppliers, and online services. Compare the complaint to the system and note the possible causes.

Test Systematically

The most efficient way of isolating the source of a failure is to test the system systematically. Begin with a visual inspection, then conduct a performance test to evaluate the system. The visual inspection should include the following:

- Compressor—Does it engage, are there any signs of overheating, is it noisy?
- Hoses and lines—Are any hoses broken or damaged, or do they show signs of obvious leakage?
- Condenser—Is there any physical damage or signs of leakage?
- Cooling system—Is the cooling fan engaged or are there signs of overheating?
- Control devices—Check electrical connections of compressor controls for loose or disconnected connectors.

Inspect all of the components for proper mounting and any signs of damage. Make any needed repairs before conducting a system performance test.

Performance Test

A performance test is simply operating the HVAC system on all settings to determine how well it performs and responds to control settings. Before starting the engine, a manifold gauge set may be attached to the system so that pressures may be read. Performance tests vary somewhat between different manufacturers; however, many are similar.

With the engine off, pressure in the system should be equal to or greater than the ambient temperature. If not, there is low refrigerant or no refrigerant in the system. If there is liquid refrigerant in the system, use a refrigerant identifier to verify that the correct refrigerant is installed and that it doesn't have an excess amount of air in it.

Next, start and run the engine. Place a thermometer in the center outlet duct, then switch the AC on. Verify that the clutch engages. If not, switch the system and the engine off and troubleshoot the cause of no clutch engagement. A clutch that rapidly cycles on and off generally indicates a low refrigerant condition. If the charge is low, add enough refrigerant to ensure proper AC clutch operation. Leak test the system to find the cause of the low refrigerant condition.

Operate the system on all settings to verify that all modes work correctly and all blower speeds work. Compare the discharge temperature to specifications in the service manual.

Verify the Test Results

Verify the test results before replacing any parts or components. If the malfunctioning component is electrical, make sure that all the electrical inputs to that component are present and at the specified levels. Make sure that all the connections are clean and tight. Never replace an electrical component before verifying all voltage signals and grounds. Keep in mind that loose and corroded connections, particularly on the ground side, cause more electrical problems than component failures do. A voltage drop of 0.1 volt or more on a ground circuit can cause trouble. Make certain to clean the connections and retest.

Make Repairs

Before beginning your repair, lay out all the tools that you will need. Be especially careful when repairing electrical parts, such as a wiring harness. Some circuits have a very narrow tolerance for resistance. The wrong gauge of wire or poor splice can cause worse problems than you started with. Always work carefully and pay attention to detail.

Verify the Repair

The final part of the troubleshooting is to verify your repair. If you retest the circuit or system, and the problem is gone, your repair is complete. However, sometimes a circuit has more than one problem, and the second one is not apparent until the first one is repaired. In these cases, resume troubleshooting from the point the repair was made. After the repairs are complete, test drive the vehicle to make sure there are no longer any symptoms present. Double-checking your repair work with a test drive can avoid frustration with your customer later on and prevent a comeback.

REFERENCE MATERIAL

There are a number of different information sources to reference when performing HVAC diagnosis and repair. The four most common sources are:

1. Original equipment manufacturer service manuals
2. Aftermarket repair manuals

3. Electronic databases
4. Underhood labels or decals

Useful service information can also be found in technical training manuals, professional trade magazines, parts catalogs, newsletters, and other publications. Although these sources usually lack the detailed procedures and specifications that you need to perform specific repairs, they are a good source of general service information and information on updates or common problems.

When using repair information, remember that accuracy is critical. Do not assume that the specifications for one model year are the same as the specifications for the same vehicle for the next model year. Find the correct specifications for the specific vehicle being serviced.

Manufacturer's Service Manuals

Nearly all the service information for HVAC systems originates with the vehicle manufacturer. Manufacturer's repair manuals are often referred to as "OEM" (Original Equipment Manufacturer) manuals, figure 2-2. Service information and specifications may be located in several different places in the manufacturer's service manuals, along with the diagnostic, repair, and component overhaul procedures. Vehicle manufacturers typically publish a new service manual every year, with service information for that year only.

Information is grouped by the system being serviced. At the beginning of each section is an index to locate the specification or procedure you are interested in. Vehicle service manuals contain the maintenance schedules, specifications, and test and repair information for all systems and components on the vehicle. Manufacturer service manuals usually will contain the

Figure 2-2. OEM manuals usually provide the most comprehensive diagnostic and repair information. (Reprinted with permission of General Motors Corporation.)

most accurate and complete service information that is available from any source. If available, they should be your source of information to aid in diagnosing and repairing HVAC systems. However, if you are working for an independent repair facility that performs repairs on many different types of vehicles, it is unlikely that these will be available to you. Most aftermarket repair facilities rely on service information provided in aftermarket repair manuals.

Aftermarket Repair Manuals

Several aftermarket companies publish repair manuals also, figure 2-3, using information obtained from OEM repair manuals, or from actual service procedures developed by disassembling and reassembling vehicles. Aftermarket repair manuals are typically written to combine service specifications and procedures for several vehicle models and years, without losing any critical information.

Most aftermarket repair manuals are written about specific systems for many vehicles rather than all systems for one vehicle. For instance, a manual may cover fluid specifications with a 10-year coverage of most domestic and foreign vehicles. Since aftermarket manuals cover a wide range of vehicles, they are generally indexed by the vehicle year, make, and model. There are also "do-it-yourself" manuals that provide multi-year coverage of all the systems for a single model. These manuals generally do not provide enough information for the professional technician and generally should not be relied upon for repair information.

Electronic Databases

In recent years, manufacturers and aftermarket companies have begun to supply information in electronic formats—

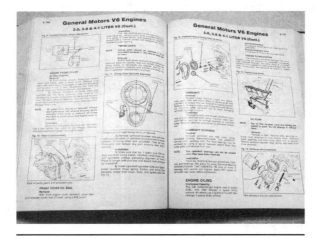

Figure 2-3. Several aftermarket companies produce repair manuals for the professional technician.

Figure 2-4. Electronic databases are becoming popular due to the large volume of service information required.

typically on computer compact disc (CD–ROM), figure 2-4. A computer and the proper software are required to access the data on the CD–ROM. Some service bay machines, such as engine analyzers, scan tools, or the alignment rack, may also have an electronic database in them. More recently, these databases are being offered on the Internet by subscription. This allows you to always have the most current information available to you. Some OEM manufacturers, as well as aftermarket information providers, are offering Internet access.

Underhood Labels

Underhood labels are a valuable source of service information. These are sometimes attached to the underside of the hood, the radiator support, a strut tower, or a component such as an air conditioning compressor, figure 2-5. The Vehicle Emissions Control Information (VECI) label, figure 2-6, provides specifications such as engine size, tune-up data, a vacuum diagram, and other data.

The EPA requires an alternative refrigerant label if the system has been retrofitted, figure 2-7. The manufacturer of new vehicles, or technicians retrofitting used vehicles, must apply an alterative refrigerant label to identify what type of refrigerant is installed in the system. The label provides the following information:

- The type, amount, and, if applicable, ASHRAE numerical designation of the alternate refrigerant
- The technician and the name and address of the shop or dealer that performed the retrofit

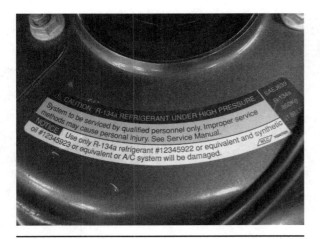

Figure 2-5. The refrigerant label under the hood supplies information about the type and amount of refrigerant, as well as the refrigerant oil required.

Figure 2-6. The Vehicle Emissions Control Information (VECI) label provides a vacuum diagram and emission control system information. (Reprinted with permission of Ford Motor Company.)

NOTICE: RETROFITTED to R-134a

Caution: System to be serviced by qualified personnel only.

R-134a Refrigerant Amount: _____ lbs. _____ oz.

Date: _____ Oil Type: _____ Amount: ____ oz.

Oil Mfg: _____ Technician: _____

Dealer Name: _____

Address: _____

City: _____ State: _____ Zip: _____

Figure 2-7. The alternative refrigerant label provides valuable information about the AC system.

- The type, manufacturer of, and the amount of refrigerant oil
- The phrase "ozone depleter" when applicable

ALTERNATIVE REFRIGERANT LABEL BACKGROUND COLORS	
Refrigerant	**Background Color**
R-12	White
R-134a	Sky Blue
Freeze 12	Yellow
Free Zone (RB276)	Light Green
Hot Shot	Medium Blue
GHG-X4	Red
R406A	Black
GHG-X5	Orange
FRIGC (FR12)	Gray

Figure 2-8. The background color of alternative refrigerant labels is unique for each refrigerant.

In a further effort to identify different refrigerants, the background color of the label is unique for each type of refrigerant, figure 2-8.

Occasionally, there is a discrepancy between the label and information found in a manual. When this occurs, the label data is usually correct.

Other Information Sources

Manufacturers sometimes need to address repair issues that are not covered in the service manual. Technical Service Bulletins (TSBs) help technicians solve unusual repair problems. A TSB may introduce new or revised repair specifications, new or revised repair procedures, repair cautions, or warnings. A TSB may describe a normal condition that your customers commonly perceive as a problem. A vehicle may have a problem caused by a substandard part that was installed at the factory. With this type of problem, the TSB directs you to verify the VIN (which identifies the manufacturing plant and model year), verify the symptom of the problem, and perform the repair with the correct replacement part. Having the symptoms and a possible repair of a problem spelled out can save a lot of diagnostic time. Being aware of pattern failures, or common repairs made to a vehicle, saves time before a vehicle enters the service bay. Researching bulletins should be part of your diagnostic procedure.

A telephone technical hotline, staffed by diagnostic and repair experts, is a valuable resource when normal procedures fail to solve a problem. There are a large number of technical hotlines in the automotive industry. Some are operated by vehicle manufacturers for the benefit of their dealerships, some are operated by aftermarket companies for the benefit of paying subscribers, and others are run by parts companies in order to support the use of their specific parts. Before using these hotlines you need to ensure that you have exhausted your other sources of information, performed all the diagnostic tests required, and thoroughly checked the system. Failure to do so will cause unnecessary expense or wasted time.

Another information resource is the Internet. There are many websites and forums for professional automotive technicians to share opinions, ask questions of other technicians, view automotive product advertisements and information, as well as give and receive troubleshooting advice. The largest such service is the International Automotive Technicians Network, www.iATN.net, with almost 40,000 members.

FINDING SPECIFIC SERVICE INFORMATION

After you retrieve a manual or database, you need to know certain information about the vehicle that you are servicing in order to find the applicable reference information needed. Usually you begin with the:

- Year, make, and model
- Type of system
- Vehicle Identification Number

You may need additional details about the vehicle as you go along, such as engine displacement.

The Vehicle Identification Number

The Vehicle Identification Number (VIN) is often used when ordering parts. The VIN is a code that identifies the year, make, engine, body, style, manufacturing plant, and other information about the vehicle. The breakdown of the numbers and letters is listed in the front section of service manuals.

The VIN is stamped into a small metal plate that is attached to the driver's side of the dashboard at the base of the windshield. It is viewed from outside of the vehicle, figure 2-9. The VIN is also on the vehicle in-

formation plate on the driver's side door pillar, and portions of the VIN may be found on other parts of the vehicle.

Service specifications may be different for the same vehicle, or even two vehicles of the same year, make, and model. These differences may be based on production changes at the factory, different markets for which the vehicle is built, or differences in other equipment on the vehicle. In these cases, the VIN is used to determine which specification applies to the vehicle in service. Which specifications apply may also depend upon the date that the vehicle was built. The production date is printed on a decal found on the driver's doorjamb. *Note that the build date should not be used to determine the model year of the vehicle.*

Troubleshooting Flowcharts

A troubleshooting flowchart lists different symptoms matched with logical, step-by-step inspection points. Flowcharts, also known as trouble trees or by other names, lead through a structured testing procedure where each step builds on the previous one. A flow-

SYMPTOM		REMEDY
No hot air flow.	Blower motor does not run.	Perform the flow chart (page 21-9).
	Blower motor runs.	Check the following: • Clogged blower outlet • Clogged heater valve • Faulty air mix door • Air mix cable out of adjustment • Faulty thermostat (section 10).
Hot air flow is low.	Blower speed does not change.	Perform flow chart (page 21-14).
	Blower runs properly.	Check the following: • Clogged blower outlet • Incorrect door position.
Function does not change.	Function control motor does not run.	Perform flow chart (page 21-18).
	Function control motor runs.	Check the heater door linkage.
Recirculation door does not change.	Recirculation motor does not run.	Perform flow chart (page 21-16).
	Recirculation motor runs.	Check the door linkage or perform flow chart (page 21-16).

Figure 2-9. The Vehicle Identification Number (VIN) is easily viewed from outside the car.

Figure 2-10. A typical diagnostic flowchart lists symptoms, possible causes, and references to the remedy or to other diagnostic procedures in the manual.

STEP	ACTION	VALUE	YES	NO
	DTC C0330 AC REFRIGERANT PRESSURE SENSOR CIRCUIT			
1	Has the Powertrain OBD System Check been performed?	—	Proceed to Step 5	Proceed to Powertrain OBD System Check
2	Observe the refrigerant pressure voltage. Is the voltage less than the specification?	0.1V	Proceed to Step 8	Proceed to Step 6
3	Is the refrigerant pressure sensor voltage greater than the specification?	4.8V	Proceed to Step 7	Refer to Diagnostic Aids
4	Disconnect the refrigerant pressure sensor while reading the sensor voltage with a scan tool. Does the scan tool read voltage near the specification?	0.0V	Proceed to Step 15	Proceed to Step 14
5	a. Disconnect the refrigerant pressure sensor. b. Connect a fused jumper between the terminals for the refrigerant pressure signal circuit and the 5-volt reference circuit at the refrigerant pressure sensor harness connector. c. Read the refrigerant pressure sensor voltage with a scan tool. Does the scan tool read voltage near the specified value?	5.0V	Proceed to Step 19	Proceed to Step 9

Figure 2-11. A trouble code diagnostic flowchart may have several different logical checks depending on the result of the previous step.

chart begins with a general check and each step narrows the choices down to pinpoint the problem. Figure 2-10 is a simple troubleshooting flowchart. Figure 2-11 is a portion of a complex diagnostic flowchart for an air conditioning fault. This flowchart branches off in several different ways depending on the results of each step.

It is important to remember that a diagnostic chart was created to help technicians follow a logical diagnostic sequence. If you skip a step in the diagnostic chart, you are, in effect, ignoring the logical sequence. Because each step was written to verify or eliminate a particular aspect of system function, and because the process is connected with other steps, skipping steps can lead to wasted time or an incorrect diagnosis.

Service Manual Illustrations

Once you have located a possible problem area and need to examine the area in detail, there are several types of reference materials available to guide your troubleshooting procedure. These may include:

1. An exploded view illustration. This shows you:
   - The relationship of components
   - The proper mounting and attachments to other components
   - The complete list of parts that a component should have
2. A specification table. This shows you:
   - Test parameters
   - Manufacturer's specifications
   - Component capacities

3. A wiring diagram. This shows you:
   - Where the circuit receives battery voltage
   - Which switches control current flow
   - Which devices use current flow
   - Where the circuit is grounded
4. A vacuum diagram. This shows you:
   - The source vacuum
   - Where the hoses should be connected
   - What devices are affected by the presence or absence of vacuum

Wiring Diagrams

A wiring diagram is an extremely useful troubleshooting tool. Manufacturers create a wiring diagram for all the vehicles that they produce. These diagrams show you, on paper, how a particular electrical circuit is constructed, figure 2-12. You will find it practically impossible to troubleshoot a problem in an electrical circuit without using a wiring diagram.

It can be difficult to match the circuits on the wiring diagram to the actual circuits on the vehicle. To make it easier, the insulation on the vehicle's wiring is color-coded for identification. The color is identified on the electrical diagram. When you are under the dash attempting to trace a wire, you will understand how important color-coding is. A wire harness may have 50 wires, which makes it hard to see the ends of the wires to determine what components the wires are connected to. With color-coding, you can trace each wire and confirm it is connected to the correct component. In the diagram, the color-code is usually abbreviated in a two-letter code, such as "BK" for black. Generally, wiring diagrams have a legend that describes the color-coding abbreviations, figure 2-13.

Electrical components, such as motors, fuses, switches, bulbs, relays, and other devices, are identified by electrical symbols on the wiring diagrams, figure 2-14. There are also common electrical symbols that identify ground, circuit breakers, contact points, and so on within a circuit. Some of these are shown in figure 2-15. The electrical symbols may vary slightly; however, they are usually similar.

Tracing electrical circuits can be somewhat difficult at first. Electrical diagrams can be rather complex and appear confusing. Sometimes it is useful to trace or draw the electrical circuit, or a portion of one electrical circuit, onto a blank sheet of paper so that you are

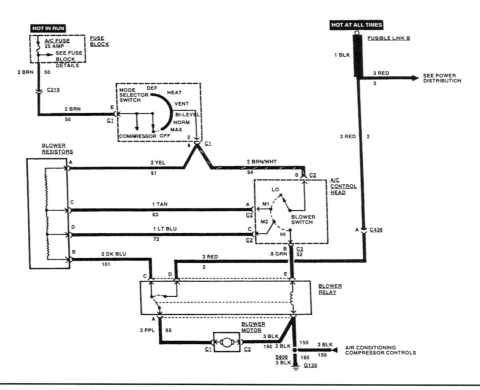

Figure 2-12. This portion of an electrical schematic shows the blower motor and relay circuits in a modern heating, ventilation, and air conditioning system. (Courtesy of General Motors.)

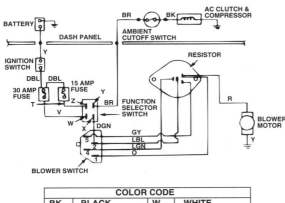

Figure 2-13. This legend identifies the color-code abbreviations found on a wiring diagram.

COLOR CODE			
BK	BLACK	W	WHITE
BR	BROWN	LBL	LIGHT BLUE
DBL	DARK BLUE	O	ORANGE
DGN	DARK GREEN	T	TAN
GY	GRAY	LGN	LIGHT GREEN
R	RED	Y	YELLOW

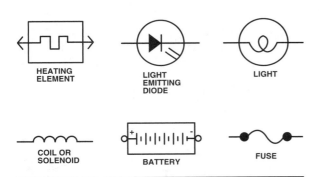

Figure 2-14. Common automotive wiring diagram symbols and the hardware they represent.

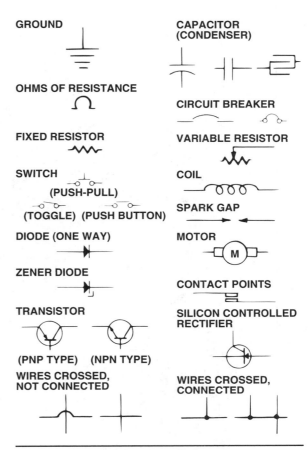

Figure 2-15. Common electrical symbols. Different manufacturers may use different symbols.

examining only one circuit at a time. It is important to remember that all circuits share these traits:

- A power source
- Load devices that perform work, such as motors, bulbs, and solenoids
- A path to ground for every branch of the circuit
- In most circuits, a control device such as a switch

When testing electrical circuits, it is important to remember the electrical principles that govern how the circuit operates. These are discussed in Chapter 4 of the *Classroom Manual*.

Some diagrams are arranged by a specific system circuit and its component. Other wiring diagrams represent the entire vehicle. Some wiring diagrams are sectioned into grids, or broken down into specific sections, corresponding to sections of the vehicle. Sometimes it is a challenge to find the exact location of a component, so manufacturers publish "component locator" illustrations which identify surrounding components for reference, figure 2-16.

Vacuum Diagrams

You will find that heating and ventilation doors are often operated by vacuum. Vacuum is applied in response to mode settings on the control panel. A series of color-coded vacuum hoses attach the control panel to the respective air doors and their vacuum motors.

COMPONENT PARTS LOCATION

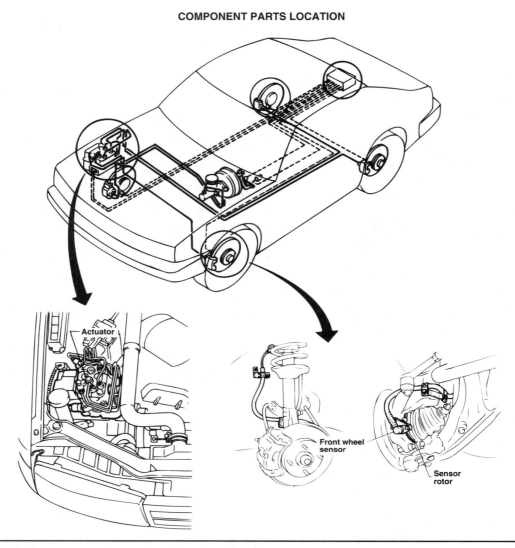

Figure 2-16. A component locator illustration identifies the exact location of an electrical component.

You will need a vacuum diagram in order to troubleshoot vacuum problems. A vacuum diagram of the system will show you how the vacuum hoses should be routed, where connections are made, and the color hose that should be connected from one point to another.

This type of vacuum diagram shows the vacuum actuators, and when they are applied for the different doors. The chart is used to determine when vacuum should or should not be applied to a specific vacuum motor, figure 2-17.

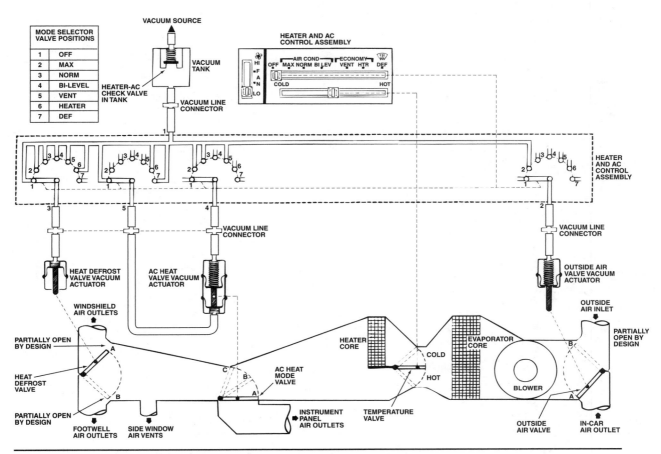

Figure 2-17. A vacuum motor test chart shows you how the heating system is laid out and how the vacuum motors are actuated. (Reprinted with permission of General Motors Corporation.)

3

HVAC Equipment, Recovery, and Charging

THE MANIFOLD GAUGE SET

The manifold gauge set is the primary air conditioning diagnostic and service tool. The gauge set may be a portable unit, or an integral part of an air conditioning charging station. The manifold gauge set enables you to:

- Monitor the pressure inside an operating air conditioning system during diagnosis
- Monitor and control the flow of refrigerant vapor into the system during recharging
- Access the system for recovery, evacuation, and service

Since refrigerant pressure is directly related to refrigerant temperature, system pressures are a major element of determining the performance of the system. The manifold gauge is used to measure system performance, and for diagnosing most air conditioning problems.

As already covered, different refrigerants cannot be mixed. All service equipment discussed in this chapter is dedicated for either R-12 or R-134a refrigerant. If you are servicing a vehicle with another type of refrigerant, you must use dedicated service equipment for that type of refrigerant. Never use dedicated equipment on another type of refrigerant or you will contaminate your service equipment and, therefore, any vehicles serviced with that equipment in the future.

The manifold gauge set service hose fittings must match the service fittings for each type of refrigerant. The R-134a gauge set has quick-disconnect couplings and the R-12 set has Schrader valve fittings, figures 3-1 and 3-2.

The Manifold Gauge Set

A portable, hand-held manifold gauge set consists of the center manifold, two or more valves, and two gauges, figure 3-3. The manifold valves are used to open the service hoses to the center hose for evacuation and recharging operations.

The left side of the manifold gauge is the low-pressure side and is color-coded blue to indicate low pressure. The right-side gauge is the high-pressure gauge and is color-coded red to indicate high pressure. Some manifold valves may be marked HI or LO instead of being color-coded. All R-134a hoses are marked R-134a and may have a thick, black stripe to further identify them as R-134a hoses. The R-134a low-side fitting is smaller in diameter to match the R-134a low-side service fitting on the vehicle. This prevents accidentally connecting the low-side hose to the high-side fitting on the vehicle. Similarly, the R-12 high-side service hose fitting is smaller than the

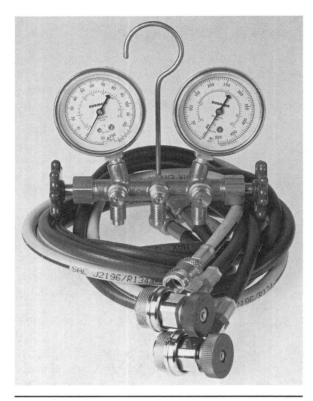

Figure 3-1. A manifold gauge set is a versatile tool for diagnosing problems in an air conditioning system. It also provides some assistance during service operations.

Figure 3-2. The R-12 gauge set has Schrader valve fittings.

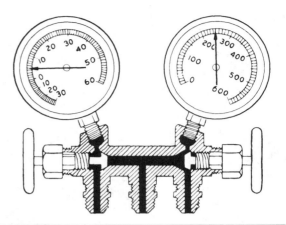

Figure 3-3. Valves and gauges on the manifold allow you to read the pressure in either the low- or the high-pressure side on an air conditioning system.

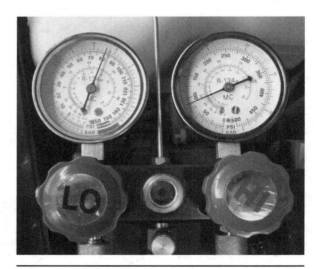

Figure 3-4. The gauge set will register the pressure in the low and high side without opening the gauge valves.

low-side service hose fitting. Some R-12 systems require that an adapter be attached to the high-side hose to connect to the high-side fitting of the vehicle.

The third hose, usually yellow in color, is used for adding and removing refrigerant from the system. The

vacuum pump, recovery unit, refrigerant supply, or oil canister are attached to the center fitting of the manifold as needed.

When both the low- and high-side valves are closed, each gauge registers the amount of pressure in the respective sides of the system, figure 3-4. When the low-side valve is opened, the low-side of the system is connected through the manifold to the center port, so that refrigerant can be added or removed. Gauge readings at that time may or may not be accurate. A gauge reading should be taken only when both valves are closed.

When the high-side valve is opened, the high side is connected to the center port of the manifold. This

Figure 3-5. The low-side gauge measures both pressure and vacuum.

Figure 3-6. This compound gauge measures both pressure and vacuum.

valve should only be opened when evacuation or recovery procedures are in progress. *The high-side gauge valve should never be opened when the system is operating as the high pressure in the system can cause injury or damage.*

Most manifold gauge sets have one low-pressure and one high-pressure gauge. The low-pressure gauge is called a compound gauge, because it registers both pressure and vacuum. The pressure side of the gauge reads in psi while the vacuum side of the gauge reads in inches of mercury (in-Hg). A typical compound gauge, figure 3-5, registers pressure by deflecting the needle clockwise from zero, and vacuum by deflecting the needle counterclockwise from zero.

A compound gauge generally reads up to 30 in-Hg (760 mm-Hg) of vacuum and up to 120 psi (830 kPa) of pressure. The high-side gauge generally reads pressure from 0 to 600 psi (0 to 4,100 kPa).

NOTE: Look at the gauge in figure 3-6. Along with R-12, R-22 and R-502 scales are displayed on the gauge. R-22 and R-502 are industrial refrigerants. The same manifold gauge set can be used in industrial as well as automotive applications. Make certain you are reading the correct scale.

Many shops use a charging station, figure 3-7, which combines the manifold gauge set with a vacuum pump for system evacuation, and houses refrigerant cylinders and scales for accurately measured recharg-

ing. Some stations perform additional functions, such as metered oil replacement, refrigerant contamination testing, and refrigerant recovery and recycling.

Shut-Off Valves

Shut-off valves are required within 12 inches of the end of each service hose to prevent refrigerant that is in the hose from venting to the atmosphere when connecting and disconnecting the hoses. Some equipment manufacturers use quick-disconnect service fittings, which shut off automatically when the hose is detached. Some shut-off valves are manual, figure 3-8. Make certain that the manual shut-off valves are closed before connecting and disconnecting service hoses to the system service fittings.

Gauge Calibration and Altitude Adjustments

Measurement tools that are frequently used tend to become unbalanced and require periodic adjustment. For instance, a pressure gauge that is not connected to an air conditioning system may show pressure readings, instead of the needle at zero. On a measurement tool, each graduation is called a caliber. When a tool is showing an incorrect reading, the tool is out of calibration.

It is simple to calibrate a pressure gauge with a small adjustment. Most low-pressure gauges are calibrated by setting the pointer to the zero mark. This is usually accomplished by removing the plastic lens cover and adjusting the calibration screw located on

Figure 3-7. The portable recovery/recycling/recharging station must be dedicated service equipment that meets EPA and SAE specifications. (Courtesy of Robinair.)

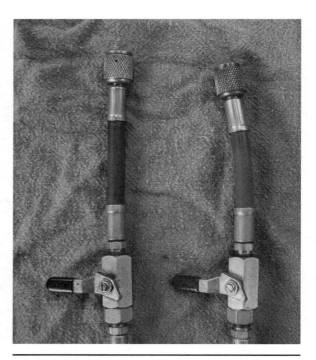

Figure 3-8. These R-12 hoses have shut-off valves installed within 12 inches from the ends of the hoses.

Figure 3-9. To calibrate a gauge, turn the screw until the gauge needle is set exactly to zero.

the gauge face, figure 3-9. Refer to the equipment manual for your particular tool to find out the calibration procedure.

Pressure is typically read in pounds per square inch (psi), or in the metric unit kilopascals (kPa), with a reading of zero starting at sea level. This is sometimes referred to in air conditioning service as pounds per square inch gauge (psig), which refers to the reading shown on a manifold gauge set. Vacuum is typically read in inches of mercury (in-Hg) or millimeters of mercury (mm-Hg).

Since atmospheric pressure varies with altitude, gauge pressure and vacuum readings also vary with altitude. As altitude increases, gauge readings for both

ALTITUDE PRESSURE VARIATIONS CHART		
Altitude (Ft. Above Sea Level)	Absolute Atmospheric Pressure (psia)	Gauge Reading Correction (psi)[1]
0	14.7	0
1,000	14.2	0.5
2,000	13.7	1.0
3,000	13.2	1.5
4,000	12.7	2.0
5,000	12.2	2.5
6,000	11.7	3.0
7,000	11.3	3.4
8,000	10.9	3.8
9,000	10.5	4.2
10,000	10.1	4.6
[1]Add correction shown to gauge readings.		

Figure 3-10. Make certain to account for altitude changes.

ALTITUDE VACUUM VARIATIONS		
Altitude (Ft. Above Sea Level)	Complete Vacuum (in-Hg)	Gauge Reading Correction (in-Hg)[1]
0	29.92	0
1,000	28.92	1.0
2,000	27.82	2.1
3,000	26.82	3.1
4,000	25.82	4.1
5,000	24.92	5.0
6,000	23.92	6.0
7,000	23.02	6.9
8,000	22.22	7.7
9,000	21.32	8.6
10,000	20.52	9.4
[1]Add correction shown to gauge readings.		

Figure 3-11. Vacuum also experiences altitude changes.

pressure and vacuum lower in value. For example, a vacuum gauge reading of 18 in-Hg at sea level is equivalent to a vacuum gauge reading of 13 in-Hg at 5,000 feet in altitude. Use the charts in figure 3-10 or 3-11 to adjust gauge readings when servicing an air conditioning system.

The Recovery/Recycling Station

It is illegal to discharge any kind of refrigerant directly into the atmosphere. Therefore, it is necessary to have equipment that will capture the refrigerant as it is be-

ing recovered and store it for recycling or disposal. This is one of the key functions of the recovery/recycling station. A recovery/recycling/recharging station also includes recharging the refrigerant. Other functions of this station include:

- A built-in source for vacuum to evacuate the system after recovery
- The ability to control the amount of refrigerant and oil being charged
- In some stations, monitoring new refrigerant from approved containers

Figure 3-12. Most shops use a combination recovery/recycling/recharging station instead of different pieces of equipment for R-134a systems.

Some of these systems may have a monitoring system for temperature, digital displays, and automated controls for easier, more accurate equipment operation. The new generation of recovery/recycling/recharging stations, figure 3-12, replaces the older style portable charging station. Due to changes in environmental and hazardous materials regulations, it is mandatory that air conditioning service shops have recycling/recovery stations for both R-12 and R-134a refrigerants.

Since different refrigerants become contaminated when mixed, each recovery/recycling station is refrigerant specific. Some stations are dual refrigerant machines that service both R-12 and R-134a; you must evacuate the service lines before you switch the refrigerant. Some dual stations have two complete systems to recover R-12 and R-134a. Most shops have dedicated, single-refrigerant machines for each type of refrigerant system that is serviced. Never mix refrigerants if you have a dedicated recycling/recovery station.

There are three types of recovery equipment:

• Recovery only
• Recovery and recycling
• Recovery, recycling, and recharging

Most equipment is dedicated to one type of refrigerant, although some equipment is capable of handling multiple refrigerants. Some stations have built-in gauges, while other units require a separate manifold gauge set to be connected to the vehicle.

A recovery only station uses a compressor to pump the refrigerant into a storage tank. When the tank is full, the refrigerant is recycled. Recycling may be performed on site, or picked up for recycling off site.

With a recovery only station, system evacuation and charging are performed using other equipment.

A typical recovery and recycling station works like an air conditioning system, figure 3-13. The compressor in the recovery and recycling station draws liquid refrigerant from the holding tank to an expansion valve and heat exchanger/oil separator. The refrigerant changes to a vapor and passes through the filter/drier core where moisture and particles are removed. The vaporized refrigerant then travels to the compressor, compressor oil separator, and heat exchanger where it is converted back to liquid. Finally, the refrigerant passes through a moisture indicator and returns to the holding tank, where it begins the process loop again. When refrigerant recycling is complete, the refrigerant is clean and moisture free. The refrigerant remains in the holding tank until ready for reuse. A charging station is then connected to the holding tank to recharge another air conditioning system. This type of equipment does not provide evacuation or recharging functions.

The recovery, recycling, and recharging station, figures 3-14a and b, provides the most convenient means to service air conditioning systems. While it provides the same recycling functions as the recovery and recycling equipment, it also incorporates system evacuation and recharging functions. Most of these machines have advanced features to make system service easier, such as exact measurement of the refrigerant removed and installed in a system, heated cylinder charging, and automatic sequences for routine functions such as evacuating and recharge. When using any of these types of equipment, it is important to read the equipment manufacturer's directions for use. Since different machines have different features, familiarize yourself with the machine before you attach it to the air conditioning system.

Do not use disposable refrigerant containers for storing recycled refrigerant. Use only DOT CFR Title 49- or UL-approved containers for recycled refrigerant. Note that these tanks must be retested every five years to ensure that they are safe, figure 3-15. Additionally, storage containers must not be filled to more than 80 percent volume of liquid refrigerant. Exceeding this percentage can potentially lead to explosion due to thermal expansion of the liquid refrigerant, figure 3-16.

Refrigerant Identification

You must identify the type of refrigerant in your possession before you begin any type of service. This applies to refrigerant in storage containers as well as that in the vehicle. A container or system labeled R-134a may be mislabeled, or may not contain pure R-134a. Do not take chances as to the type of refrigerant or

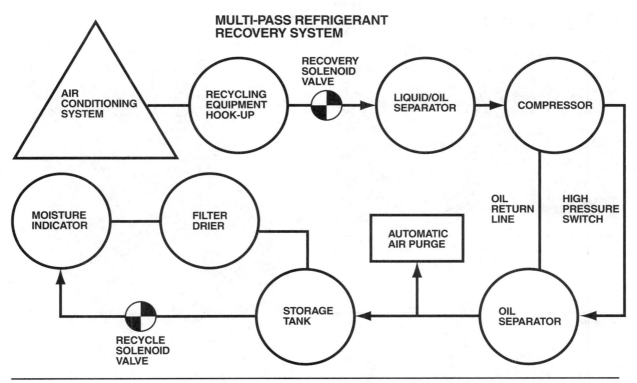

Figure 3-13. A typical multi-pass refrigerant recovery and recycling station. After recycling, refrigerant remains in the storage tank until ready for use.

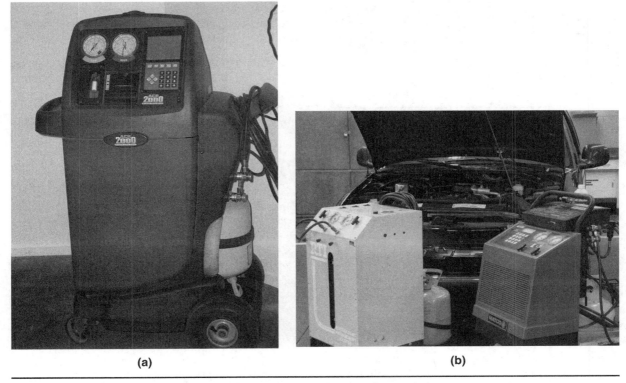

Figure 3-14. A typical single-pass recovery, recycling, and recharging station.

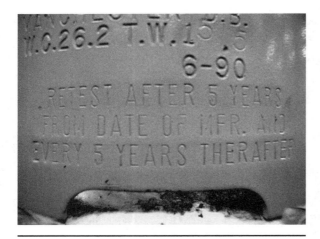

Figure 3-15. Note that recovery tanks must be tested every five years from their original production date.

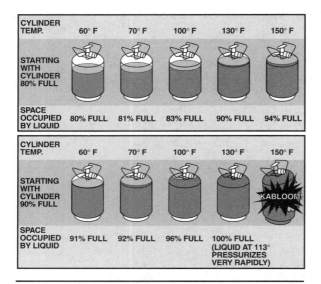

Figure 3-16. Refrigerant expands as it warms. NEVER fill a refrigerant storage container to more than 80 percent of its volume.

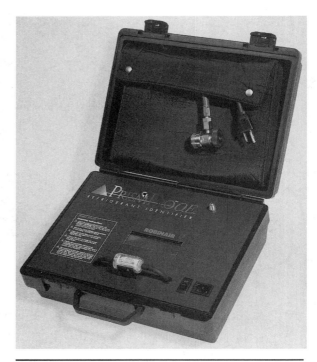

Figure 3-17. A refrigerant identifier confirms the refrigerant purity.

whether it is contaminated or not. You must check it yourself, or you run the risk of contaminating all systems, equipment, and other refrigerant that any contaminated refrigerant comes in contact with.

Refrigerant identifiers are available in portable, hand-held units, figure 3-17, or as part of an AC service station. Currently there is no way to separate different refrigerants. Contaminated refrigerant is sent to a recycler to be disposed of. The use of a refrigerant identifier is detailed in Chapter 1 under special tools.

As stated, you must identify the purity of refrigerant in storage containers before you attempt to use any of it.

Recycled refrigerant often may be contaminated with air. Recycled refrigerant is checked for excess air by carefully measuring the container pressure of a temperature-stabilized container, figure 3-18. To check for excess air:

1. Store the container of recycled refrigerant at 65°F (18.3°C) or above for a period of 12 hours. Make certain the container is protected from direct sunlight.
2. Attach a calibrated pressure gauge, with one psi divisions, to the container and determine the container pressure.
3. Use a calibrated thermometer to measure the temperature of the air within four inches of the container.
4. Compare the container pressure and air temperature readings to the chart in figure 3-19 to determine if the refrigerant is contaminated with excess air.
5. If the pressure readings exceed the maximum pressure, slowly vent a small amount of vapor from the top of the tank into the recovery/recycling equipment until the pressure is less than the maximum limit.
6. If the container pressure continues to exceed the maximum pressure limit, the refrigerant must be recycled.

Figure 3-18. Compare the readings in the photo to the chart in figure 3-19. Does this refrigerant contain excess air?

RECOVERING THE SYSTEM

Any time the AC system must be opened for service, the refrigerant must first be recovered from the vehicle's system. (Remember: it is unlawful to knowingly vent refrigerant to the atmosphere.) The procedure

Figure 3-20. Attach the recovery equipment to both the low- and high-side service ports.

listed and shown below is typical of the procedure for most recovery units. Remember to check the procedure for the type of equipment that you are using.

1. Attach the recovery equipment to the low-side and high-side service ports on the vehicle, figure 3-20.
2. Open both service valves on the recovery equipment hose, figures 3-21 and 3-22.
3. Start the engine and operate the AC system for about two minutes. This helps heat up the refrigerant in the system to aid in the recovery process. (If the system is nonoperational, you may skip this step.)
4. Open both valves on the recovery equipment tank, figure 3-23.
5. Check the pressure on the gauges to ensure that there is refrigerant in the system, figure 3-24.

MAXIMUM CONTAINER PRESSURE					
Temperature		R-12 Pressure		R-134a Pressure	
°F	°C	psi	kPa	psi	kPa
70	21.1	80	552	76	524
75	23.9	87	600	83	572
80	26.7	96	662	91	627
85	29.5	102	703	100	690
90	32.2	110	758	109	752
95	35.0	118	814	118	814
100	37.8	127	876	129	889
105	40.6	136	938	139	958
110	43.4	146	1,007	151	1,041

Figure 3-19. Measure the container pressure to check recycled refrigerant for excess air.

Figure 3-21. Open the high-side service fitting.

Figure 3-22. Open the low-side service fitting.

Figure 3-23. Open both valves on the recovery tank.

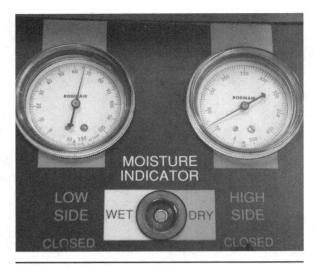

Figure 3-24. Check the system pressure on the gauges to ensure that the system contains refrigerant.

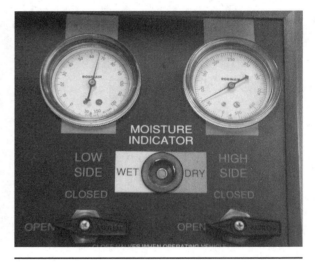

Figure 3-25. Open both the low-side and the high-side valves on the recovery unit.

6. Open both the low-side and high-side valves on the recovery unit if so equipped, figure 3-25.
7. Slowly open the oil drain valve on the equipment to remove any oil from the previous system service, figure 3-26.
8. Press the recover switch on the unit to start the recovery process, figure 3-27.
9. After the recovery unit shuts off automatically, the initial recovery process has been completed and the low-side gauge on the recovery unit should show about 10 to 17 in-Hg, figure 3-28.
10. Monitor the low-side gauge of the recovery unit for a period of a couple of minutes. Observe the

Figure 3-26. Slowly open the oil drain valve on the equipment to remove any oil from a previous recovery.

Figure 3-27. Start the recovery process on the recovery unit.

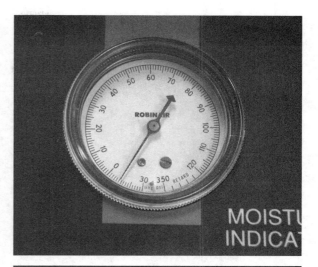

Figure 3-28. After the recovery unit shuts off, the low-side gauge should indicate between 10 and 17 in-Hg.

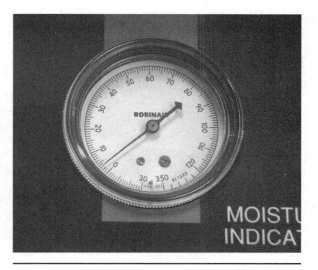

Figure 3-29. Monitor the low-side gauge. If the pressure rises above 0 in-Hg, repeat the recovery process.

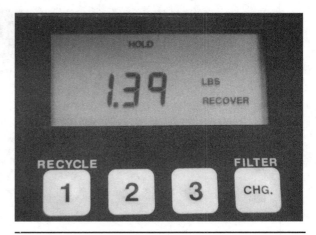

Figure 3-30. If your recovery unit has the capability, check the amount of refrigerant removed from the system.

gauge and, if the gauge rises above 0 psi, repeat the recovery process, figure 3-29. Usually the recovery process will need to be repeated several times to ensure that all the refrigerant has been removed from the vehicle's system.

11. If your equipment has the capability, check the amount of refrigerant recovered from the system, figure 3-30.

Figure 3-31. Open the oil drain valve and measure the oil removed from the vehicle.

12. Open the oil drain and measure the oil that was removed from the system, figure 3-31. You may need to replace this amount of oil if a significant amount was removed from the vehicle.

EVACUATING THE SYSTEM

Any time the refrigerant system is opened, it must be purged of moisture and air before it is recharged. Water contamination in an air conditioning system reduces system efficiency. Water mixed with R-12 forms hydrochloric acid, which corrodes system components. Even a single drop of moisture in a refrigerant system can cause serious damage.

Evacuating a refrigeration system removes all moisture and air. However, evacuation does not remove oil or any foreign substances, which can be removed only by flushing the system or components. Evacuation works by reducing the vapor pressure inside the system, which reduces the boiling point of the moisture to below ambient temperature. The moisture then boils into a vapor that can be removed from the system with a vacuum pump. See the chart in figure 3-32 for the boiling points of water at different pressures. The following evacuation procedures apply to the use of a manifold gauge set and a vacuum pump. If you are using an air conditioning station, refer to the equipment directions for proper use.

CAUTION: The system's refrigerant must be completely recovered before beginning evacuation. Allowing liquid refrigerant to enter the vacuum pump can damage or destroy the pump.

The Evacuation

The air conditioning system must be evacuated anytime the system has been opened. Perform the evacuation procedure as follows:

1. Attach the low-side and high-side hoses to the system, and attach the center (yellow) service hose to the vacuum pump, figure 3-33.
2. Turn the vacuum pump on, and open both manifold valves, figure 3-34.
3. The low-side gauge should read at least 20 in-Hg (508 mm-Hg) vacuum within five minutes, and the high-side gauge needle should be pulled down slightly below its zero mark. If the high-side gauge needle does not move, check for a restriction on the system high side, figure 3-35.

BOILING POINT OF WATER UNDER VACUUM		
Vacuum Reading (in-Hg)	Pounds per Square Inch Absolute Pressure (psia)	Water Boiling Point°
0	14.696	212°F (100°C)
10.24	9.629	192°F (89°C)
22.05	3.865	151°F (66°C)
25.98	1.935	124°F (51°C)
27.95	0.968	101°F (38°C)
28.94	0.481	78°F (26°C)
29.53	0.192	52°F (11°C)
29.82	0.019	1°F (−17°C)
29.901	0.010	−11°F (−24°C)

Figure 3-32. The boiling point of moisture is reduced below the ambient temperature when the system pressure is reduced.

Figure 3-33. Attach the low-side and high-side hoses and open both service valves.

Figure 3-35. After approximately five minutes, check the low-side gauge. Vacuum should be at least 20 in-Hg.

Figure 3-34. Start the vacuum pump and open both the low-side and high-side valves on the gauge set or the charging station.

Figure 3-36. Continue to evacuate for 20 minutes after the vacuum has reached 28 to 30 in-Hg.

4. If the system does not drop to the required vacuum, it is leaking. Find and repair the leak before continuing the evacuation process.
5. Keep the pump running for a minimum of 20 minutes after the vacuum has reached 28 to 30 in-Hg of vacuum, figure 3-36. It must pull down enough to make the water boil. On humid days, it will take longer for the water to boil.
6. When the evacuation is complete, close both the low-side and high-side service valves and observe the vacuum for a loss of vacuum, figure 3-37. A small rise in the vacuum is normal; however, the vacuum should hold in the system. If it does not, it indicates that the system has a leak and should be repaired before charging.

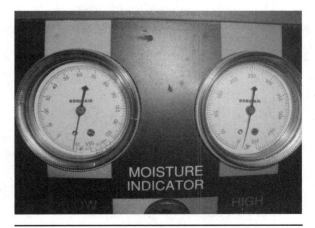

Figure 3-37. After the evacuation is complete, close the service valves and observe the low-side gauge. It should only move slightly after two minutes. If it continues to rise, the system is leaking and must be repaired before recharging.

CHARGING THE SYSTEM

System charging is the process of installing refrigerant into the air conditioning system using a manifold gauge set or a charging station. Before beginning this procedure, consult the factory shop manual for the vehicle that you are servicing. For example, you need to know the type of air conditioning system, its capacity, and the oil charge and type if you need to add oil to the system.

With recent changes in environmental safety laws, more shops are purchasing combination recovery/recycling/recharging equipment. Although less common, charging with 12-ounce cans, figure 3-38, is still performed in some shops.

NOTE: At one time these were referred to as one-pound cans. Refrigerant was originally sold in 16-ounce cans, but the price of refrigerant gradually went up. Instead of raising the price, manufacturers made the refrigerant cans smaller. When recharging, it is important to remember that although they are called one-pound cans, the containers hold only 12 ounces. This author does not recommend using these to charge with. There is no way to accurately measure the amount of refrigerant being charged into the system. As the capacity of R-134a systems have gotten smaller, they are much more sensitive to overcharging or undercharging. Accuracy of the charge is critical for proper system performance.

Following are a few general tips on charging the air conditioning system:

- Remember that any container of refrigerant has both liquid and vapor inside, figure 3-39. When

Figure 3-38. A one-pound can of refrigerant.

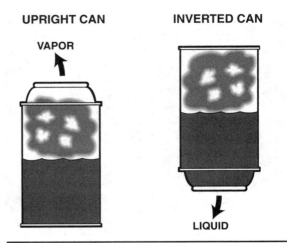

Figure 3-39. An upright can releases vapor; an inverted can releases liquid refrigerant.

the container is upright, pressurized vapor is forced into the service hose as the refrigerant boils. When you turn the container over, pressurized liquid is forced through the nozzle instead. Large refrigerant containers and charging station set-ups have two-way valves that let you choose whether to draw vapor from the top of the container or liquid from the bottom.

- There are two ways to speed the charging process. If you are using small cans of refrigerant, shake the can or warm it slightly with heat from the engine fan while you are dispensing the refrigerant. If you warm the refrigerant while you are dispensing it, the pressure will increase and help propel the refrigerant into the system. Most charging stations have heaters that warm the refrigerant.

- You must know the system capacity so you do not overfill it. Even a quarter-pound overcharge can damage some systems. Factory systems have the capacity noted on a label underhood.

- If you do not know the capacity and a sight glass is provided, add refrigerant in vapor form until the bubbles just disappear in the sight glass. Then add an additional half-pound. Remember that bubbles may appear when the clutch cycles off and then on again, so allow the system time to stabilize before checking the sight glass for bubbles.

- If you are charging directly from a bulk container, measure the amount of refrigerant added by placing the container on a scale and measuring the weight change while you are charging. Most charging stations can be preset to deliver a specific amount of refrigerant. Do not overcharge the system.

- NEVER open the high-side service valve while the compressor is running. This would release system pressure through the gauge set and into the refrigerant container. This is dangerous because it can rupture the container, spraying you with refrigerant and causing personal injury.

RECHARGING THE SYSTEM

When a system has been evacuated and you are recharging, you want to get as much of the refrigerant into the system as possible before you engage the compressor. Without refrigerant, there is no oil, or any means to circulate the oil. Never run the compressor without lubrication.

A storage container of refrigerant has both liquid and vapor in it. Liquid is heavier than vapor, so the liquid refrigerant settles at the bottom of the container, and the lighter vapor is at the top. When you are charging from a one-pound can, holding the can upright provides a vapor charge. Inverting the can provides a liquid charge. You must be careful not to charge liquid into the compressor.

NOTE: The type of air conditioning system the vehicle has, and the location of the low-side service fitting, determine whether you can charge by liquid or vapor. Remember to check the manufacturer's service manual before charging.

With liquid charging, liquid refrigerant is added to the system through the high-side service fitting with the compressor off. The engine must be off when you liquid charge. Liquid charging is performed first. Liquid refrigerant is heavier than vapor and fills the system faster. With liquid, you can charge approximately 12 ounces before the system pressure and container pressure equalize. With a vapor charge, you can charge only approximately four ounces before the two pressures equalize. After the pressures have equalized, you must run the compressor. A running compressor creates suction in the low side and pulls the refrigerant vapor out of the container and into the system.

Make certain you add the liquid refrigerant to the high side only so it does not contact the compressor. Liquid refrigerant charged to the low side can damage the compressor. With a reed valve compressor, if liquid refrigerant freezes the reed valves, they become brittle and can break.

NOTE: The only exception to the liquid refrigerant to the high-side-only specification is if the low-side service valve is on or before the accumulator. The accumulator stores liquid refrigerant; therefore, it is safe to charge liquid refrigerant into the accumulator. However, this is the ONLY exception. If the low-side service fitting is after the accumulator in the system, you must add liquid refrigerant to the high side to avoid damage to the compressor.

After the system and the container pressure are equalized, you can vapor charge the system to its capacity. Refrigerant vapor is added to the system through the low-side service fitting with the compressor running. Vapor charging is always performed after liquid charging. Using the drum and scale method, recharge the system as follows:

1. Attach a manifold gauge set and evacuate the system. When the evacuation is complete, close the service fittings to maintain the vacuum, figure 3-40.
2. Disconnect the center (yellow) service hose from the vacuum pump and attach to the refrigerant drum, figure 3-41.
3. Open the tank refrigerant valve and place the refrigerant drum upside down on the scale and record the weight, figure 3-42.
4. Open the manifold gauge high-side service valve and allow liquid refrigerant to flow until the system pressure is equal to the refrigerant tank pressure, figure 3-43.
5. Close the high-side service valve on the manifold gauge set, figure 3-44.

Figure 3-40. The system must be evacuated first if it has been opened. Refer to system evacuation.

Figure 3-41. After evacuation, connect the center hose (usually yellow) to the refrigerant drum.

Figure 3-42. Open the refrigerant tank valve, invert the refrigerant drum, and place it on the scale.

6. Turn the refrigerant drum upright so refrigerant vapor will be drawn from the top of the tank, figure 3-45.

7. Start the vehicle and turn the AC system on.

8. After the compressor engages, open the low-side manifold gauge valve and allow the compressor to draw in vapor refrigerant, figure 3-46.

9. When the correct amount of refrigerant has been added to the system, close the low-side valve on the manifold gauge set, figure 3-47.

10. Close the refrigerant tank valve and reopen the low-side valve on the manifold gauge set to allow the compressor to draw in the refrigerant that was left in the hose, figure 3-48.

11. Close the low-side manifold gauge valve and allow the system to stabilize.

12. Perform a system performance test before disconnecting the manifold gauge set.

13. Remove the manifold gauge set and replace all service caps, figure 3-49.

Figure 3-43. Allow refrigerant to flow until both the low-side and the high-side gauges are equal and the refrigerant stops flowing into the vehicle.

Figure 3-44. Open the high-side gauge service valve only. Note that the vehicle is NOT RUNNING.

Figure 3-46. After starting the vehicle and turning the AC on, open the low-side gauge service valve and allow the compressor to draw in vapor refrigerant until the system is full.

Figure 3-45. After liquid charging is complete, close the high-side gauge valve and turn the refrigerant drum upright to finish charging the system with vapor.

Figure 3-47. After the correct amount of refrigerant has been drawn into the system, close the low-side service valve on the manifold gauge set.

Figure 3-48. After the correct amount of refrigerant has been drawn into the system, close the refrigerant tank valve.

Figure 3-49. After the system performance test, remove manifold gauge hoses and install caps on service fittings.

The important points to remember are:

- Do not allow any air to enter the system. If a hose is opened when switching containers, the hose must be purged. Always close the shut-off valve in the hose to prevent this.
- To protect the compressor, charge as much refrigerant as possible into the system before you engage the compressor.

- Never run the compressor with the manifold high-side valve open.
- If liquid refrigerant is allowed to enter the compressor, it is possible to break a suction reed valve. The key point in determining whether to liquid charge or vapor charge is where the low-side service fitting is located. If charging into the accumulator or before the accumulator, it is safe to charge with liquid. If the service valve is close to the compressor, it should be vapor charged.

PART TWO

Diagnosing Components and Air Conditioning Systems

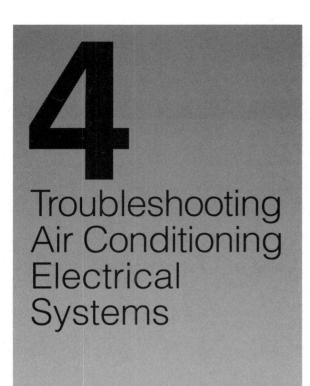

Troubleshooting Air Conditioning Electrical Systems

TROUBLESHOOTING ELECTRICAL SYSTEMS

This chapter covers basic electronic troubleshooting for automotive heating, ventilation, and air conditioning (HVAC) systems.

Getting Started

Many failures in air conditioning systems involve the electrical side of the system. Before you begin diagnosing the system, make certain that you are properly prepared.

1. Obtain the system specifications and service information, including the electrical and vacuum diagrams.
2. Familiarize yourself with how the system should respond to each input.
3. Familiarize yourself with the operation of the appropriate test equipment.
4. Begin with the basics. A good visual inspection combined with the customer complaint, followed by an attempt to recreate the problem, will help you get started in the right direction and eliminate wasted time.
5. Conduct a system performance test following the manufacturer's specifications.
6. As you narrow the problem area, perform a troubleshooting procedure that traces the circuit and component operation.

Electrical Diagnosis Procedure

There are three basic reasons that an electrical part or subassembly fails:

1. The part or assembly is defective.
2. The electrical circuit is open or incomplete.
3. The control system for the component is faulty, preventing component operation despite instructions from the driver.

Electrical diagnosis consists of an organized procedure that uses information and testing to find the cause of the failure. The five basic steps of an electrical diagnosis procedure are:

1. Verify the complaint. Find out exactly what the system is doing or not doing.
2. Reference a wiring diagram and service manual to determine exactly how the system should operate.
3. Systematically test the system.
4. Repair the system.
5. Verify the repair.

This procedure is especially useful in tracing power supply problems to individual components. The same procedure can be used to troubleshoot problems in computerized systems. Because these systems use low signal levels, the quality of connections is much more important. Where possible, use a scan tool to localize the problem to specific sensor circuits.

Verify the Complaint

The correct troubleshooting diagnosis begins with an evaluation of the customer's complaint. When evaluating the complaint, consider the following points:

- What are the symptoms of the problem?
- When did the trouble begin?
- What were the weather and operating conditions at the time of the failure?
- Do these same symptoms occur each time the system is operated?
- If the problem is intermittent, what circumstances cause the problem to repeat itself?

- Which parts of the system could cause the problems described by the customer (air delivery, refrigeration system, or controls)?

If you cannot easily duplicate the symptoms described by the customer, test the affected circuits and components. *If you cannot duplicate the problem then you cannot repair the problem. Any repairs made will be guesses with no actual verification if the problem has been repaired.*

Identify How the System Should Operate

Refer to a wiring diagram to learn how the circuit should work. You cannot test a circuit unless you understand how it is supposed to work. Follow the current flow to read an electrical diagram. Most manufacturers arrange their schematics to show power at the top and ground at the bottom of the diagram, figure 4-1. Some diagrams include symbols, components, connectors, and switch continuity position identifications.

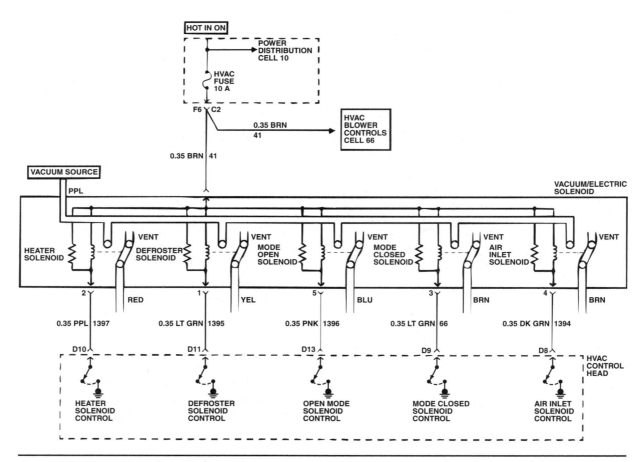

Figure 4-1. Most wiring diagrams are arranged vertically with the power supply at the top and the ground connections at the bottom. (Reprinted with permission of General Motors Corporation.)

Some aftermarket automotive publishers redraw all manufacturers' diagrams into a single format. This eliminates the difficulty of familiarization with each separate manufacturer's diagram style. A wiring diagram establishes:

- The fuse or fuses that supply the circuit.
- Controls, switches, and connectors that may be faulty and prevent operation.
- The signal to the PCM, which is necessary for normal operation. However, the diagram does not show the other inputs that may affect whether the PCM energizes the AC compressor control relay.

Once you understand the circuit operation, your next step is to locate the components or circuits that may be causing the problem. For example, the AC compressor circuit shown in figure 4-2 cannot operate unless:

- The fuses are good.
- The AC selector mode is in any AC mode, and not in the OFF, VENT, or HEATER mode.
- The AC compressor cycling switch is closed.
- The AC high-pressure cut-off switch is closed.
- The AC compressor control relay is energized by the PCM.
- The ground connection is complete.
- All the wiring is complete and does not have excessive resistance.

All this information shows the value of having an accurate wiring diagram on hand. You must learn to read diagrams properly to determine which switches and circuits you need to evaluate.

Basic Electrical Test Procedures

Troubleshooting electrical systems requires skill because you must understand and interpret the results from your electrical test. Performing the electrical tests themselves, however, is not difficult. The basic tests covered in the section are:

- Power supply checks
- Voltage tests
- Continuity and resistance tests
- Amperage tests
- Short to ground tests
- Relay tests
- Special equipment tests

Be careful when selecting test equipment for today's electronic circuits and systems. Sometimes the wrong type of tester can overload the circuit being tested and damage electronic components—even the onboard computer. Digital Volt-Ohm Meters (DVOMs) are specifically designed to work with electronic systems. Consult appropriate service publications for recommendations on test equipment to use.

Power Supply Checks

Typically, power supply checks begin with general area tests and proceed to specific area tests, allowing you to narrow the possible source of a problem as you troubleshoot.

Locate Junctions of Power Supply

When you troubleshoot problems related to the power supply, it is often useful to identify the branches and junctions of the circuits that you are testing, figure 4-3. A junction (also known as a common point) is a point connected to two or more branch circuit paths. If power is available at the junction, it is available to the branch circuits.

Examples of junctions include the positive and negative terminals of the battery, which are common power and ground points to the entire electrical system. The positive bus bar in the fuse box and the metal body of the vehicle are common power and ground points to most of the electrical system. The side of the ignition switch that receives current when the key is turned to RUN is common to the branches of the electrical system that are powered only when the engine is running.

Perform Area Test and Additional Electrical Test

Junction diagnosis is useful because it allows you to assume that both branches from a common point are receiving power. If one branch is operational, then power is available at the other branch, even if the other branch is not operational. If the cycling clutch pressure switch is operational, then the circuit is complete through the fuse, selector switch, and wiring to that junction. It is usually easier to go to a junction in the middle of the circuit, and choose a point that is easier to get to. You may have to perform various electrical tests depending on the nature of the problem. A few common electrical test procedures are described in the next section. Don't forget to check the appropriate grounds in each circuit as well. Quite often a poor ground connection is responsible when a component fails to operate.

Available Voltage Test

When there is current flow in a circuit with one or more loads, the voltmeter reading after each load always shows a voltage drop. This is because the initial available voltage decreases whenever a load is between the test point and the battery positive terminal. Each load decreases the voltage available to additional loads that are further along the circuit.

When components are not drawing current, the available voltage should be equal to the source voltage, or about 12.6 volts. When the components are not drawing current, the voltage in a circuit is usually called the no-load or open circuit voltage.

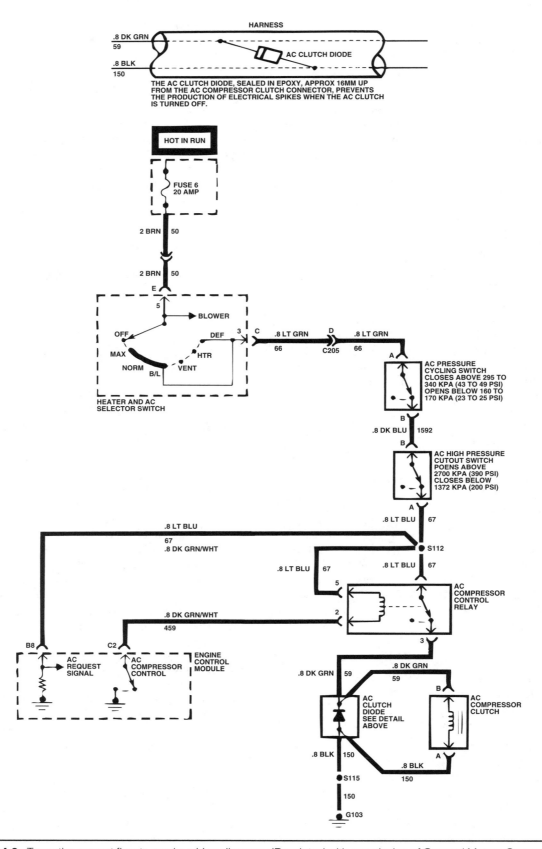

Figure 4-2. Trace the current flow to read a wiring diagram. (Reprinted with permission of General Motors Corporation.)

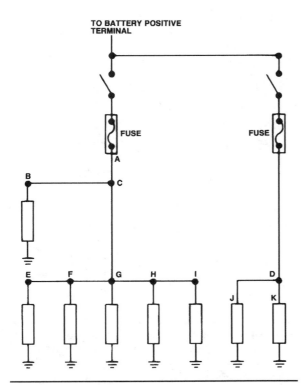

Figure 4-3. Point A is common to junctions B and C, but not to D. Junction D is common to junctions J and K, but not to E through I.

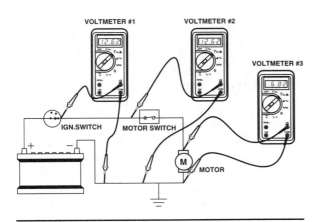

Figure 4-4. These available voltage tests pinpoint the area of high resistance.

Available Voltage at Points in a Circuit

High-resistance faults can be detected by checking available voltage with current flowing in the circuit. Connect the voltmeter positive lead to a test point and ground the voltmeter negative lead. For example, if the blower motor is not running fast enough, an available voltage test can pinpoint the fault. Figure 4-4 shows

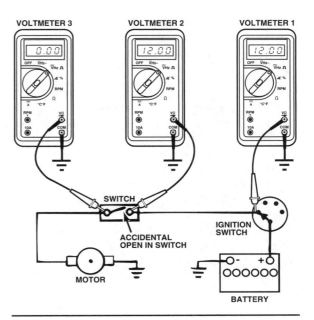

Figure 4-5. When no current is flowing due to an open circuit, a few no-load voltage tests pinpoint the problem.

how such a loaded circuit test can indicate that the circuit, and not the motor, is at fault. A corroded switch connection has reduced the voltage available to the motor so that the motor cannot run at the correct speed.

When no current is flowing, a no-load available voltage test can pinpoint an open in a circuit. Figure 4-5 shows a circuit being tested for available voltage.

- Voltmeter readings 1 and 2 show that the system voltage is available at these test points.
- Voltmeter reading 3 is zero volts, indicating that the circuit is open at some point between voltmeter point 2 and 3.

Voltage Drop Test

Voltage drop is the amount of voltage that an electrical component uses. The voltage drop is the amount of resistance (ohms) multiplied by the amount of current (amps). A high-resistance connection causes a high voltage drop. High resistance increases the voltage drop at the point of high resistance and decreases the voltage available at other points in the circuit because of the decreased current flow.

Excessive current flow in the circuit also has a higher voltage drop in a connector or switch. High amperage in a circuit is caused by a short to ground, or internally shorted components.

Perform a voltage drop test while current is flowing through the circuit under normal operating conditions. Voltage drop tests are especially useful for pinpointing faults that are caused by heat and vibration. Voltage drops can be calculated indirectly, or they can be measured directly. An unwanted voltage drop indicates unwanted resistance in the circuit or component.

Measuring Voltage Drops

In most cases you can measure voltage drops using a DVOM, figure 4-6. Place the voltmeter positive lead on one side of the load nearest the battery positive. Place the voltmeter negative lead on the other side of the load on the ground side. The voltmeter reads the voltage drop across the load. Figure 4-7 shows the voltage drop readings for an entire circuit. You can see that the sum of the voltage drops equals the source voltage.

A single voltage drop test can be useful if you know what the normal drop should be. For example, the voltage drop across the switch in figure 4-8 should be no more than 0.1 volt. If it exceeds that, there is a problem in the switch or connections at the switch.

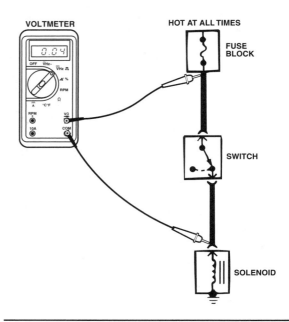

Figure 4-8. This single voltage drop test is used when you know what the normal voltage drop should be. In this case, there should be no more than one volt drop across this switch.

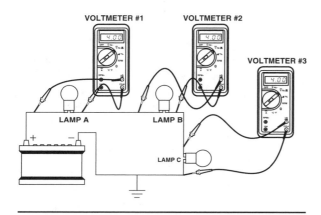

Figure 4-6. Voltage drops can be measured directly by connecting a voltmeter across the load.

Continuity and Resistance Testing

Continuity and resistance testing are similar. Generally, continuity testing is used to determine whether an electrical circuit is complete. Continuity testing is performed with a voltmeter or ohmmeter. An ohmmeter is used to perform resistance testing, which determines the amount of electrical resistance present and if the electrical path through a component is complete.

Continuity Testing

Continuity testing is very similar to no-load voltage testing. Both tests reveal if the system voltage is being applied to a part of a circuit. A continuity test is performed with the voltmeter connected as shown in figure 4-9. At any point in the circuit before the motor, the voltmeter should indicate the source voltage present. Voltmeter 3 indicates that no voltage is available at the power side of the motor. Therefore, a loss of continuity is indicated somewhere between the switch and before the motor.

Continuity testing can also be performed with an ohmmeter. You need to isolate the circuit before testing for continuity. Isolating a circuit means there is no current flow in any portion of the circuit being tested, figure 4-10. Perform a continuity test with an ohmmeter as follows:

1. Isolate the circuit by disconnecting the circuit at its power source or its ground source. In many

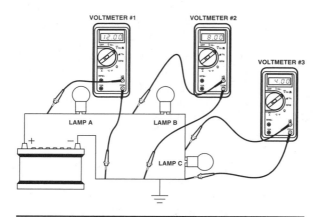

Figure 4-7. Voltage drops can be calculated from a series of available voltage readings.

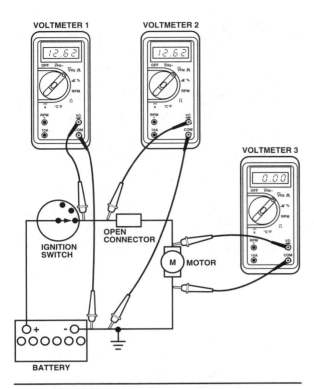

Figure 4-9. To test continuity in this motor, connect the voltmeter in parallel with the circuit.

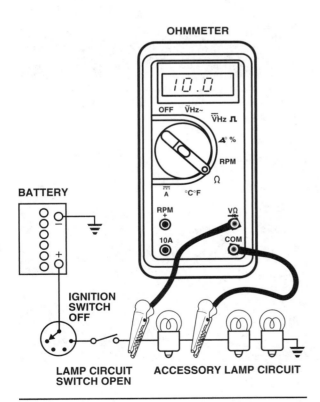

Figure 4-10. The circuit must be open or "isolated" to test for continuity with an ohmmeter.

cases, it is easier to disconnect the power source, because many circuits have multiple grounds.
2. If your ohmmeter has more than one resistance scale, set the ohmmeter to the highest scale.
3. Connect one ohmmeter test lead to the disconnected end of the circuit and connect the other lead to the other end of the circuit.
4. Observe the ohmmeter reading.
   a. If the ohmmeter reads infinite resistance, the circuit is open.
   b. If the ohmmeter reads an amount of resistance, the circuit is continuous. The amount of resistance varies depending on the loads in the circuits.

Resistance Testing

An ohmmeter is also used to test circuits or components for resistance. This is particularly useful when checking load devices that have a specific resistance, such as solenoids, clutch coils, and relay coils. To test the resistance of a load device, disconnect its wiring and attach the ohmmeter leads to the power and ground connections of the load device, figure 4-11. Compare the ohmmeter reading to the specifications for the component to determine if the component is good or bad.

Resistance tests were commonly used to test diodes, which are frequently found in air conditioning circuits. However, since the introduction of high-impedance DVOMs, resistance testing is no longer used. Most high-impedance DVOMs have a special function that is used to test diodes, figure 4-12. This function applies more voltage to the diode being tested to ensure that the diode is forward biased (turned on) when testing it.

Figure 4-11. Measuring the resistance of the compressor clutch coil.

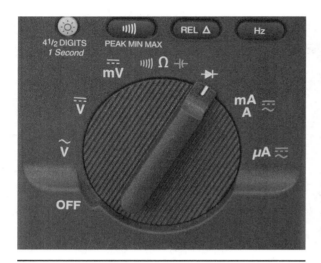

Figure 4-12. Most DVOMs have a diode test range to test diodes.

Figure 4-13. Remove or isolate the diode from the circuit and connect the DVOM to each end of the diode.

To test a diode using this function:

1. Isolate the diode by disconnecting one or both ends of the diode from the circuit, figure 4-13.
2. Select the diode test function of the DVOM, figure 4-14.
3. Touch the meter leads to each end of the diode and observe the reading on the meter, figure 4-15. The meter will read either OL or a voltage reading of approximately 0.5 to 0.7 volts.
4. Reverse the leads of the meter, and observe the reading on the meter, figure 4-16. The meter reading should show the opposite reading from the previous reading.
5. If one reading is approximately 0.5 to 0.7 volts and the other reading is OL, then the diode is good. If both readings are OL or showing voltage, then the diode is defective and must be replaced.

IMPORTANT: If the diode was removed from the circuit for testing, it must be reinstalled in the same position and direction after testing.

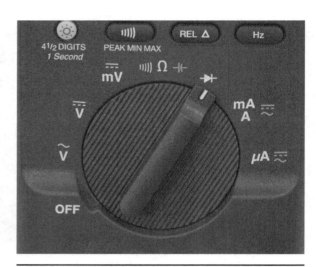

Figure 4-14. Select the diode test range on the meter.

Figure 4-15. With the leads connected one way you should get a reading of approximately 0.5 to 0.7 volts.

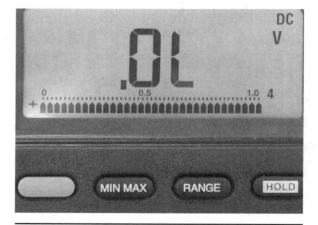

Figure 4-16. Reverse the leads to the diode and the meter should read OL. If it reads OL both ways, the diode is open. If it reads voltage both ways, the diode is shorted.

While resistance testing is useful for testing some load devices, it can be misleading if used to test switches, wiring, or other low-resistance components in a circuit. This is because an ohmmeter puts out a very small current and cannot sufficiently "load" a switch, wire, or low-resistance device. Use a continuity or voltage drop test on these components.

Voltage drop is the preferred alternative to resistance testing in most cases. Resistance in circuits may not show up until full circuit current is applied to the circuit. Cuts in wires that reduce the effective wire diameter, or defects in the contacts of switches that reduce the contact area, severely reduce the current capabilities of the circuit, but may have no trouble at all in carrying the output current from your ohmmeter. By performing a voltage drop test on a "live" circuit, resistance in a section of wire or across a switch can be accurately diagnosed.

Amperage Testing

Ammeters are used to test the current flow in circuits. An ammeter must always be connected in series with the circuit, figure 4-17. Additionally, some ammeters require that you observe polarity—the positive ammeter lead must be connected toward the power source, and the negative lead must be connected toward the ground, figure 4-18. Some meters can be damaged if the meter polarity is accidentally reversed. A DVOM will not be damaged; however, it will display a negative current flow.

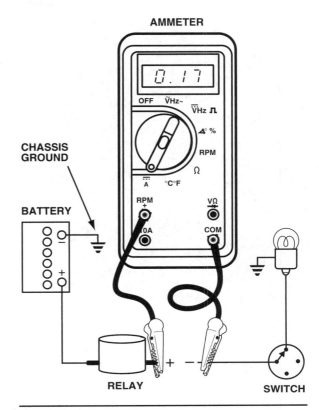

Figure 4-18. The polarity of ammeter leads must be observed, or the meter could be damaged.

Always set your ammeter to the highest current scale, or higher than the expected current in the circuit. This protects the ammeter from excessive current that can damage the meter or blow a fuse in the meter. Take an initial current reading from the circuit. If the current is below the maximum scale reading of the lower range on the meter, you may switch to that lower ammeter range for more accurate results.

Inductive ammeters, which clip around a wire, measure current flow without disconnecting or disturbing the circuit, figure 4-19. This feature is extremely useful when performing diagnosis, because circuits may be tested without disturbing wiring or connections that may be defective. Also, inductive ammeters are more tolerant of mistakes—if you place the ammeter inductive probe on a wire with the polarity reversed, it shows a negative current reading on the ammeter; however, it will not damage the meter.

Compare the measured circuit current with the manufacturer's specifications for the circuit. Along with the manufacturer's specifications, keep in mind that:

- No current indicates an open circuit.
- Lower-than-normal current indicates a high-resistance fault. Too much resistance in the circuit is causing a reduction in circuit current.

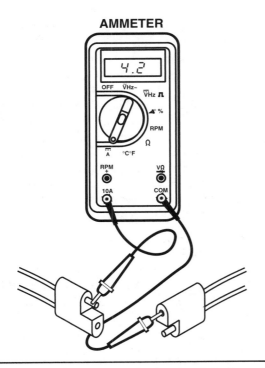

Figure 4-17. An ammeter must be connected in series with the circuit being tested.

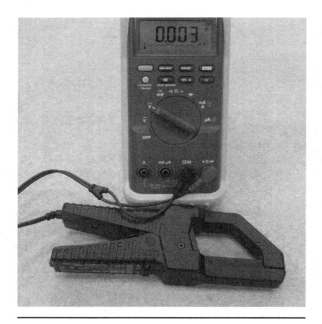

Figure 4-19. An inductive amp probe connects to your DVOM and allows you to measure current without opening the circuit. It also allows you to measure high current that your meter cannot.

- Higher-than-normal current flow indicates a low-resistance fault, such as a short to ground. High current flow in a circuit can be caused by a binding or defective motor.

Checking for Shorts to Ground

One of the most difficult electrical problems to trace is a short to ground in a circuit. This usually happens when a voltage carrying wire chafes and touches the sheet metal of the vehicle or another wire. You can test for a short to ground with a test light, ohmmeter, or a special tool called a short finder. In each case it is likely that a fuse or fusible link has also blown as a result of the short. This test pinpoints the exact location of the unwanted ground.

Testing with a Test Light

A test light allows you to locate shorts to ground without risking sparks or wiring damage. The load imposed by the bulb substitutes for the load of a normal system component.

1. Remove the fuse and disconnect the load.
2. Connect a test lamp across the fuse terminals, figure 4-20. Make certain that current is reaching the fuse receptacle. If the test light is lit, then the short to ground is present.
3. Beginning near the fuse block, wiggle the harness from side to side. Continue this action at points about six inches apart, while watching the test lamp.

Figure 4-20. With the load disconnected, install a test light in place of the fuse to check for a short. If the test light lights, it indicates a short to ground.

4. When the test lamp goes out, you have located the spot of the grounded circuit.
5. Repair the circuit, remove the test lamp, reinstall the fuse, and reconnect the load.
6. Operate the circuit to verify the repair.

Testing with an Ohmmeter

Shorts to ground can also be detected with an ohmmeter. To use an ohmmeter, the circuit must be disconnected from the battery. If battery voltage is present it can damage the meter.

1. Remove the blown fuse and disconnect both the battery and the load.
2. Connect one lead of the ohmmeter to the fuse terminal on the load side of the circuit, figure 4-21.
3. Connect the other lead of the ohmmeter to ground. If the ground is present, the meter will read some resistance value.
4. Wiggle the affected wire or harness and observe the meter. When the meter reading changes to OL you have located the spot of the ground in the circuit.
5. Repair the circuit, disconnect the ohmmeter, reinstall a new fuse, and test the operation of the circuit to verify the repair.

Testing with a Short Finder

A short finder is a special tool consisting of test leads with an attached circuit breaker and separate inductive meter. These tools can locate shorts to ground in the wiring behind sheet metal, interior panels, carpet, or upholstery.

1. Remove the blown fuse, but leave the battery connected.
2. Connect the short finder leads across the fuse terminals, figure 4-22.

Figure 4-21. With the load disconnected, an ohmmeter can be used to detect a short to ground. Remove the fuse, connect one lead of the ohmmeter to the unpowered side of the fuse, and connect the other lead to ground. If a short to ground is present the meter will show some continuity.

Figure 4-22. The short detector is installed in place of the fuse. It creates a pulsing magnetic field that can be detected with a meter supplied with the tool.

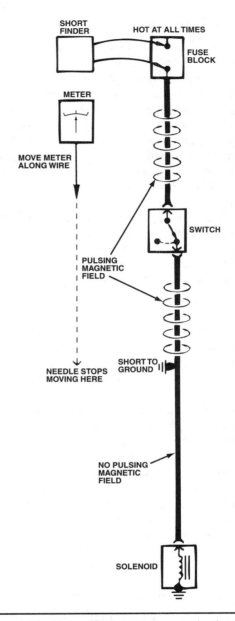

Figure 4-23. A short finder creates a pulsating magnetic field before, but not after, the short to ground.

3. Close all switches in series with the circuit you are testing.
4. Turn the short finder on. The short finder pulses current into the circuit, creating a magnetic field around the circuit wiring between the fuse block and the short to ground, but not after the short.
5. Beginning at the fuse block, slowly move the meter along the circuit wiring, figure 4-23. The meter shows current pulses through the sheet metal and body trim. As long as the meter is between the fuse block and the short to ground, the needle moves with each current pulse. However,

as soon as you move the meter past the short, the needle stops. Inspect the wiring in that area for a short to ground.

SPECIALIZED ELECTRICAL TEST EQUIPMENT

Various electronic tools have been developed in recent years to simplify troubleshooting on computer-controlled electrical systems. These tools make troubleshooting faster and easier. Familiarize yourself with these tools so you can understand the test procedure and interpret the test results accurately.

Using a Scan Tool

A scan tool connects to and communicates with the on-board computers of a vehicle. With the appropriate service information, retrieved trouble codes can be quickly deciphered and appropriate diagnostic tests can be followed. The scan tool relays selected information to the technician through a digital display. A scan tool is powered by battery voltage through the cigarette lighter, through the DLC, or through a direct connection to the battery.

Scan tool capabilities vary. Units with built-in memory can be used only on certain vehicles. Others have interchangeable software cartridges that allow the tool to be used on many systems. Some scan tools allow you to override the vehicle's computer and control the engine and air conditioning operating conditions, or switch the engine into a programmed test mode.

Independent Manufacturer's Scan Tools

Independent equipment manufacturers offer hand-held scan tools, figure 4-24. The scan tool is able to retrieve and read stored diagnostic trouble codes (DTCs). It can monitor a circuit called the serial data link and transmit a continuous stream of information concerning the status of various parts of the engine and other systems that are computer controlled.

In addition to certain tests, some scan tools can check specific sensor circuits or activate the circuits of actuators, such as the air conditioner compressor relay, and test their operation. Scan tool manufacturers continue to develop up-to-date data cartridges available for use in a single scan tool. This provides the specific information needed to read the data stream for each vehicle, without the expense of buying separate testers.

Vehicle Manufacturer's Scan Tools

Automotive manufacturers provide testers for use with their specific vehicles and electronic control systems. For example, DaimlerChrysler markets a diagnostic tester that has three general test modes:

1. The diagnostic mode that displays trouble codes.
2. The circuit actuation mode that operates system actuators.
3. The switch mode that checks the operation of switches and sensors that send information to the computer.

All manufacturers have developed their own testers that are used on their vehicles. These scan tools generally can perform more functions, such as reprogramming of control modules, and more comprehensive

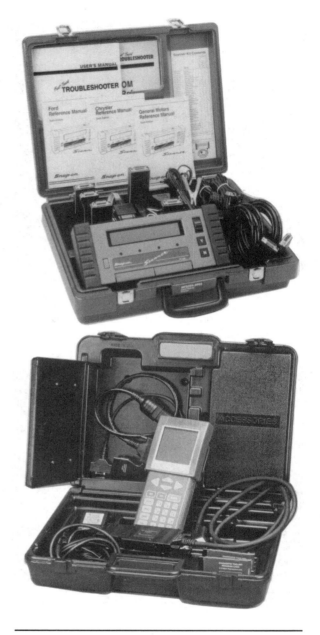

Figure 4-24. Electronic scan tools communicate with the PCM to read any stored trouble codes.

testing than the aftermarket scan tools. However, in most cases, they are manufacturer specific and will not work on other makes of vehicles. In most cases this limits their use to dealership technicians. The aftermarket scan tools usually do not have as much capability as the manufacturer scan tools; however, they are designed to work on a wide variety of vehicle makes and models. Each shop or technician needs to decide what capabilities they need in a scan tool and carefully choose the one that is best suited to their needs.

Vehicle Test and Diagnostic Connectors

All late model vehicles have a test or diagnostic connector to attach tools or diagnostic equipment. These connectors access circuits, the onboard computers, and/or stored trouble codes. The onboard computers receive and process inputs from several circuits and systems on the vehicle, and direct the appropriate response back to the components.

To assist with diagnosis, a test connector is located on the vehicle, usually under the instrument panel. This connector may be called the Assembly Line Diagnostic Link (ALDL) or the Diagnostic Link Connector (DLC). Until 1996 this connector could have many different configurations and locations. This made it difficult sometimes for technicians to find or access the connector. In 1996 the connector was standardized, consisting of 16 pins, figure 4-25, and should be located under the instrument panel on the driver's side of the vehicle. These links connect to a scan tool and allow the scan tool to communicate with the vehicle's onboard computers to retrieve trouble codes and access the data stream, if available. Some systems also have the capability of displaying diagnostic codes by flashing codes through a light on the dash or through a control panel display. These abilities vary widely from make, model, and vehicle year, so consult the service information for that vehicle to determine this capability.

ELECTRICAL SWITCH DIAGNOSIS AND TESTING

Heating and air conditioning systems use many electrical, pressure, or temperature actuated switches for system control. It is important to understand how to troubleshoot these devices. As you diagnose, keep in mind the three functions that switches perform:

1. Switches control the flow of current in a circuit by turning it on or off.
2. Switches can direct the flow of current within a circuit.
3. Switches may be used for signal circuits to a module or computer.

Be careful when you select test equipment for electronic circuits and systems. You can damage the circuit being tested or change the test results if you select the wrong type of test equipment. Before you test any switch, use a voltmeter to confirm that voltage is reaching it. Your voltmeter should read within one volt of battery voltage. A lower reading indicates a problem in the circuit between the battery and the switch being tested. Next, test the switch output. The switch is closed if the voltage reading is the same as the input voltage. This is when a scan tool can be very useful by allowing you to quickly check the state of various switches in the system, figure 4-26. The input voltage to the switch should be almost the same as the output voltage from the switch when the switch is closed. If not, the switch or connections to the switch are defective and need to be repaired.

Using a test light adds current to show resistance better. However, using a test light on a signal circuit can give the wrong results. If the circuit begins at a computer, it may be a circuit with high resistance in the computer. Using a test light pulls the voltage to ground without lighting the bulb. Always use a DVOM on these types of circuits.

PIN
NO. ASSIGNMENTS

1. MANUFACTURER'S DISCRETION
2. BUS + LINE, SAE J1850
3. MANUFACTURER'S DISCRETION
4. CHASSIS GROUND
5. SIGNAL GROUND
6. MANUFACTURER'S DISCRETION
7. K LINE, ISO 9141
8. MANUFACTURER'S DISCRETION
9. MANUFACTURER'S DISCRETION
10. BUS – LINE, SAE J1850
11. MANUFACTURER'S DISCRETION
12. MANUFACTURER'S DISCRETION
13. MANUFACTURER'S DISCRETION
14. MANUFACTURER'S DISCRETION
15. L LINE, ISO 9141
16. VEHICLE BATTERY POSITIVE

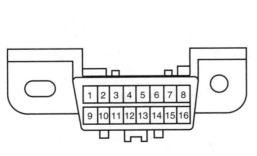

Figure 4-25. The 16 pin DLC is found on all 1996 and newer vehicles. Certain pins are common to all vehicles and certain pins can be used by the manufacturers at their discretion.

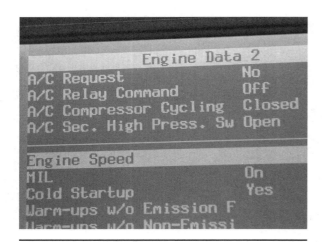

Figure 4-26. The scan tool can be very useful in allowing you to quickly verify the status of various AC switches.

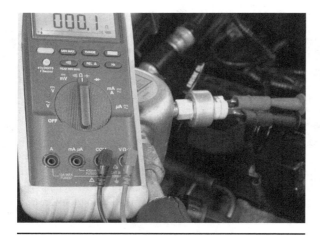

Figure 4-27. This photo shows the pressure cycling switch being checked for continuity. A low reading indicates that the switch is closed.

When testing a switch out of the circuit, use an ohmmeter to check for continuity and resistance. The ohmmeter will show if the switch has continuity as well as the amount of resistance of the contacts, figure 4-27. You must be absolutely accurate when testing electrical components. If the resistance is not quite zero, but close to it, the switch may have too much resistance and need to be replaced.

Air Conditioning Selector and Blower Motor Switch Testing

Air conditioning selector switches and blower motor switches have multiple terminals and more than one switch position. Quite often their function is dependent on proper operation of the other switches or relays.

Such switches require the use of a continuity diagram, figure 4-28. Continuity diagrams may be provided in published service information, or you may have to construct one from the switch's electrical diagram. Once you have the continuity diagram, test the switch as follows:

1. Disconnect the switch connector and test the terminals involved in each switch position in turn, figure 4-29. When several terminals are involved in one switch position:
   a. Hold an ohmmeter lead on one terminal.
   b. Use the other hand to probe each of the remaining terminals used in that position, one at a time, noting the ohmmeter reading at each terminal.
   c. The reading should be zero or very nearly zero for each test point requiring continuity in the switch position tested, figure 4-30.
2. Before moving to the next switch position, check all the other terminals to make sure they read infinite resistance (no continuity).
3. Repeat this procedure for all remaining switch positions. If the switch fails any part of the test, replace it.

Compressor Clutch Electrical Troubleshooting

The compressor clutch is an electromagnetic device used to mechanically connect the torque of the belt-driven compressor pulley to the compressor driveshaft. Clutch operation is covered in Chapter 8 of the *Classroom Manual*. Service procedures for mechanical failure are covered in Chapter 8 of this *Shop Manual*. This section details various symptoms of compressor clutch electrical failure and their probable cause.

Failure to Engage

Clutch failures can result from a variety of causes, both electrical and mechanical. The following section details electrical problems that may prevent the clutch from engaging.

Let's begin with open safety switches. A safety switch prevents compressor operation when compressor damage could result. These conditions are:

- Low refrigerant pressure
- Low refrigerant charge
- Excessively high refrigerant pressure
- High coolant temperature
- High compressor temperature

The other types of switches that can prevent compressor operation are switches or sensors used to monitor

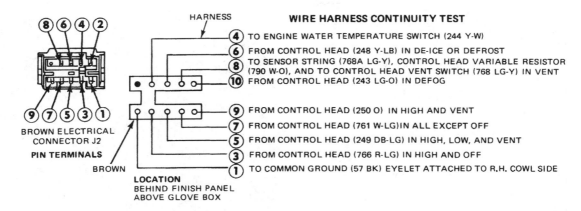

WIRE HARNESS CONTINUITY TEST

(4) TO ENGINE WATER TEMPERATURE SWITCH (244 Y-W)

(6) FROM CONTROL HEAD (248 Y-LB) IN DE-ICE OR DEFROST

(8) TO SENSOR STRING (768A LG-Y), CONTROL HEAD VARIABLE RESISTOR (790 W-O), AND TO CONTROL HEAD VENT SWITCH (768 LG-Y) IN VENT

(10) FROM CONTROL HEAD (243 LG-O) IN DEFOG

(9) FROM CONTROL HEAD (250 O) IN HIGH AND VENT

(7) FROM CONTROL HEAD (761 W-LG) IN ALL EXCEPT OFF

(5) FROM CONTROL HEAD (249 DB-LG) IN HIGH, LOW, AND VENT

(3) FROM CONTROL HEAD (766 R-LG) IN HIGH AND OFF

(1) TO COMMON GROUND (57 BK) EYELET ATTACHED TO R.H. COWL SIDE

BROWN ELECTRICAL CONNECTOR J2

PIN TERMINALS

BROWN

LOCATION
BEHIND FINISH PANEL
ABOVE GLOVE BOX

Figure 4-28. You need a continuity diagram to test complex switches.

Figure 4-29. Connect the ohmmeter to the switch you are testing. As the switch is moved through the different positions the meter should show continuity or no continuity.

Figure 4-30. If the switch is good the meter should show very low resistance readings.

driveability. These may prevent compressor operation under high engine loads. They typically could include:

- Power steering pressure switch (PSPS)
- Constant run relay
- Wide-open throttle switch (WOTS)
- Time delay relay

Blown fuses can prevent clutch engagement. Generally, blown fuses are the result of higher-than-normal current flow in the circuit.

Open electrical connections, or wiring on either the positive or ground side, may appear as a failed component or failed operation of part of the AC system and prevent compressor clutch engagement.

A defective cycling switch can keep the compressor engaged all the time, not let it engage at all, or cause erratic cycling patterns. And finally, a defective clutch relay or faulty electronic controller can result in symptoms similar to a defective cycling clutch switch.

Clutch Troubleshooting Procedure

You can tell if the clutch is operating by moving the mode selector to any air conditioning position with the engine running—typically AC, MAX AC, some BI-LEVEL positions, and DEFROST. You should hear a click and a momentary change in engine speed when the clutch engages. If the clutch is not engaging:

1. With the ignition on and engine running, turn the AC on. Check for voltage at the clutch coil.
2. If voltage is present, check for voltage on the ground wire, if applicable.

3. If there is no voltage on the ground, check the air gap between the driveplate and pulley. If the gap is within specifications, replace the clutch coil.

4. If there is no voltage to the clutch coil, use a wiring diagram to test the circuit. Make certain that you understand how the system is supposed to operate before you begin testing. Some systems do not have power to the clutch until the engine is running.

5. If the fuse was blown, remove the electrical wiring connector from the clutch coil. Use an ohmmeter to measure resistance of the coil, or connect an ammeter and measure the current flow, figure 4-31. Compare this reading to the manufacturer's specifications. Low resistance will allow too much current to flow and high resistance will lower the current flow.

6. If there is no power to the ground wire, use a wiring diagram to test the circuit. An additional switch could be in the ground circuit.

CAUTION: Do not operate the system for more than 60 seconds when jumping a switch. The switch may be open to prevent compressor damage, such as when the refrigerant is low.

Figure 4-31. Measuring the current flow in the compressor clutch coil is sometimes more accurate than measuring resistance.

5

Air Conditioning Systems Diagnosis and Testing

SYSTEM IDENTIFICATION

There are almost as many different types of air conditioning systems as there are vehicle makes and models. However, air conditioning system identification is not difficult. Typically, an automobile manufacturer uses a simpler, less expensive system for economy cars, and a more sophisticated system for luxury cars. While this is true for the controls portion, the basic refrigeration system changes very little.

All modern automotive refrigeration systems use compressors, condensers, evaporators, and devices that control the flow of refrigerant into the evaporator. There may also be a device that controls the flow from the evaporator. Expansion devices are the restrictions that control the flow into the evaporator. Suction-throttling devices and variable displacement compressors control flow from the evaporator. Identifying these components will help you understand and troubleshoot the air conditioning system you are servicing.

Expansion Devices

In Chapter 6 of the *Classroom Manual,* we detailed the two types of expansion devices that control refrigerant flow into the evaporator:

- The thermostatic expansion valve (TXV)
- The fixed-orifice tube or variable-orifice valve (FOT or VOV)

Thermostatic Expansion Valve

The thermostatic expansion valve (TXV) regulates the flow of refrigerant into the evaporator by varying the opening in response to temperature and pressure changes in the evaporator. The TXV is typically located at the evaporator inlet. It may also be located in the evaporator case or the engine compartment. The H-block valve is also located at the evaporator inlet. The inlet line is easily identified because it is smaller and warmer than the outlet (suction) line. Systems with the TXV also have a receiver-drier.

Orifice Tube Systems

As with the TXV, the orifice tube is located at the refrigerant inlet; however, it is not always easy to find. The orifice tube may be found at the evaporator inlet, at the condenser outlet, or in the line in between.

Unlike the expansion valve, the fixed-orifice tube does not vary the opening to regulate the flow of refrigerant. The rate of flow is determined by the pressure differential between the high and the low side, and the size of the orifice. Instead of a receiver-drier, orifice tube systems have an accumulator on the suction side of the evaporator.

Suction-throttling Devices

As detailed in earlier chapters, suction-throttling devices regulate minimum evaporator pressure by controlling the flow of refrigerant from the evaporator. Suction-throttling devices are found on some late model Lexus, Nissan, and Toyota vehicles that have AC systems with automatic temperature controls. The Nissan suction-throttling valve (STV) is located at the evaporator outlet. On Lexus and Toyota models, the evaporator pressure regulator (EPR) valve is located in the suction line between the evaporator and the compressor.

To diagnose a suction-throttling device, you must know whether the valve should be open or closed, and then determine which position the valve is in. When the valve is open, the temperature is the same on both sides of the valve. When the valve is closed, the valve outlet is colder because of the pressure drop. The normal regulated pressure is about 28 psi (194 kPa). If the evaporator pressure is lower, the valve should close to raise the pressure. If the pressure is above the pressure specification, the valve should open. If the pressure is within specification, the valve is in the correct position.

The STV works like a coolant thermostat. If the coolant temperature is too low, the thermostat should be closed. If the temperature is too high, the thermostat should be open. If the temperature is correct, the thermostat position is correct at that time.

Variable Displacement Compressors

The variable displacement compressor also maintains a minimum evaporator pressure. If evaporator pressure drops below the minimum pressure, the compressor displacement reduces. As with the STV system, the compressor runs continually.

Identifying Temperature Control Systems

There are many different types of controls used to regulate the operation of heating, ventilation, and air conditioning systems. Manufacturers use manual, semiautomatic, and fully automatic control systems to control the operation.

Manual control systems can be identified by the controls, which are driver-operated, push-button, slide, or rotary controls, figure 5-1. The operator makes all the decisions for blower speed, temperature, and operating mode.

Semiautomatic control systems are the same as manual ones, except the desired temperature is set, figure 5-2. Instead of adjusting to hot or cold, the actual desired temperature is selected. The operator makes the decisions for blower speed and operating mode.

Fully automatic systems are electronic, and usually have digital temperature readouts and setting fea-

Figure 5-1. Manual control systems require that the driver select the desired temperature setting and fan speeds.

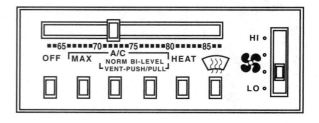

Figure 5-2. The driver sets the exact temperature on a semiautomatic control system. (Reprinted with permission of General Motors.)

Figure 5-3. Automatic control systems usually have a digital display. In the AUTO mode, all the driver has to do is select the desired temperature setting.

tures, figure 5-3. When on AUTO, the blower speed, temperature, and operating mode are set automatically. If cooling is needed, the air is discharged at the panel vents. If there is a large difference between the discharge air and the temperature in the car, the blower speed will be on high. As the temperature difference decreases, so does the blower speed. The controls also allow the operator to override or to change modes or blower speed. Some systems have the capability for dual zone control of air discharge, figure 5-4. This allows a different setting for the driver and passenger.

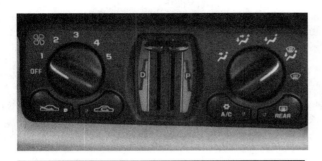

Figure 5-4. Dual zone systems allow the driver and passenger to independently control the discharge duct temperature.

When testing the control portion of a vehicle, the system should be checked for proper blower speeds in all settings and the proper operation of all operating modes.

1. Set the controls to AC and blower to LO. The air should be coming from the panel vents.
2. Move the blower speed switch slowly up to the HI position to confirm it works on all settings.
3. With the blower still on HI, change the mode to MAX or RECIRC. When the inside air door opens, you should be able to hear a difference in the sound of the blower.
4. Change the mode to BI-LEVEL. The air should be split between the floor and the panel vents, and the inside air door should close for outside air.
5. Move the mode to DEFROST; the air should switch to the defroster vents. When the

HEATER mode is selected the air should be delivered to the floor vents, with the AC off.
6. The VENT mode is typically used for bringing in outside air through the panel vents, with the AC off.

Follow the manufacturer's test procedure for the specific vehicle and system you are servicing. Often the Owner's Manual is a good source to determine the correct operation of the various modes.

INSPECTING THE AIR CONDITIONING SYSTEM

Inspecting the air conditioning system should be part of the vehicle's routine maintenance service. Periodic service checks ensure that the system is operating at peak efficiency. The following checks should be performed annually before hot weather, or prior to troubleshooting a problem, figure 5-5.

1. Inspect the condenser for leaves, mud, or other debris that can obstruct airflow. Some aftermarket bug screens reduce airflow more than bugs do.
2. Test the controls for proper operation.
3. Inspect and/or replace drive belts and cooling system hoses at the intervals specified by the vehicle manufacturer.
4. Make certain that all mechanical components are correctly mounted and secure. Incorrect or loose mountings can break a component or cause noise.

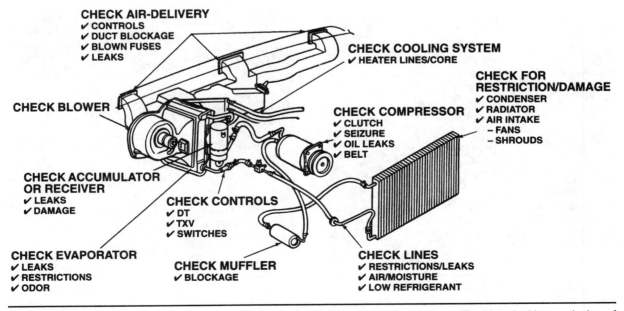

Figure 5-5. Basic checks in a visual inspection of a typical AC refrigeration system. (Reprinted with permission of ACDelco.)

5. Check the evaporator case drain tube, figure 5-6. A restricted or plugged drain tube holds moisture and allows bacteria to grow. This can cause a foul smell. It can also cause windshield fogging or water dripping on the floor on the passenger side. In extreme cases, water may run from the floor vents during turns.

6. Inspect the fittings and hoses for signs of oil, which indicates a refrigerant leak, figure 5-7.

Follow the manufacturer's test procedure for the specific vehicle and system that you are servicing.

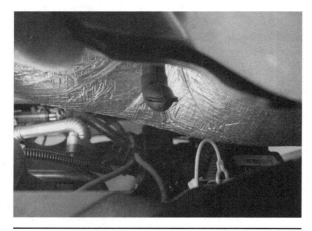

Figure 5-6. The evaporator drain tube usually can be accessed from under the vehicle. Make sure that the drain is not blocked with debris.

Figure 5-7. Inspect the lines and fittings for signs of oil and dirt. If they appear oily, leak test these fittings. (Courtesy of INFICON.)

AIR CONDITIONING PERFORMANCE TEST

After inspecting the physical condition of the heating, ventilation, and air conditioning, conduct a system performance test. Check the system operation in different modes for airflow and blower operation. Then conduct the performance test as follows:

1. Adequately ventilate your shop area. Connect the appropriate hoses to the exhaust system of the vehicle.

2. With the engine running, measure and record the ambient temperature in the area a few inches in front of the condenser, figure 5-8.

3. Connect a manifold gauge set to read system pressures on both the high and low side of the system. Keep both valves on the gauge set closed. When you connect the gauge set to a system that has not been operating, the pressure should read the same. If there is pressure only on one gauge, the other gauge may not be fully connected. The system is empty if both pressures are obviously less than the ambient temperature, figure 5-9.

4. Place a thermometer in the center dash duct, figure 5-10. Set the controls to MAX or RECIRC, and the blower on HIGH. Close all of the doors and windows.

5. Start the engine, and let it idle for a few minutes. Raise the engine speed to about 1,500 rpm. Note the temperature at the dash duct; it should range from 35° to 45°F (2° to 7°C).

Figure 5-8. Measure and record the ambient temperature a few inches in front of the condenser.

Figure 5-9. Install a gauge set to verify that the system contains refrigerant. Generally the pressure should be higher than the ambient temperature or at least 50 psi.

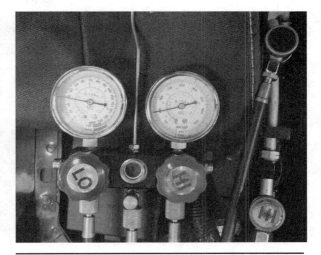

Figure 5-11. After running at 1,500 rpms for a couple of minutes, record the low- and high-side pressures on the gauge set.

Figure 5-10. Place a thermometer in the center AC duct.

6. Measure both the high and low pressure on the gauge set, figure 5-11.
7. Compare the measured high- and low-pressure readings and the center duct temperature to a chart if the manufacturer provides one, figure 5-12.

This performance test has a reduced heat load because of the recirculating air. This helps to compensate for the reduced airflow across the condenser. To increase the heat load, change the control setting to NORMAL or OUTSIDE air. This increases the heat load because warmer outside air is brought in. Under shop conditions, with the hood up, the air being brought in is even hotter than the ambient air. Air heated by the engine is inducted into the outside air door. This approach can be used to increase the heat load on a system when the ambient temperature is not hot enough. When testing an AC system at 70°F ambient temperature, a marginal system may adequately cool the air. Increasing the heat load can help determine the system operation.

TEMPERATURE AND PRESSURE MEASUREMENTS

Temperature and pressure are directly related in AC systems. As the ambient temperature increases, the high pressure must also increase to have a heat transfer at the condenser. The temperature of the vapor must be higher than the ambient temperature to allow enough heat to be removed for condensation. Also, higher ambient temperatures, and high humidity, usually mean a higher heat load on the evaporator. This means a larger quantity of heat has to be removed at the condenser.

The high-side pressure is directly related to the amount of heat that needs to be removed, and the heat transfer at the condenser. Low pressure indicates the boiling point, or temperature of the evaporator. If the pressure is too high, the boiling point and temperature of the evaporator are too high. Low-side pressure that is too low indicates the evaporator is too cold and may ice, or that there is not enough boiling refrigerant in the evaporator to remove an adequate amount of heat.

Using the ambient temperature you recorded earlier, use the pressure temperature chart, figure 5-13, to compare your temperature with normal specifications.

RELATIVE HUMIDITY	AMBIENT AIR TEMP.		RIGHT CENTER OUTLET AIR TEMP.		LOW SIDE PRESSURE		HIGH SIDE PRESSURE	
%	F DEG.	C DEG.	F DEG.	C DEG.	PSIG	kPa	PSIG	kPa
20	70	21	43	6	32	221	175	1207
	80	27	44	7	32	221	225	1551
	90	32	50	10	32	221	275	1896
	100	38	51	11	33	228	275	1896
30	70	21	45	7	32	221	190	1310
	80	27	47	8	32	221	235	1620
	90	32	54	12	34	234	290	2000
	100	38	57	14	38	262	310	2137
40	70	21	46	8	32	221	210	1448
	80	27	50	10	32	221	256	1758
	90	32	57	14	37	255	305	2103
	100	38	63	17	44	303	345	2379
50	70	21	48	9	32	221	225	1551
	80	27	53	12	34	234	270	1882
	90	32	60	16	41	283	326	2241
	100	38	89	21	49	338	380	2620
60	70	21	60	10	32	221	240	1855
	80	27	66	13	37	255	290	2000
	90	32	63	17	44	303	340	2344
	100	38	75	24	55	379	395	2724
70	70	21	52	11	32	221	255	1758
	80	27	59	15	40	276	305	2103
	90	32	67	19	48	331	355	2448
	100							
80	70	21	53	12	36	248	270	1862
	80	27	62	17	43	286	320	2206
	90	32	70	21	52	356	370	2551
	100							
90	70	21	55	13	40	278	286	1965
	80	27	65	18	47	324	335	2310
	90							
	100							

Figure 5-12. Performance test results for a typical CCOT refrigeration system. (Reprinted with permission of ACDelco.)

R-134a PRESSURE-TEMPERATURE CHART			
Ambient Air Temperature (°F)	Humidity	Low-Side Pressure (psi)	High-Side Pressure (psi)
70	Low	25 to 30	140 to 190
	High	28 to 35	165 to 220
80	Low	26 to 33	150 to 200
	High	30 to 36	190 to 260
90	Low	31 to 37	170 to 220
	High	37 to 45	210 to 290
100	Low	35 to 44	195 to 245
	High	38 to 48	230 to 320
110	Low	40 to 50	235 to 285
	High	42 to 52	260 to 350

Figure 5-13. The average R-134a pressure-temperature readings during a performance test. The high-side pressure of R-12 systems will be lower at higher temperatures than a similar system using R-134a.

The pressure readings may vary due to variations in system design. Consult a factory service manual for exact specifications.

The low-side pressure has a range based on the type of system. How low it goes is determined by the controls used to prevent icing. A thermostatic control switch allows the pressure to go lower than a pressure cycling switch. A pressure cycling switch normally opens in the range of 20 to 25 psi, while a thermostatic switch allows the low pressure to go as low as 15 psi.

The high-side pressure has a large range that is considered normal. High-side pressure varies with many factors, such as heat load and heat transfer. You will probably see pressures on the high side of normal without driving the vehicle, due to lower airflow across the condenser. When diagnosing AC problems using pressures, it is important to understand how the pressure reacts to operating conditions.

Low-side pressure is the result of the amount of refrigerant metered into the evaporator, and the efficiency of the compressor pulling it out. Low low-side pressure is usually a result of not enough refrigerant being metered into the evaporator. This can be caused by a low charge or restriction in the system. A low heat load on the evaporator, which allows the evaporator to get too cold and begin icing, may also cause low low-side pressure.

High low-side pressure is usually a result of reduced compressor efficiency. This can be caused by high-side pressure that is too high. Also, the compressor is not as efficient at low engine rpm as it is at higher rpms. Another cause of high low-side pressure is if too much refrigerant is metered into the evaporator by a flooding expansion valve. High-side pressure is determined by how much heat has to be removed, heat transfer at the condenser, and compressor efficiency.

As the ambient temperature rises, the heat load on the evaporator goes up, and the temperature in the condenser also has to rise to achieve the heat transfer. As the humidity of the air increases, the heat load on the evaporator also increases. These conditions are factored into the pressure charts for different ambient temperatures.

The heat transfer at the condenser is usually the cause of high-side pressure that is too high. The number one cause of poor heat transfer is lack of airflow across the condenser. The vehicle is dependent upon fans to move enough air when you are testing in a stall. It may be necessary to drive the vehicle at 30 mph to get the ram air necessary to determine if lack of airflow is the reason for the poor heat transfer.

The AC system has limited interior space. The upper two-thirds of the condenser is for the high-side vapor to condense back into a liquid. If the vapor is not condensing, there is more vapor in the same amount of space. Anything that reduces the amount of space

available for condensing increases the pressure. This is because additional heat transfer is needed to condense the vapor in the even smaller available space in the condenser. Other factors that reduce the vapor area of the condenser include an overcharge of refrigerant, air, or an excess of refrigerant oil.

Another cause of excessive high-side pressure is contamination with a different refrigerant. Mixing R-12 and R-134a raises the condensing pressure of the mixture. Pressures rise even higher when R-22 is mixed with R-12. At 150°F, the pressure of R-12 is 235 psi (1,620 kPa), R-134a is 263 psi (1,813 kPa), and R-22 is 381 psi (2,627 kPa). This is an important reason to use a refrigerant identifier. Another cause for excessive high-side pressure is excessive air in the refrigerant. When refrigerant is recovered the recovery unit should automatically vent air or it needs to be manually vented from the recovery tank. It is not uncommon to find excess air in recovered refrigerant. Once again, a refrigerant identifier will determine if the recovered refrigerant has excess air in the refrigerant. If no identifier is available, the temperature-pressure relationship charts must be used, figure 5-14.

A flooding expansion valve also raises high-side pressure because it allows too much refrigerant into the evaporator. There is now more heat being picked up in the hoses, which increases the heat load. However, the high-side pressure does not rise by a large amount under this circumstance.

As compressor efficiency is reduced, the high side decreases, and the low side increases. The function of the compressor is to pull down the low side and push up the high side. When the compressor is failing, it does not do either job well. Always look at both the high-side and low-side pressures when diagnosing a problem.

All of the following conditions were tested at 80°F (26.67°C) with low humidity. As the temperature and humidity increase, the pressures also increase.

CONDITION # 1
Refer to figure 5-15.

Low Side:	LOW @ 5 psi
High Side:	LOW @ 120 psi
Evaporator Outlet:	COOL to WARM
Discharge Air:	WARM

Since both sides are low, there is not enough refrigerant being metered into the evaporator, and a low heat load is causing the low high-side pressure. This could be caused by a low charge or restriction in the liquid portion of the system. Symptoms may also include a pressure cycling switch that is cycling on and off very rapidly. If you bypass the pressure cycling switch, the pressures will drop even lower. A restriction often has

CALCULATION EXAMPLE
Maximum Chart Pressure 5% Contamination

CFC-12	96 psig	(SAE Ref. Chart Pressure)
	x 1.05	(Multiplication Factor)
	= 100.8 psig	(Contaminated Ref. Press.)
HFC-134a	91 psig	(SAE Ref. Chart Pressure)
	x 1.05	(Multiplication Factor)
	= 95.5 psig	(Contaminated Ref. Press.)

MAXIMUM ALLOWABLE NCG AIR CONTAINER PRESSURE RECYCLED CFC-12 (SAE J1989)

TEMP °F	PSIG	TEMP °F	PSIG	TEMP °F	PSIG	TEMP °F	PSIG	TEMP °F	PSIG
65	74	75	87	85	102	95	118	105	136
66	75	76	88	86	103	96	120	106	138
67	76	77	90	87	105	97	122	107	140
68	78	78	92	88	107	98	124	108	142
69	79	79	94	89	108	99	125	109	144
70	80	80	96	90	110	100	127	110	146
71	82	81	98	91	111	101	129	111	148
72	83	82	99	92	113	102	130	112	150
73	84	83	100	93	115	103	132	113	152
74	86	84	101	94	116	104	134	114	154

PRES kg/sq cm

MAXIMUM ALLOWABLE NCG AIR CONTAINER PRESSURE RECYCLED HFC-134a (SAE J2211)

TEMP °F	PSIG	TEMP °F	PSIG	TEMP °F	PSIG	TEMP °F	PSIG	TEMP °F	PSIG
65	69	76	85	88	105	99	127	110	151
67	71	78	88	89	107	100	129	111	153
67	73	79	90	90	109	101	131	112	156
68	74	80	91	91	111	102	133	113	158
69	75	81	93	92	113	103	135	114	160
70	76	82	95	93	115	104	137	115	163
71	77	83	96	94	118	105	139	116	165
72	79	84	98	95	118	106	142	117	168
73	80	85	100	96	120	107	144	118	171
74	83	86	102	97	122	108	146	119	173
75	85	87	103	98	125	109	149	120	176

PRES kg/sq cm

Figure 5-14. SAE specifications for maximum allowable container pressures for recycled refrigerants. (Reprinted with permission of ACDelco.)

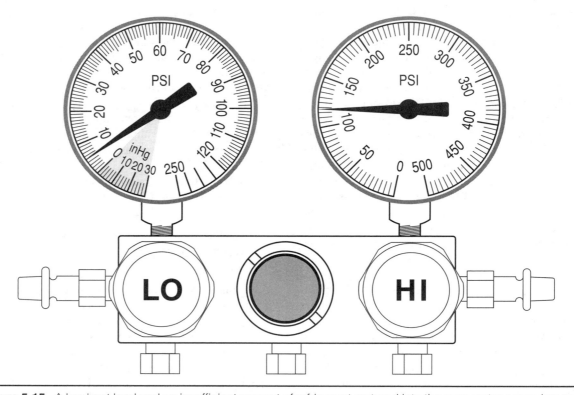

Figure 5-15. A low heat load and an insufficient amount of refrigerant metered into the evaporator cause low pressure on both sides.

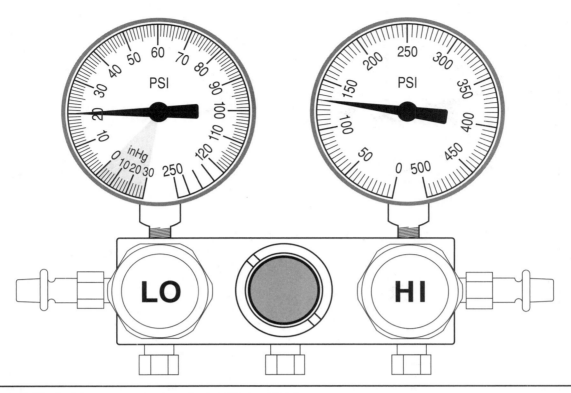

Figure 5-16. An icing evaporator is reducing this heat load.

a vacuum reading, while a low charge is above 5 psi. If the system is equipped with a sight glass, bubbles indicate a low charge or a restriction before the sight glass.

CONDITION # 2
Refer to figure 5-16.

Low Side:	LOW @ 20 psi
High Side:	LOW @ 130 psi
Evaporator Outlet:	FROSTED
Discharge Air:	COLD with REDUCED AIRFLOW

This problem does not occur until the heat load on the evaporator is reduced. The typical customer complaint is that the discharge air from the ducts slows down after the vehicle has been driven for a while. It seems to be worse on cooler days. An icing evaporator is reducing the heat load. This problem is caused by a faulty device used to prevent evaporator icing, such as a pressure cycling switch or thermostatic control switch. The device is not opening. It may also be a suction-throttling valve that is stuck open or a variable displacement compressor that is not modulating. To confirm this problem, reduce the heat load on the evaporator by either disconnecting the blower motor or putting the fan speed on LOW. Set the controls to recirculating air and keep the engine on fast idle.

CONDITION # 3
Refer to figure 5-17.

Low Side:	NORMAL @ 28 psi
High Side:	LOW @ 125 psi
Evaporator Outlet:	WARM
Discharge Air:	WARM

The normal low-side pressure with a warm tailpipe means that an inadequate amount of refrigerant is being metered into the evaporator. This indicates either a low refrigerant charge, or a restriction in the liquid portion of the system. The normal low-side pressure may be the result of a suction-throttling valve that has closed to maintain proper evaporator pressure. A variable displacement compressor also maintains a normal low-side pressure.

CONDITION # 4
Refer to figure 5-18.

Low Side:	HIGH @ 60 psi
High Side:	LOW @ 120 psi
Evaporator Outlet:	COOL to WARM
Discharge Air:	WARM

A faulty compressor can display these symptoms. Other symptoms may include a compressor that is noisy or very hot to the touch. Before condemning the

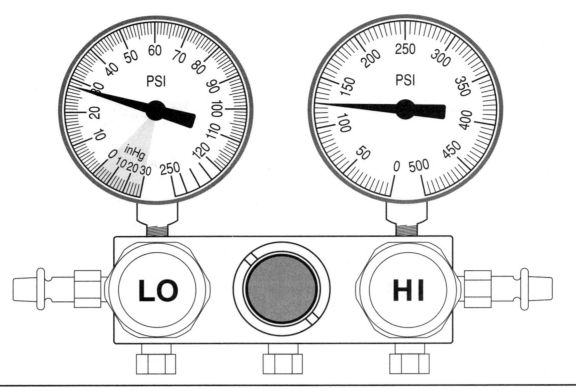

Figure 5-17. A low refrigerant charge, or a restriction in a liquid line, is preventing refrigerant from entering the evaporator.

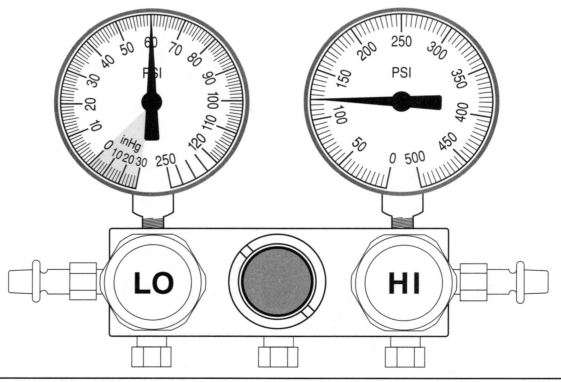

Figure 5-18. Many components may be responsible for this problem.

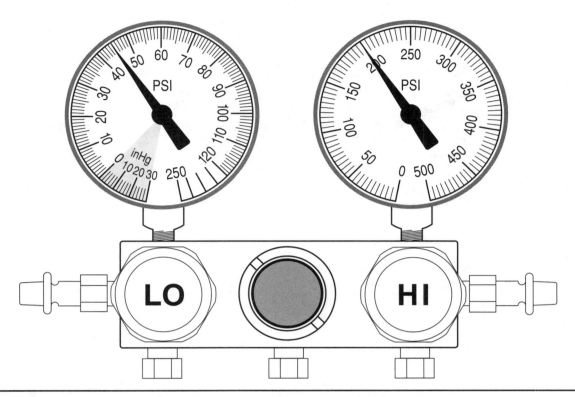

Figure 5-19. These readings indicate the evaporator has too much refrigerant in it.

compressor, confirm that there is no slippage at the clutch drive hub or belts. If the compressor is cycling off at the high pressure, check the thermostatic control or pressure cycling switch. These symptoms can also be caused by a suction-throttling valve that is stuck in the closed position. Check for a cold spot on the suction-throttling valve, which indicates a restriction.

CONDITION # 5
Refer to figure 5-19.

Low Side:	HIGH @ 45 psi
High Side	NORMAL @ 200 psi
Evaporator Outlet:	COOL
Discharge Air:	COOL

Either there is too much refrigerant being metered into the evaporator, or the compressor is not pulling it out. The suction hose and the compressor will feel cold if the evaporator is being flooded. A flooding expansion valve is usually the result of the sensing bulb sensing a warm temperature. Check the connection of the sensing bulb at the evaporator outlet. The connection should have a wide metal band making good contact between the bulb and the outlet pipe, and should be covered with insulating material. A stuck closed suction-throttling device or a faulty compressor may

be the reason the compressor is not pulling the refrigerant out. This is a common complaint with the variable displacement compressor.

CONDITION # 6
Refer to figure 5-20.

Low Side:	NORMAL @ 30 psi
High Side:	NORMAL @ 190 psi
Evaporator Outlet:	COLD to COOL
Discharge Air:	COOL

Check the controls and blend door if the evaporator outlet is cold. Discharge air that is cold when the vehicle is first started, and warms up as the engine warms, indicates a control problem. Contaminated refrigerant is a possibility if the discharge air is only cool. Recover, evacuate, and recharge the system. Retest the system with the new refrigerant charge.

CONDITION # 7
Refer to figure 5-21.

Low Side:	LOW to NORMAL @ 15–25 psi
High Side:	HIGH @ 395 psi
Evaporator Outlet:	WARM
Air Discharge:	WARM

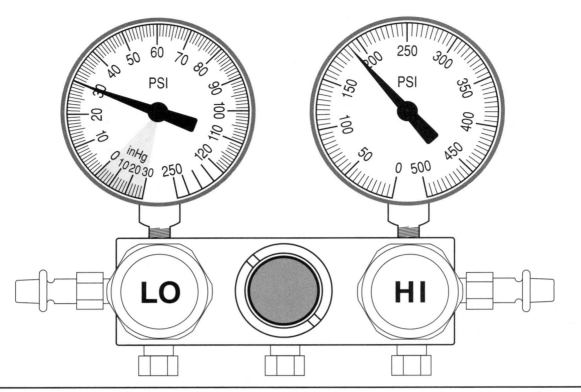

Figure 5-20. A problem with the controls, or contaminated refrigerant, may be the cause of these readings.

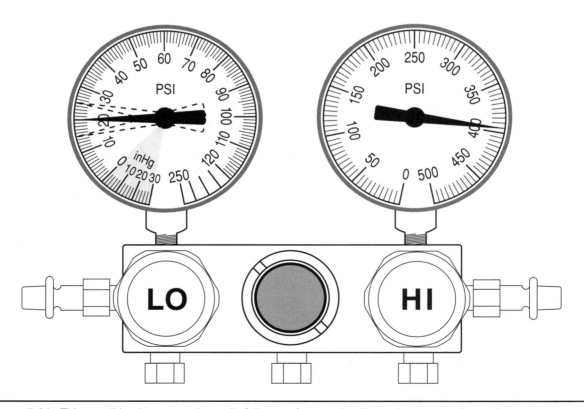

Figure 5-21. This condition is rare, and usually follows a front-end collision that causes body damage, or a compressor failure.

A restriction in the high-side vapor area reduces the condensing area, increasing discharge pressure. A restriction also reduces high-side pressure after the restriction, and refrigerant flow through the orifice tube or expansion valve. If the high-side service port is after the restriction, the high pressure will not be obvious. The compressor may cycle off if a high-pressure cut-off switch is located before the restriction. This condition is rare, and usually follows a front-end collision that causes body damage, or a compressor failure. The restriction can be found by a sudden drop in temperature at the point of the restriction.

CONDITION # 8
Refer to figure 5-22.

Low Side:	HIGH @ 45 psi
High Side:	HIGH @ 325 psi
Evaporator Outlet:	WARM or SLIGHTLY COOL
Discharge Air:	WARM or SLIGHTLY COOL

This is a condensing problem. The number one cause is not enough airflow across the condenser. Inspect for leaves or debris blocking the airflow. If the condenser is clear, check for debris in front of the radiator. A fan may be put in front of the vehicle to increase airflow; however, it may not be effective with many of the designs on new vehicles. Spraying the condenser with cold water may also help isolate the cause. The most effective method is to connect the gauge set and drive the vehicle to get ram air. There are transducers available that allow you to read and record pressures with a hand-held DVOM.

Other causes include factors that reduce the vapor area, such as an overcharge of refrigerant or oil, or air in the system. All of these occupy space, which leaves less room for condensing. The problem of excess oil is more prevalent in systems that have been retrofitted. Another possibility is the wrong type of refrigerant, or contaminated refrigerant in the system. To verify these possibilities, recover, evacuate, and recharge the system. While charging, watch the pressures before the entire refrigerant is charged into the system. If the pressures start to go high before the specified amount is charged, stop and test the system for proper operation. Many retrofit systems operate best with less than the recommended refrigerant charge.

CAUTION: Do not recover the refrigerant into your recovery tank until you have tested for contamination with a refrigerant identifier.

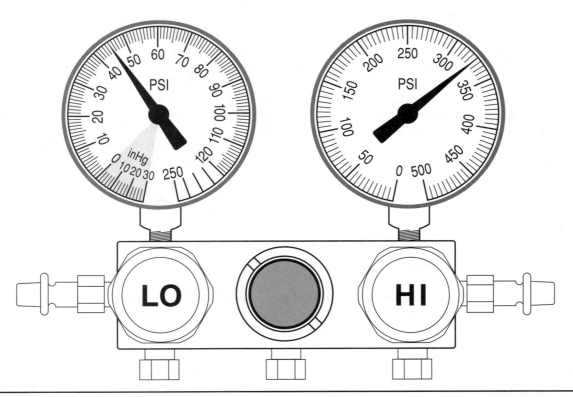

Figure 5-22. Insufficient airflow across the condenser is usually the cause of this problem.

SYSTEM DIAGNOSIS

Proper diagnosis requires more than just looking at pressures. To verify many problems you must check other items to help confirm your diagnosis.

Diagnosis by Temperature

Temperature is an important tool in diagnosing. To learn what is "hot" or "cold," touch different components on a properly operating system. The discharge hose is very hot when the high-side pressure is high. The receiver-drier or liquid line is cooler, but still hot. The temperature is cold after the expansion valve or orifice tube, and the evaporator outlet or accumulator is also cold. The evaporator outlet on an expansion valve system is not as cold as the evaporator outlet on an orifice tube system. This is because liquid refrigerant does not leave the evaporator on expansion valve systems. A restriction in the liquid portion is cold, and may have frost. Any restriction causes a temperature drop at that point. Familiarize yourself with the temperature of components on a properly operating system. After you have learned what is "normal," a quick touch may speed up or confirm your diagnosis.

Diagnosing by Sight

You can detect many faults by simply observing the system operation:

- See if the compressor clutch engages. Check the compressor drive belt for proper position and tension.
- Some receiver-drier systems have a sight glass to check the condition of the refrigerant.
- Look for frost as an indication of a restriction.
- Inspect fittings. Dirt and oil indicate leaks.
- Observe cooling fan operation and placement of air dams around the condenser and radiator.

Sight Glass Diagnosis

On receiver-drier systems, a sight glass allows a visual check of the refrigerant state of charge. Sight glass locations vary by design. The sight glass is always in the liquid line portion of the system between the receiver-drier and the expansion valve. It is commonly built into the receiver-drier, figure 5-23, but may also be in the liquid line. Only systems with expansion valves and receiver-driers use a sight glass. Systems with orifice tubes do not.

R-12 Sight Glass

Since refrigerant is colorless, the sight glass should be clear. The sight glass also looks clear when the

Figure 5-23. Many receiver-driers are equipped with a sight glass on the top of the unit.

system is empty, or when the compressor is not engaged. An R-12 system must have a high heat load when using the sight glass to diagnose. Do not diagnose using the sight glass when the ambient temperature is below 70°F.

A low refrigerant level, which allows vapor to enter the system through the pickup tube in the receiver-drier, is indicated by a stream of bubbles in the sight glass. As the system loses more refrigerant and takes in more vapor, the bubbles start to look like foam. An empty system has oil streaks on the sight glass. The oil is on the glass, and is being moved by the vapor passing, figure 5-24. If the refrigerant in the sight glass is a red or yellow color, the system contains leak-detecting dye. The dye should be left in to help find future leaks.

R-134a Sight Glass

Some, but not all, R-134a systems have a sight glass. An accurate sight glass reading on an R-134a system requires certain conditions. The heat load cannot be too high. Make a sight glass check when:

- Ambient temperature is below 95°F (35°C).
- Engine speed is at 1,500 rpms.
- The controls are set for COLD and RECIRCULATE.
- The blower is on HIGH.
- High-side pressure is below 240 psi (1,655 kPa).

It is normal to see an almost transparent flow of bubbles. A constant flow of bubbles indicates a low refrigerant charge. The sight glass reading should be used only as an indication of further testing needed. Do not

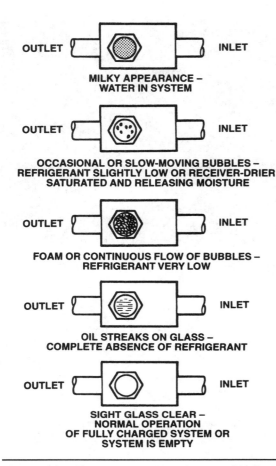

OUTLET — INLET

**MILKY APPEARANCE –
WATER IN SYSTEM**

OUTLET — INLET

**OCCASIONAL OR SLOW-MOVING BUBBLES –
REFRIGERANT SLIGHTLY LOW OR RECEIVER-DRIER
SATURATED AND RELEASING MOISTURE**

OUTLET — INLET

**FOAM OR CONTINUOUS FLOW OF BUBBLES –
REFRIGERANT VERY LOW**

OUTLET — INLET

**OIL STREAKS ON GLASS –
COMPLETE ABSENCE OF REFRIGERANT**

OUTLET — INLET

**SIGHT GLASS CLEAR –
NORMAL OPERATION
OF FULLY CHARGED SYSTEM OR
SYSTEM IS EMPTY**

Figure 5-24. Typical sight glass views and indicated problems. (Reprinted with permission of ACDelco.)

charge an R-134a system using the sight glass as an indicator of adequate charge.

Diagnosing by Sound

An air conditioning system can produce two types of noise that may be useful in diagnosing problems:

1. Mechanical noise
2. Refrigerant noise

Mechanical Noise
Mechanical noise is made by moving parts that:

- Have defective bearings
- Are improperly lubricated
- Are colliding with other moving parts
- Are loose in their mountings

Locating the noisy part and correcting the problem require additional troubleshooting.

Refrigerant Noise
A common service complaint is hissing noise when the engine is turned off after the AC was operated. This

noise is refrigerant flow through the orifice tube. This is a normal condition. In some cases manufacturers have relocated the orifice tube further away from the evaporator to reduce this noise.

Compressor Clutch Noise
Compressor pulley bearing noise depends on the type of pulley being used. Some clutch assemblies mount on the end of the compressor driveshaft. The pulley bearings are used when the clutch is disengaged. When the clutch is engaged, the assembly is locked together, and the compressor front bearing is being used. A faulty pulley bearing on this style is noisy when the compressor is disengaged. The noise goes away when the compressor is engaged. The compressor stays engaged if the bearings are seized.

The more common style has the pulley bearings mounted on the front housing of the compressor. These bearings are in use whenever the pulley is turning. The drive hub is mounted to the end of the compressor driveshaft. When disengaged, the pulley bearings are being used. When engaged, they are still in use but have a heavier load on them. A faulty pulley bearing on this style tends to be louder when the compressor is engaged.

Compressor Noise
A clicking, knocking, or rumbling noise when the compressor is engaged usually indicates internal compressor damage. A rumbling noise can also be caused by a loose clutch or loose compressor mounting bracket. A faulty idler pulley bearing makes the same noise, so you need to confirm that the noise is from the compressor.

Check the belt tension. It is possible for the belt to set up a harmonic vibration, usually at specific rpms.

Blower Motor Noise
Most blower motors have armature shafts that are supported by brass or bronze bushings. As these bushings wear, two types of problems are likely to occur:

1. If a bushing is poorly lubricated and worn to the point that it causes the shaft to drag, current draw to the motor increases. If the drag is severe, the circuit fuse may blow. If the drag is intermittent, or heat related, the blower may operate when cool, but stall or blow the fuse when hot.
2. Defective bushings can cause motor squeal, shaft vibration, or noise due to the fan rubbing against the fan housing. These noises often increase as the speed of the fan increases.

An unbalanced cage fan causes blower vibration. Debris in the fan, or blades that are bent or cracked, may cause the cage fan to become unbalanced. Check the

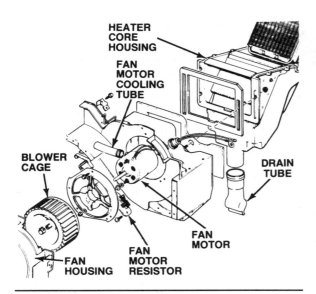

Figure 5-25. An unbalanced cage causes blower vibration.

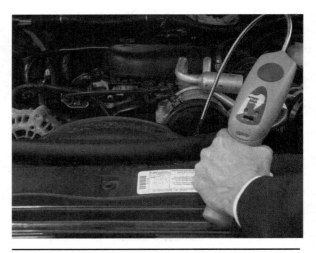

Figure 5-26. Checking the compressor shaft seal for leaks. (Courtesy of INFICON.)

fan and the motor, figure 5-25. Blower motors are usually replaced rather than repaired.

Compressor Pumping

Compressor pumping noises can be transmitted into the vehicle if a hose is lying against the body. Make sure that all hoses are mounted properly. Most systems use a muffler in the system to help prevent compressor "moan" when operating.

REFRIGERANT LEAK DETECTION

Leaking refrigerant is the main cause of air conditioning service problems. The refrigerant is held in the system under high pressure, and a leak results in a loss of refrigerant, which decreases cooling capacity. Leaks are indicated by insufficient cooling, low readings on the test gauges, and an accumulation of dirt and oil at the location of the leak. A leak test is part of routine service.

Refrigerant leaks are often found where parts of the system are joined together, especially if the joints are made of different materials. Parts that move in relation to each other are also especially vulnerable. Refrigerant is heavier than air and tends to sink. Concentrations of leaking refrigerant are therefore most likely to be found underneath components (especially around the evaporator). Always check the entire system in case there is more than one leak. Common leakage points include:

- *Compressor seals.* Shaft seals can wear over time, allowing refrigerant to leak, figure 5-26.
- *Refrigerant line connections.* These lines and hoses are subject to expansion and contraction

from rapid heating and cooling. They also endure vibration and movement between the compressor and the relatively motionless auto body. Spring-lock connectors are especially subject to movement within the connector.
- *Component pinhole leaks.* Leaks in components such as the accumulator, receiver-drier, evaporator, and condenser may occur. Oily spots are a common indication of pinhole leaks.

A large leak in the system is usually fairly easy to locate. Look for oily residue on hoses, connections, or seals. A large amount of oil in one location indicates the likely leak sight. Confirm the exact location with a leak detector. A large leak can be difficult to pinpoint because it floods the surrounding area with refrigerant. Many detectors have a button to desensitize the tester to aid in locating large leaks.

A leak in the evaporator can usually be found by "sniffing" at the evaporator drain with the detector. If this is not accessible, it may be possible to remove the blower resistor block to gain access to the evaporator.

Condenser leaks usually have oil in the area of the leak. It is also possible that they leak only when the high-side pressure is high. It may be necessary to run the AC to build up pressure, turn off the engine, and test while the pressure is still high.

Leak Detection Tools

An electronic leak detector, figure 5-27, has a wand with a probe at the end. As the wand is moved along the refrigeration system, the probe draws in a small sample of air, and examines it electronically. Some detectors have an audible alarm and illuminate a light when the refrigerant is detected. Others have a continuous audi-

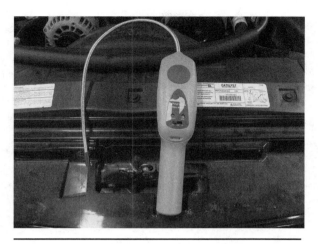

Figure 5-27. An electronic leak detector samples the air and sounds an alarm if refrigerant is detected. (Courtesy of INFICON.)

ble tone that changes with detection. Always use the detector according to the manufacturer's instructions.

Some electronic detectors are programmed for use with R-12 only or with R-134a only. Other leak detectors can detect multiple types of refrigerant. Always verify that the detector is the correct one for the system that you are servicing.

Since the electronic detector is very sensitive, refrigerant in the air may set it off before the actual leak is discovered. Blow out the area with shop air before beginning. Do not conduct the testing where there is any wind blowing as this may carry away refrigerant. To locate a refrigerant leak with an electronic leak detector:

1. Calibrate your leak detector if required. Confirm that it is responding to refrigerant by passing it by a known leak, such as a gauge hose connection.
2. Slowly move the probe along the refrigerant lines and system components. Never directly touch a component with the tip of the wand. You want to keep the probe approximately 1/4 inch away from the component being tested. You may obtain incorrect readings if the probe contacts the component. Move the probe about 1/2 inch per second, figure 5-28. Remember that refrigerant is heavier than air and tends to accumulate under leaking joints or seals, or behind the compressor pulley near the front seal.
3. After you locate a leak, use shop air to blow out the area and then retest. It is important to know the exact location. If there is a possibility of a leak in two close locations, place a piece of paper between them to act as a dam so you can isolate the leak.

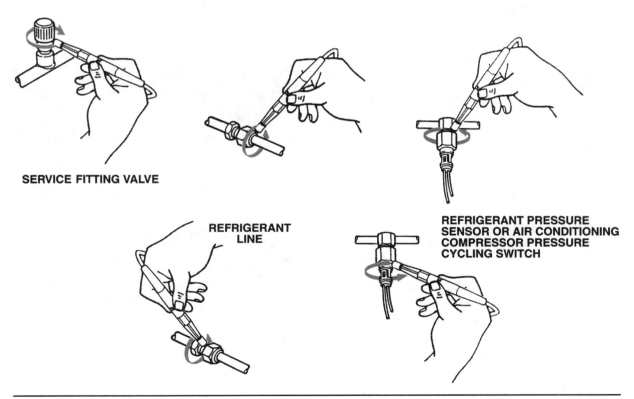

SERVICE FITTING VALVE

REFRIGERANT LINE

REFRIGERANT PRESSURE SENSOR OR AIR CONDITIONING COMPRESSOR PRESSURE CYCLING SWITCH

Figure 5-28. Accurate refrigerant leak testing with a halogen leak detector. (Reprinted with permission of General Motors Corporation.)

4. Do not keep the probe tip in contact with escaping refrigerant any longer than needed to establish that there is a leak. The sensitive components of the detector may be damaged by overexposure to refrigerant.

5. As you move the probe around the refrigeration system, the beeping will get faster and louder as the probe nears the leak. The larger the leak that is detected, the faster and louder the beeper will sound.

Dye Leak Detection

Dye leak detection involves adding fluorescent dye to the system, which mixes with the system lubricant. As with the lubricants, the dyes are dedicated for R-12 or R-134a, or both. Make certain to use the correct dye for the system that you are servicing. Dye leak detection is available as a straight dye to add to the system, or premixed with refrigerant in a 14-ounce can. Dye is now installed at the factory by many manufacturers, as well as in the oil charge of rebuilt compressors. To add dye to the system:

1. Attach a manifold gauge set to the high- and low-side service fittings.

2. If the dye leak detection includes refrigerant, add the solution to the system as you would normally add a can of refrigerant.

3. If the dye leak detection does not include refrigerant, connect the center hose to one end of the dye injector, and the other end to the refrigerant bottle. Now add the dye with the refrigerant, figure 5-29.

4. Many of the newer dye injection kits do not require the use of a manifold gauge set to inject the dye, figure 5-30.

5. It takes liquid refrigerant to wash the dye into the system. You need to charge with liquid until the dye has entered the system. This presents a problem when adding refrigerant at the low-side service port at the compressor. Control the flow into the low side with the hand valve on the gauge set. After the dye is in the system, revert back to vapor charging. Remember to control the flow until all the liquid is out of the hoses.

6. Operate the air conditioning system for at least 15 minutes. Turn off the engine.

7. Inspect all joints for signs of the dye using a black light. Special glasses are available to enhance the reading, figure 5-31.

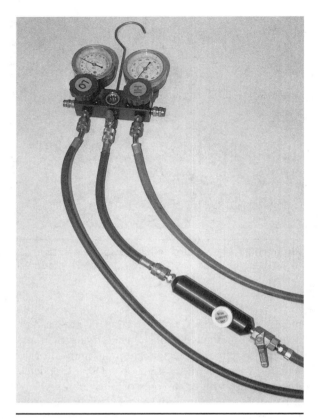

Figure 5-29. The dye injector is filled with dye and attached inline on the manifold gauge set service hose.

Figure 5-30. Many dye injection kits allow you to inject dye without having to connect a manifold gauge set.

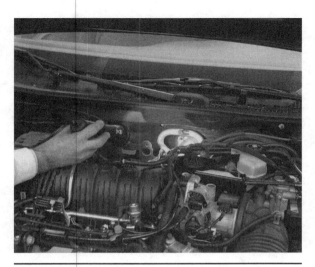

Figure 5-31. After injecting the dye and running the AC system, use a black light to look for leaks.

8. If there is no immediate indication of a leak, leave the vehicle parked for 24 hours and recheck. It may be necessary to have the vehicle come back in a week to retest it. Once the leak is found, perform necessary repairs. The dye remains in the system until the lubricant oil is changed.

6

Component Diagnosis and Service

The decision to disassemble parts or portions of the air conditioning system is not one to be taken lightly. Most major component replacement jobs are both time-consuming for the technician and expensive for the customer. Specific tools, skills, training, and certification are required.

Needless replacement of refrigerant components often results in unnecessary expense to your customer without actually fixing the problem. Proper equipment and procedures must be used to prevent the release of refrigerant into the atmosphere during service. Use the repair procedures outlined in this chapter, along with accurate specifications and model-specific instructions provided by the vehicle manufacturer, to ensure an accurate diagnosis and successful repair.

Chapter 8 of this *Shop Manual* covers compressor diagnosis, repair, and replacement. This chapter details servicing the other refrigeration components of the AC system. The following sections explain the possible reasons for replacing each air conditioning component, the symptoms these parts exhibit when they have failed, and how to accurately diagnose a failure to isolate the defective component. Typical procedures for removing and replacing defective AC components are also included.

DIAGNOSIS AND REPAIR PROCEDURES

Before starting major repairs to the air conditioning system, go through a checklist to make sure you are prepared to complete the repair successfully. The sample checklist that follows may seem lengthy, but it becomes an easy-to-use guide once it is practiced a few times. Creating and using a checklist develops sound shop practices and increases the probability of repairing the problem on the first attempt. Another checklist is used after repair work is completed to verify the repair, make sure the system functions properly, and eliminate the need for any additional service.

Before the Repair

Items to include on a preliminary checklist can be divided into five categories:

1. Information
2. Diagnosis
3. Materials
4. Tools
5. Cleaning

Using this type of checklist saves time because it ensures that the repair work goes smoothly without being interrupted to locate a part, tool, specification, or other item.

Information

The first step is to identify the problem and the system. This includes the following procedures:

- Discuss the symptoms with your customer. Then attempt to recreate the problem in the shop or on a road test.
- Identify the type of AC system. Determine if it is a manual or automatic, uses an expansion valve or orifice tube, and what type of compressor is used.
- Use your electronic refrigerant identifier to identify the type of refrigerant in the system, whether it is R-12, R-134a, or some other alternative.
- Determine what kind and grade of refrigerant oil the system uses, whether it is mineral oil, PAG, or Ester oil, figure 6-1.
- Locate the shop manual or other technical information, including an electrical diagram, for the system being serviced.

Diagnosis

The next step is to locate the source of the problem. Include the following procedures on your checklist.

- Perform a complete visual inspection of the AC system and its components, including the fans, belts, wiring, evaporator drain tube, and other related items.
- Connect a manifold gauge set and take a static reading of the pressures. Compare these readings to the values shown in figure 6-2, then switch the AC on and read the operating pressures.
- Verify that the compressor comes on and that the clutch cycles properly as the system operates if it is a cycling clutch system.
- Listen for any abnormal noises from the compressor, clutch, pulley, or fan.

R-134a	
Temperature (°F)	Vapor Pressure (PSIG)
−15	0
−10	2
0	7
10	12
20	18
25	22
30	26
35	30
40	35
45	40
50	45
60	57
70	71
80	86
90	104
100	124
110	146

Figure 6-2. R-134a static pressures.

- Use a thermometer to check the discharge air temperature.
- Compare the discharge air temperature change with changes in the control panel settings.
- Follow the diagnostic procedure recommended by the manufacturer to pinpoint the cause of any malfunction.
- Access the self-diagnostic program, if equipped, and perform a diagnostic trouble code (DTC) check on the electronic system.
- Perform the appropriate test to confirm the diagnosis.

Materials

Once the defective component is identified:

- Gather all the materials needed to replace it. This includes all the required replacement components, seals, gaskets, fasteners, and other incidental parts needed for the job.
- Verify the fit of the replacement parts. Remember, not all components are universally applicable; make sure you have the correct replacement.
- Have an adequate supply of the correct type of refrigerant, refrigerant oil, and flushing compound.
- Have the proper size caps or plugs, figure 6-3, for sealing the system openings when refrigerant components are opened.

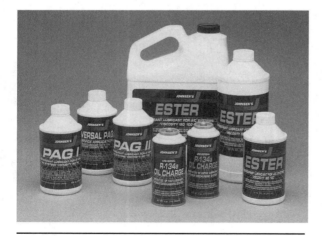

Figure 6-1. Different types of refrigerant use different types of lubricating oil.

Figure 6-3. Use caps saved from previous repairs to seal lines when they are opened.

Tools

Most major AC repairs require special tools or equipment in addition to standard service tools. Include the following on your checklist:

- Acquire a refrigerant identifier.
- Have all the necessary tools for the specific air conditioning repair being performed.
- Make certain any special tools recommended by the manufacturer are available.
- Make sure all tools are clean, in good condition, and ready to use.

Cleaning

An AC system is prone to contamination any time a refrigerant component is loosened or removed. Before beginning repairs:

- Clean the outside of the lines, fittings, and components to prevent system contamination when connections are opened.
- Clean the work area such as the bench top before placing AC components on it.

After the Repair

After repairs are made, use the following checklist to make sure the procedure was performed correctly and completely:

- Verify that replacement parts are installed according to instructions from the manufacturer.
- Add the specific amount of refrigerant oil to the new parts to compensate for the residual oil in the components being replaced, figure 6-4.

OIL REPLACEMENT GUIDE		
Compressor	2 oz	60 ml
Evaporator	2 oz	60 ml
Condenser	1 oz	30 ml
Accumulator	2 oz	60 ml
Lines	1 oz	30 ml
Receiver-Drier	1 oz	30 ml

Figure 6-4. Many manufacturers have an oil replacement chart that can be used to determine how much oil to add when replacing a component.

- Tighten all nuts, bolts, and other fasteners to the torque settings specified by the manufacturer.
- Check that all hoses, assemblies, and wiring harnesses are in place, correctly routed, and securely attached.

Flushing

If a system has been contaminated with metal particles from compressor failure or contaminated refrigerant or oil, it may require flushing. Flushing procedures vary by manufacturer; some manufacturers use a flushing solvent, while other manufacturers only recommend flushing with refrigerant. Make sure that you follow the manufacturer's recommendations concerning flushing.

- Thoroughly flush the system, according to procedures recommended by the manufacturer, to remove any debris or foreign particles if required by the repairs performed.
- Replace the receiver-drier or accumulator if specified by the manufacturer.

Recover and Recharge

- Recover the refrigerant and recharge the system following guidelines from the manufacturer.
- Replace refrigerant oil equal to the amount lost during recovery as specified by the manufacturer.

CAUTION: It is important to note that you must follow manufacturer specifications when you are replacing the refrigerant oil. The oil capacity specification is usually stamped on the compressor. This is the total system capacity. Make certain that you do not add more than the total system capacity. Use the oil amounts included here as a general guide. Model-specific instructions and capacities should be included with a replacement compressor. When in doubt, contact your tool supplier or compressor manufacturer for additional oil capacity information.

Leak and Performance Test

- Perform a leak test to make sure the system is free of leaks.
- Conduct a performance test to verify proper system operation.

IDENTIFYING SYSTEMS, REFRIGERANTS, AND OILS

Properly identifying the type of AC system, the refrigerant installed, and the refrigerant oil used is critical to a successful repair.

System Type

It is important to identify the type of system being worked on because it determines the diagnostic process used to isolate the defective component. Identifying the system involves establishing:

- If the system is manual or automatic
- What type of expansion device is used
- What type of compressor is used

Manual or Automatic

To quickly confirm if the system is manual or automatic, look at the control panel. If the temperature control has a slide lever or knob to adjust temperature, it is likely manual. Automatic systems generally use digital displays or other means of setting the exact temperature selection, figure 6-5. See Chapter 11 of the *Classroom Manual* for a discussion of these systems.

MANUAL

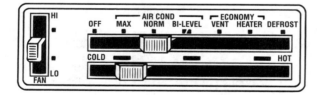

AUTOMATIC

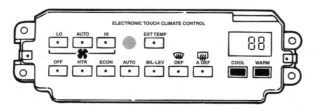

Figure 6-5. Manual AC heat control levers range from cold to hot, while automatic AC system controls allow a specific temperature selection. (Reprinted with permission of General Motors Corporation.)

Expansion Device

Check under the hood and locate the expansion device. Expansion valves may be easily seen on or near the firewall at the evaporator inlet. Some expansion valves are located inside the evaporator case and cannot be seen from under the hood. If this is the case, look for a receiver-drier located between the condenser and the evaporator, figure 6-6.

An orifice tube may not be easily visible, because it installs inside the evaporator inlet line or in the liquid line between the condenser and the evaporator. Look for indentations just beyond a fitting in the line, figure 6-7, or look for an accumulator on the outlet side of the evaporator to confirm if the system uses an orifice tube, figure 6-8.

Type of Compressor

It is important to determine the type of compressor that is being used on the vehicle. The type of compressor

Figure 6-6. Thermostatic expansion valve systems will have a receiver-drier located between the condenser and the evaporator.

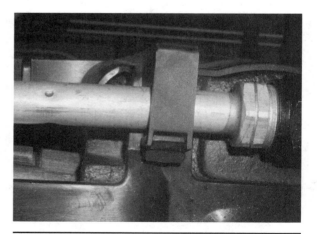

Figure 6-7. A dimple in the liquid line just beyond a fitting usually indicates the presence of an orifice tube.

Figure 6-8. A fixed-orifice tube system has an accumulator between the evaporator and the compressor.

used determines the operating characteristics of the refrigeration system. If the vehicle is equipped with a cycling clutch compressor, the compressor should cycle on and off as it operates to maintain the correct evaporator temperature. If the compressor is a variable displacement or a scroll compressor, it may run all the time whenever AC is selected. The evaporator temperature will be controlled by the TXV or the control valve that determines the displacement of the compressor based on the demand.

Determining the type of compressor used is a critical step before you begin your diagnosis of the system.

Refrigerant and Refrigerant Oil

It is absolutely imperative to know the type of refrigerant in the system before beginning repairs. The type of refrigerant in the system being serviced determines the materials, tools, equipment, and replacement parts needed to make the repairs. Remember that mixing refrigerants contaminates the system, manifold gauges, and recovery/recycling equipment as well. Correctly identify the refrigerant and oil to avoid costly mistakes.

Refrigerant Identification

The first step in identifying the refrigerant type is to look for the original AC system label, figure 6-9, or a retrofit label, figure 6-10. However, labels are not always in place, correctly filled out, or accurate. This is

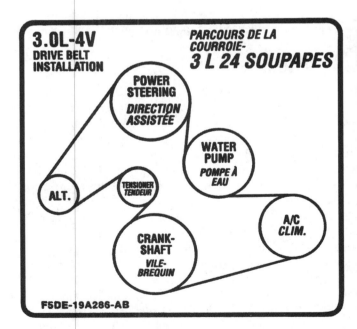

Figure 6-9. The original air conditioning label identifies the type of refrigerant, the charge amount, and refrigerant oil type.

NOTICE: *RETROFITTED TO R-134a*
RETROFIT PROCEDURE PERFORMED TO SAE J166
USE ONLY R-134a REFRIGERANT AND SYNTHETIC
OIL TYPE:_____ PN:_____OR
EQUIVALENT, OR A/C SYSTEM WILL BE DAMAGED.

REFRIGERANT CHARGE/AMOUNT:_____
LUBRICANT AMOUNT:_____ PAG ☐ ESTER☐

RETROFITTER NAME: _____ DATE:_____
ADDRESS: _____
CITY:_____ STATE:____ ZIP: _____
PART NUMBER 21030857   DO NOT REMOVE

Figure 6-10. Retrofit labels help identify the type of refrigerant in a system.

especially true if the system was charged with a non-approved alternate refrigerant as a quick fix for an R-12 system failure.

The next step in correctly identifying the refrigerant type is to check the refrigerant with your refrigerant identifier. Electronic refrigerant identifiers typically use a nondispersive, infrared technology to determine the refrigerant type. Some identifiers are capable of evaluating the purity of a particular refrigerant. These identifiers test the percentage of refrigerant, and whether it has been contaminated by water or air. This helps form an accurate diagnosis of needed repairs.

Consult your service manual to confirm the type of refrigerant required by the year, make, and model of the vehicle being serviced. If you are servicing an original R-12 system you might want to check for retrofit bulletins for the make and model that you are working on. Depending on the scope of repairs, it may be practical to retrofit an R-12 system to R-134a at this time. See Chapter 12 of this *Shop Manual* for more information on retrofitting.

Refrigerant Oil

Identification of refrigerant oil cannot be confirmed with test equipment. The type of oil used in a particular system is specified in the vehicle service manual. As with refrigerants, refrigerant oils should not be mixed. Different types of oils are not compatible. The mineral oil used with R-12 will not provide protection in a system using R-134a. In addition, different manufacturers use many types of PAG oil. Different grades of PAG oil are not compatible. Always follow the manufacturer's recommendations.

Keep oil containers tightly closed when not in use. Refrigerant oil absorbs moisture vapor from the air and introduces it into the AC system. In fact, water can be used as a tool in identifying the type of oil in a compressor. Although you cannot visually tell the difference between different oils, you can perform a simple test to

tell if the oil is PAG or Ester. Add a few drops of oil from your compressor to a cup of water. Because PAG oil attracts moisture, it will become soluble. If the oil remains separated from the water, you know it is Ester oil.

Oil Replacement

Remember to choose the manufacturer-specified oil type for the particular vehicle and system that you are servicing. As mentioned in previous chapters, replacement of components and service of the AC system require the addition of refrigerant oil. This is necessary because some oil may have been lost due to a system leak, or component failure, and the proper amount of oil is critical in ensuring adequate compressor lubrication. Compressor oil checking is covered in Chapter 8 of this *Shop Manual*. Guidelines for adding refrigerant oil to other replacement components, the condenser, evaporator, receiver-drier, accumulator, and lines are included in the replacement procedures. Always consult your factory service manual for specific instructions about the amount and type of oil for all components.

In general, measure and replace the same amount of oil that is trapped in any old component that you remove. Completely drain the oil from the old part into a graduated container to measure the quantity of trapped oil, figure 6-11. Then, refer to the vehicle service manual to verify the proper amount of replacement oil. Typical AC component refrigerant oil requirements are shown in figure 6-12. Be sure to drain the oil from the component. Some parts, especially accumulators, may require drilling a hole into the housing to drain the oil. When the information given shows a range, the exact amount depends on the system application.

HOSE AND LINE SERVICE

Chapter 6 of the *Classroom Manual* discusses the different types of rigid and flexible hoses used on current AC systems. Due to the high pressures produced in the system and because the system operates in an environment of high temperatures and nearly constant vibration, it is important to take extreme care and make sure that all connections are tight and all fittings are in good condition. Dirt and moisture easily enter the system if connections are loose or left opened during the repair or replacement of lines and components.

Most air conditioning reliability problems occur when there is movement and extreme temperature differences between components. Both of these conditions are found in the refrigerant lines, especially the flexible hoses. Flexible refrigerant hoses link assemblies and stationary components like the evaporator and condenser. Keep the following tips in mind when working with rigid lines and flexible hoses.

Figure 6-11. Drain parts being replaced to measure the oil lost during the procedure.

OIL REPLACEMENT GUIDE		
Compressor	2 oz	60 ml
Evaporator	2 oz	60 ml
Condenser	1 oz	30 ml
Accumulator	2 oz	60 ml
Lines	1 oz	30 ml
Receiver-Drier	1 oz	30 ml

Figure 6-12. If the manufacturer does not list oil replacement amounts, these can be used as guidelines.

- As a rule, the radius of all bends in a flexible hose should be kept to at least 10 times the diameter of the hose. Sharper bends reduce the flow of refrigerant and reduce performance.
- Route flexible hoses so they are at least three inches (76 mm) from the exhaust manifold or other heat sources.

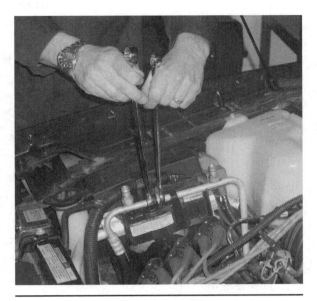

Figure 6-13. Always use a backup wrench when loosening or tightening line fittings.

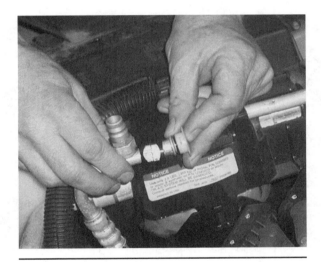

Figure 6-14. Always cap the line immediately after disconnecting to prevent contamination from entering the system.

- Inspect all flexible hoses at least once a year to make sure they are in good condition, properly routed, and securely attached.
- Use two wrenches when loosening or tightening fittings, figure 6-13.
- If the refrigerant system must be opened, have everything needed, such as tools, parts, and caps or plugs, on hand before beginning the repair. This prevents the system from being open longer than necessary. Cap or plug all lines and fittings as soon as they are opened to prevent contaminates from entering the system, figure 6-14. All

line replacement parts should be left sealed until just before installation.

- When removing refrigerant lines, avoid additional bending or twisting of the line if it is to be reinstalled.
- While servicing refrigerant lines, look for failures elsewhere in the system that may have caused the line failure.
- Always replace the O-ring that seals the fitting. Never reuse an O-ring. Lubricate the O-ring with mineral oil only; do not use PAG oil or other lubricants.

Be aware that some refrigerant lines are an integral part of a component assembly. If in doubt, check with the parts supplier regarding whether a replacement unit comes with a refrigerant line attached to it. Do not attempt to repair lines or hoses unless the manufacturer has an approved repair process.

Refrigerant Hose Failure

Vibration is the leading cause of hose failure because the constant movement fatigues the hoses, lines, and fittings, figure 6-15. However, hoses, lines, and con-

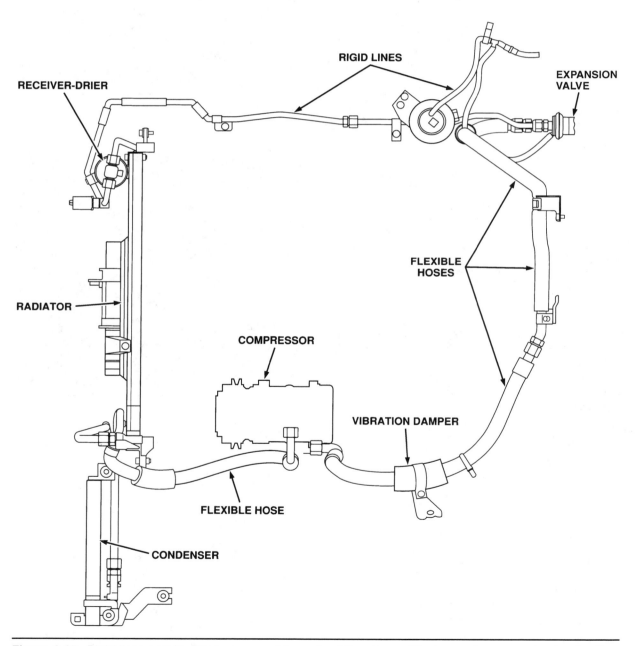

Figure 6-15. Rigid lines and flexible hoses used throughout the air conditioning system are prone to vibration-related failure.

nections fail for other reasons as well. Refrigerant hose and line failure may result from:

- Vibration
- High pressure
- Collision damage
- Chemical attack
- Improper installation

Use the following inspection procedures to isolate and identify hose problems.

Vibration

If excessive vibration is the suspected cause of a refrigerant hose failure, perform the following checks:

- Check the engine and transaxle mounts for secure attachment, proper alignment, and good cushioning. Make sure that the rubber is not spongy or broken.
- Check the rubber bushing in the engine strut on front-wheel-drive vehicles.
- Make sure that mounting bolts and brackets for the AC compressor are securely in place, the unit is properly aligned, and lines and hoses leading to the compressor are properly routed.
- Look for incorrectly mounted or loose AC component assemblies, such as the receiver-drier, evaporator, and condenser.

High Pressure

Internal hose damage results if the AC system pressure exceeds the maximum pressure that a hose is designed to withstand. With excessively high system pressure, perform the following checks:

- Check the entire length of the hose for splits, bubbles, and signs of swelling. These may indicate exposure to extremely high pressure, which is often caused by a stuck pressure relief valve.
- Determine what caused the excessive high pressure.
- Determine why the pressure relief valve has failed.
- Check around fittings and connections for any signs of oil that might indicate a leak.

Collision

If you suspect the vehicle has had collision damage repaired, perform a thorough inspection to make sure all AC components are correctly installed and in good condition. Check for:

- Obvious visual damage and correct mounting and alignment of components that may have been removed during body repair.
- Leaks at assemblies, hoses, and fittings that may have been strained by the force of the collision.

If the system was opened to make body repairs, it is likely contaminated. Recover the refrigerant, then flush and recharge the system. Flushing procedures are detailed later in this chapter.

Chemical Attack

Some common underhood chemicals react with the outer covering of flexible AC hoses. This weakens the hose and eventually leads to failure. Clean the surface of the hoses and check for:

- Stains, soft spots, or swelling caused by engine oil, transmission fluid, engine coolant, battery acid, and other substances that can attack refrigerant hoses.
- Spongy hoses that offer little resistance when squeezed. These are likely damaged. Hoses can also deteriorate from the inside due to heat or chemical aging. Inspect hoses annually, as well as every time the vehicle is in for AC service.

Repair the source of any underhood fluid leak and replace hoses as needed when damage is found.

Improper Installation

An AC hose is unnecessarily stressed if it is incorrectly installed or routed, a condition that results in premature failure. Perform the following checks:

- Look for twists, kinks, or bends along the length of the refrigerant lines and hoses.
- Make sure hoses and lines are correctly routed to prevent damage from heat, abrasion, or vibration. Look for hoses positioned on or near hot parts of the engine.
- Verify that all hose, line, and component mounting brackets, clamps, and tie-wraps are securely installed.
- Look for properly installed aftermarket accessories. Use tie-wraps, mounting brackets, and abrasion-resistant materials as necessary to prevent repeated damage.

Refrigerant Hose and Line Service

A majority of all leaks occur at hose and line fittings as a result of a faulty seal. When checking for leaks in these areas, remember that refrigerant is heavier than air, so it is likely to accumulate beneath the actual point of leakage.

Feel the hose for oil contamination, which may indicate a refrigerant leak. Older hoses are particularly prone to leaks, due to both their construction and their age. Replace the hose if an oil leak is detected.

Hose Replacement

When you replace a faulty R-12 hose, install a barrier hose suitable for R-134a. When R-12 hoses need replacement, it may be a good time to retrofit the system. See Chapter 12 of this *Shop Manual* for retrofit information.

Always replace barrier hoses; never repair them. The reason is permeability. When a hose is repaired, the ability to totally seal the refrigerant inside the refrigerant hose is jeopardized. Therefore, the standard industry practice is to replace hoses, rather than repair them. If a hose breaks or splits, or is otherwise damaged, the entire section of flexible hose must be replaced with the same type of barrier hose.

Line Replacement

Rigid refrigerant line failure is usually the result of a collision, overtightening, incorrect installation, or internal or external corrosion. Inspect carefully and replace any rigid lines that show signs of damage. For best results, replace with new lines from the manufacturer designed specifically for the model application. In some instances, when the line is no longer available or it is not practical to replace the entire line, such as with vehicles equipped with rear air conditioning, repair kits are available, figure 6-16.

These repair kits are designed to repair the aluminum portion of lines. To repair a line using this method:

1. Cut the line at the damaged spot. It must be in a straight section of the line or this repair method cannot be used, figure 6-17.
2. Clean 3/4 inch on each end of the line. Avoid making longitudinal scratches on the line, figure 6-18.
3. Apply sealing compound to each end of the line, figure 6-19.
4. Select the proper size connector and install on the line. Rotate the connector to spread the sealing compound, figure 6-20.

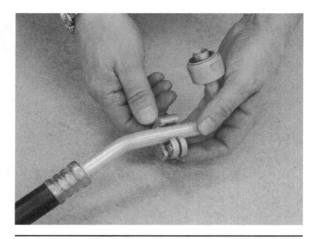

Figure 6-17. Cut the line at the damaged area. It must be in a straight section.

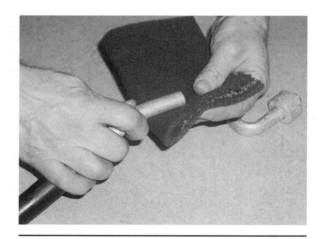

Figure 6-18. Clean 3/4 inch on each end of the line that was cut.

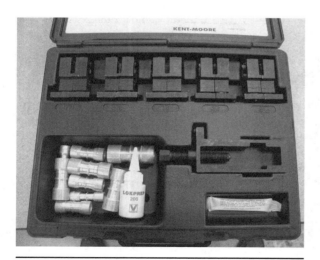

Figure 6-16. This repair kit is used to repair metal lines that are damaged.

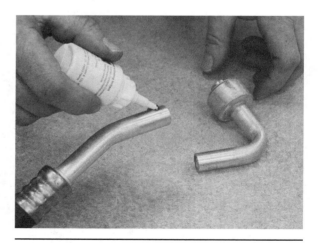

Figure 6-19. Apply sealing compound to each end.

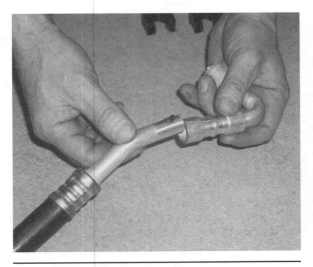

Figure 6-20. Select the proper size connector and install it on the line. Twist the connector to spread the compound.

Figure 6-22. Holding the tool with a breaker bar, tighten the forcing screw.

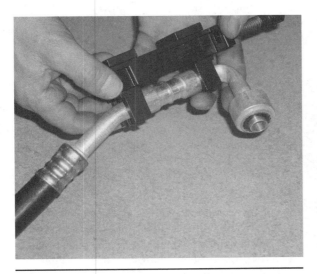

Figure 6-21. Using the correct size jaws, install the tool over the connector.

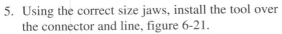

Figure 6-23. Tighten the forcing screw until the coupling is completely collapsed.

5. Using the correct size jaws, install the tool over the connector and line, figure 6-21.
6. Holding the tool with a breaker bar, turn the forcing screw with a ratchet, figure 6-22.
7. Continue to turn the forcing screw until the collar is completely collapsed in the center, figure 6-23.
8. Remove the tool, inspect the repair, and leak test the repair site after recharging, figure 6-24.

Line Fitting Repair

Sometimes you can repair minor fitting leaks without replacing the line or hose. However, the fitting must be loosened or disconnected to repair a connection leak.

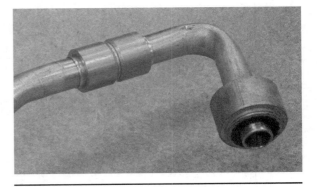

Figure 6-24. Inspect the repair, reinstall, recharge, and leak test the joint.

Therefore, it is necessary to recover the refrigerant from the system. *DO NOT* attempt to make repairs without recovering the refrigerant first.

Flare fittings are often restored simply by slightly loosening the fitting, then retightening it. After tightening, use compressed air to clear any residual refrigerant from around the joint. Evacuate and recharge the system, then check the fitting with a leak detector.

With O-ring connections, it may be necessary to separate the fitting and replace the O-rings to repair a leak. Thoroughly clean the joint surface and lightly lubricate the new O-ring with 525-viscosity mineral oil. Also cap the open lines and ports when the fitting is disconnected to prevent contamination from entering the system. Make sure replacement O-rings are compatible with the type of refrigerant used in the system. After tightening the connection, evacuate and recharge the air conditioning system. Recheck the fitting with a leak detector.

O-Ring Replacement

Whenever a fitting is opened, a new O-ring must be installed. Although O-rings look the same, there are important variations in their composition. O-rings may be captured or noncaptured depending on the fitting design. As shown in figure 6-25, a captured O-ring has a thicker diameter than the noncaptured O-ring. A captured O-ring installs on a fitting that is grooved to seat the O-ring. A noncaptured O-ring installs on a straight male fitting.

As discussed in Chapter 6 of the *Classroom Manual*, O-rings are made of a variety of materials and some are only compatible with certain refrigerants. They also come in a variety of different colors used to help identify the type of material that the O-ring is made from. Review the *Classroom Manual* if you are unsure if you are using the correct O-ring.

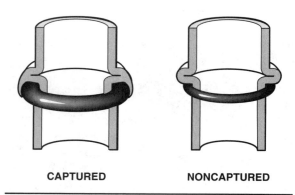

CAPTURED   **NONCAPTURED**

Figure 6-25. Captured O-rings are seated in a groove, while noncaptured O-rings install on a straight fitting. (Reprinted with permission of General Motors Corporation.)

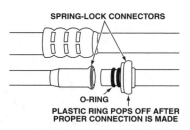

Figure 6-26. Many manufacturers use spring-lock couplings to connect refrigerant lines. (Courtesy of DaimlerChrysler Corporation.)

Spring-lock Coupling

Manufacturers have been using spring-lock couplings on refrigerant line connections since the early 1980s, figure 6-26. Rather than threading together, the coupling uses a garter spring enclosed in a cage to lock the two pieces of the fitting together. O-rings are used to seal the connection. A special tool is inserted to expand the spring and separate the coupling, figure 6-27.

If a spring-lock coupling is the source of a refrigerant leak, damaged O-rings or a weak spring is the likely cause. Both are repairable, providing the lines are in good condition. The refrigerant must be recovered before servicing the coupling. New O-rings should be installed whenever the coupling is opened. Many technicians also make it a practice of replacing the springs whenever a coupling is opened.

Weak or damaged springs can be carefully removed with a small pick or screwdriver and replaced if needed, figure 6-28.

SYSTEM FLUSHING

Some manufacturers recommend flushing when the system has been contaminated with an alternate refrigerant, a desiccant bag failure occurs, the oil is contaminated, or gross overcharge of oil exists. Compressor failure that contaminates the system with metal particles may also require flushing; however, flushing will not always do a thorough job of removing metal debris. Some manufacturers require the installation of an in-line filter to remove metal debris from the system. Recommendations vary by manufacturer whether to flush with chemical solvents or use a closed-loop flushing process that only uses refrigerant to flush the system. There is some disagreement, even among professionals, whether chemical flushing is appropriate. Be sure to follow the manufacturer's recommendations.

Flushing Solvents

There are many types of solvents available on the market for flushing AC systems. Be aware that some flushing agents previously used, such as R-11 and R-113, are CFC compounds, which are now illegal to use.

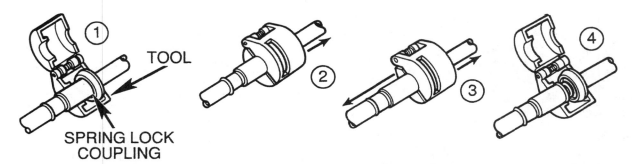

Figure 6-27. Special tools are used to disconnect and connect spring-lock couplings. (Courtesy of DaimlerChrysler Corporation.)

Dura-141, which can be used in place of R-11 and R113, is the trade name of a non-CFC solvent. Other flushing agents are also available and different manufacturers recommend various agents. Check the appropriate service manual for specific recommendations.

Be careful when choosing a flushing solvent, and always follow the recommendations of the manufacturer. The solvent cleanses the system of impurities while removing some debris. It may also absorb moisture that may be in the system. Each solvent should be supplied with a safety data sheet. Be sure to read this information, then use the product as directed.

Flushing Equipment

Select the proper flushing agent for the AC system being serviced. Consult the equipment instructions and add the recommended quantity of the flushing agent to fill the tank of the machine, figure 6-28. The type of equipment being used will determine which components may be flushed, figure 6-29. Exact procedures vary by equipment and system, so it is important to follow both the machine operating instructions and the vehicle service manual procedures. With any type of

flushing equipment, the refrigerant must be recovered from the system before connecting the machine. In general, an AC system flush is performed as follows:

1. Recover the refrigerant from the system and connect the flushing equipment as instructed by the manufacturer. Some connections are made at the service fittings, while others require an opening created by disconnecting a component, figure 6-30.

Figure 6-29. The FLUSHWORKS™ manufactured by Cliplight is one of the few flushing methods recommended by a major vehicle manufacturer. (Courtesy of Cliplight Manufacturing Company.)

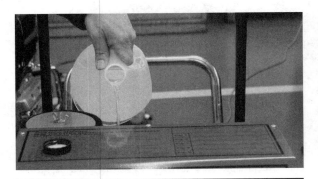

Figure 6-28. Using the appropriate flushing solvent, fill the flushing machine with fresh flushing solvent. (Courtesy of Cliplight Manufacturing Company.)

Figure 6-30. Disconnect the components to be flushed. Usually these would be the evaporator and the condenser. (Courtesy of Cliplight Manufacturing Company.)

2. Remove the expansion device and the receiver-drier or accumulator if the entire system is to be flushed. Also, remove or bypass the receiver-drier, if specified by the manufacturer.
3. If flushing only a major component, connect the equipment in the reverse direction of refrigerant flow to back-flush the part and force out debris, figure 6-31.
4. Following the equipment manufacturer's procedures, flush the component for the recommended time period, figure 6-32.
5. After flushing of the component is complete, purge the component for the specified time period, figure 6-33.
6. After purging is completed, disconnect the equipment from that component and connect to the next component to be flushed, figure 6-34.
7. Replace the receiver-drier or accumulator.

Figure 6-31. Connect the flushing equipment so that the component will be reverse flushed. (Courtesy of Cliplight Manufacturing Company.)

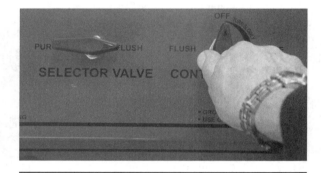

Figure 6-33. After flushing is complete, purge the component for the required time period specified by the equipment manufacturer. (Courtesy of Cliplight Manufacturing Company.)

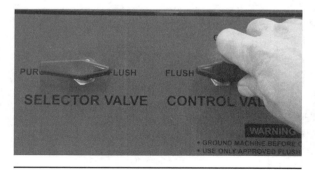

Figure 6-32. Follow the equipment manufacturer's recommendations and flush the component for the prescribed amount of time. (Courtesy of Cliplight Manufacturing Company.)

Figure 6-34. After purging of each component is complete, disconnect the equipment from that component and connect to the next component to be flushed. (Courtesy of Cliplight Manufacturing Company.)

8. Replace the expansion device.
9. Add the appropriate amount of the correct refrigerant oil.
10. Evacuate, recharge, and leak test the system. Then conduct a system performance test.

CONDENSER AND EVAPORATOR SERVICE

Due to their location under the hood, the condenser and the evaporator are susceptible to collision damage. The condenser is vulnerable to flying rocks and other road debris as well. Eventually, condensers and evaporators develop cracks at seams and other points of chemical and mechanical stress as a result of age and wear. In addition, the condenser is prone to developing restrictions as a result of heavy contamination from compressor failures. Replace a condenser or evaporator if it has:

- Collision damage
- Irreparable leaks
- Clogging or debris that cannot be removed by flushing
- Corrosion damage from acids due to moisture contamination

Symptoms of a plugged or defective condenser include:

- Excessive high-side pressure. The pressure relief valve may be venting excess pressure. Also look for frost on the liquid line, which may indicate a restriction at the bottom of the condenser.
- Severe compressor damage, which causes debris to circulate into and contaminate the condenser. After a compressor failure, some condensers can be cleared by flushing and then reused. However, many newer multi-pass condensers cannot be completely flushed and must be replaced if they become clogged or restricted.
- Refrigerant loss and oily spots on the condenser, which indicate leakage points.
- Areas of localized frost. Frost buildup indicates the point of a restriction.

Evaporators generally do not become restricted because the orifice or expansion valve stops most of the contaminates before they can enter the evaporator. Thoroughly inspect the evaporator for signs of physical damage and leakage.

When replacing a plugged or contaminated condenser or evaporator, flush the system to remove any debris. Installing an inline filter as part of a contamination repair reduces the chance of further system failures due to residual debris. These filters, figure 6-35, which install on the outlet side of the condenser before the expansion device, can hold a significant volume of debris and still allow adequate refrigerant flow.

Figure 6-35. Inline filters can be installed to prevent debris from a previous compressor failure from damaging the new compressor.

Installing an Inline Filter

There are a variety of inline filters available that can be installed in a system that has suffered a compressor failure. Filters are available for installation in metal liquid lines or in hose assemblies. The filter is installed between the condenser but before the expansion device. In some cases the filters are available with a built-in orifice tube so that they can be installed in place of the orifice. In general these filters are installed as follows:

1. Find a location in the liquid line that provides adequate clearance and has a straight section of tubing, figure 6-36.
2. Cut the liquid line and remove enough of the line to allow the inline filter to be installed, figure 6-37.
3. Install the filter without the O-rings and tighten the fittings firmly. This avoids damaging the O-rings, figure 6-38.
4. Remove the filter and install the O-rings at each fitting, figure 6-39.
5. Tighten each fitting to the specified torque, evacuate, recharge, and leak test the filter, figure 6-40.

Figure 6-36. Locate a straight section of the liquid line to install the inline filter.

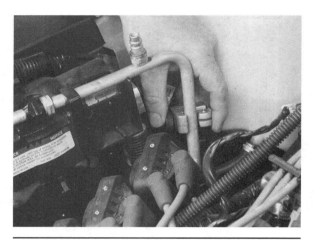

Figure 6-37. Cut the liquid line, allowing enough room for installation of the filter.

Figure 6-40. After the O-rings have been installed, evacuate, recharge, and leak test the fittings.

Figure 6-38. Install the filter without the O-rings and tighten the fittings firmly.

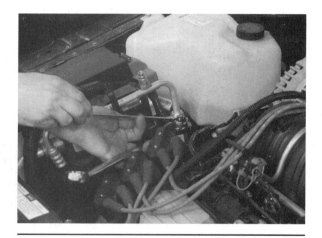

Figure 6-39. Remove the filter and install the O-rings.

Evaporator Replacement

Each model of vehicle has a different procedure for removing the evaporator. Follow the service manual instructions for the model being repaired. The following evaporator replacement procedure is provided as a general guideline.

1. Recover the refrigerant using an approved recovery/recycling machine.
2. Disconnect the negative battery cable.
3. Retain and measure the amount of refrigerant oil lost during recovery. Check the oil for signs of debris or other contamination. If contaminated, replace the receiver-drier or accumulator. Replacing these components is a good idea during any major service or component replacement.
4. If the evaporator and heater core are combined in a single unit, as in many General Motors vehicles, drain the cooling system also.
5. Disconnect any electrical harnesses, cables, and vacuum hoses that attach to the evaporator housing, figure 6-41.
6. Disconnect the refrigerant hoses at the evaporator. Cap or plug the hoses to prevent system contamination.
7. Unbolt and remove the evaporator. This may require extensive disassembly of the ventilation system plenum or module, figure 6-42. Refer to the appropriate service manual for specific instructions.
8. Drain residual oil in the evaporator into a graduated container and measure it.
9. Remove the replacement evaporator from its packaging and add the specific amount of new refrigerant oil to the unit.

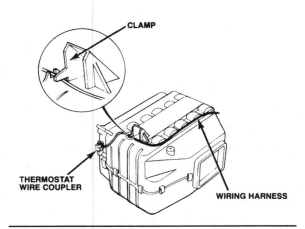

Figure 6-41. Carefully remove any electrical wiring, vacuum hoses, or cables that attach to the evaporator housing.

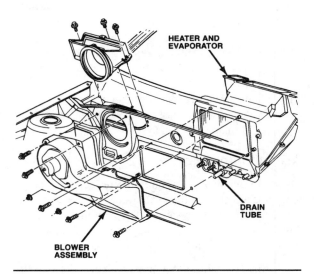

Figure 6-42. Extensive disassembly of the instrument panel and other passenger compartment items is often required to remove the evaporator.

10. Install the new evaporator using new O-rings. Coat the O-rings with clean 525 refrigerant oil before connecting and tightening the fittings.
11. Connect the negative battery cable.
12. Evacuate and recharge the system. Follow the specified procedures regarding checking and adding new refrigerant oil.
13. Leak test and performance test the system.

Condenser Replacement

Condenser replacement is usually much easier than replacing the evaporator because less disassembly is involved to access the unit. Use the following as a general procedure for removing and installing a condenser.

1. Recover the refrigerant using an approved recovery machine.
2. Disconnect the negative battery cable.
3. Check the oil recovered for signs of debris or contamination.
4. On many vehicles, the radiator and fan shroud must be removed to access the condenser. If necessary, drain the coolant.
5. Remove any other components, such as engine covers, splash shields, sensors, and fan that prevent or limit access to the condenser.
6. Disconnect the refrigerant lines at the condenser. Cap or plug the hoses to prevent system contamination.
7. Remove the condenser mounting fasteners and lift the unit from the chassis, figure 6-43. If the receiver-drier mounts on the condenser, disconnect it from the system and remove it along with the condenser.

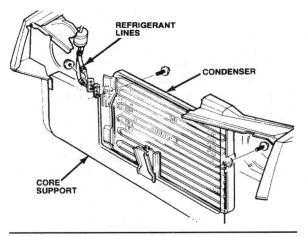

Figure 6-43. With the refrigerant lines disconnected, remove the fasteners and lift the condenser from the vehicle.

8. Drain the residual oil from the condenser into a graduated container and measure it.
9. Remove the new condenser from its protective wrapper and add the specified amount of new oil to the unit.
10. Position the new condenser in the chassis and loosely install the mounting hardware. Coat your new O-rings with 525 mineral oil before installation. Install and tighten the fittings, then tighten the condenser mounting bolts.

11. Install the fan shroud, fan, radiator, or other components that were removed to gain access.
12. Install the radiator hoses, fill the radiator with coolant, and bleed the cooling system as needed.
13. Connect the negative battery cable.
14. Evacuate and recharge the system, leak test, and performance test the system.

Accumulator Service

The accumulator is a low-pressure refrigerant storage unit located between the evaporator and the compressor on orifice tube systems. The accumulator has a desiccant bag and oil-metering orifice. Replace the accumulator when any of the following occurs.

- Any AC failure that spreads debris through the system.
- Moisture contamination from a system that has been open for an extended period of time.
- Loose desiccant spreading through the system.
- Leakage from the accumulator or its connections.
- If service is being performed and the accumulator is more than five years old.

The accumulator is a sealed assembly that is typically replaced as a unit. Although rebuilt accumulators are available for many models, they are generally purchased from a remanufacturer, rather than being rebuilt in the shop. The desiccant bag can be replaced to service some accumulators; however, a defective accumulator is generally replaced as a complete unit. Transfer the cycling clutch switch, cut-off switch, or other devices mounted on the old accumulator to the replacement accumulator. Always use new O-rings when transferring switches. Do not open the accumulator until you are ready to install it on the vehicle. When the accumulator is opened, the desiccant material will immediately start to absorb moisture.

Receiver-Drier Service

The receiver-drier is a high-pressure storage device located between the condenser outlet and the expansion valve on a thermostatic expansion valve (TXV) system, figure 6-44. The mounting position of the receiver-drier varies. Some are located on the outlet side of the condenser, while others are somewhere in the line between the condenser and expansion valve. A desiccant bag in the receiver-drier removes moisture from the circulating refrigerant. Similar to an accumulator, a receiver-drier is replaced when:

- Contaminated with moisture or debris.
- Leaks develop at the housing or fitting connections.
- Damaged by collision.
- Other parts, such as the compressor, evaporator, condenser, and expansion valve are replaced, or the system is flushed due to contamination.
- The AC system is exposed to outside air for a long time due to disassembly or refrigerant loss.

On some receiver-drier assemblies, the desiccant bag is replaceable separately. However, most are not serviceable and are replaced as a unit when defective. As with an accumulator, any switches or sensors fitted to the receiver-drier are removed and transferred to the replacement unit.

Expansion Device Service

Air conditioning systems use a thermostatic expansion valve (TXV) or an orifice tube, figure 6-45. Each type of expansion device has unique service requirements, and exact service procedures vary by make and model as well. Have accurate factory service information and specifications on hand when working with a TXV or orifice tube. Following are general procedures that apply to most expansion device repairs.

Expansion Valve

The TXV regulates the amount of refrigerant that enters the evaporator. The TXV measures temperature and pressure at the evaporator outlet, and then uses this information to control the position of a metering valve. The valve is in line to the evaporator, so the position of the valve determines the amount of refrigerant that flows to the evaporator. Typically a TXV fails due to:

- Clogging of the input screen due to debris
- Clogging of the valve as a result of debris getting past the screen
- Clogging or restriction of the metering valve due to moisture in the system
- Corrosion resulting from acids formed when moisture reacts with refrigerant
- Damage to or leaks in the capillary tube or bulb

The symptoms of an expansion valve malfunction depend on the nature of the failure. Typically, when an expansion valve fails, the valve is stuck either closed

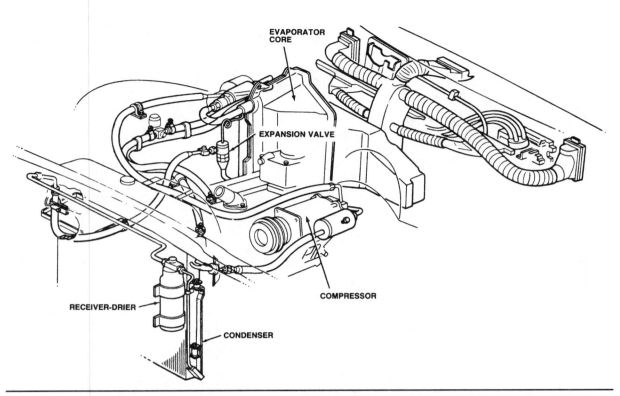

Figure 6-44. The receiver-drier, a high-pressure storage device, is located between the condenser and the expansion valve.

or open. When the expansion valve is closed, the evaporator is starved of refrigerant, and refrigerant floods the evaporator when the valve is stuck open. A faulty expansion valve may also be the cause of intermittent AC system operation. Symptoms of a stuck closed expansion valve starving the evaporator include:

- Warm or only slightly cool discharge airflow.
- Low gauge readings on both the low side and the high side.
- Sweating or frost formation on the expansion valve body.
- Evaporator outlet is warm.

Be aware that a low refrigerant charge also produces the same symptoms. Sweat or frost on the valve may also be caused by a clogged TXV inlet screen that is restricting refrigerant flow. Always make sure the system is fully charged before attempting to diagnose component failures by symptoms. Symptoms of a stuck open expansion valve flooding the evaporator with refrigerant include:

- Warm or only slightly cool discharge air
- High low-side gauge readings and a cool and sweaty compressor suction line

- Normal or slightly higher high-side pressure gauge readings

NOTE: Evaporator flooding may also be caused by a damaged capillary tube or sensing bulb that cannot sense conditions at the evaporator outlet.

A sticking expansion valve that operates intermittently may cause intermittent air conditioning system operation. Intermittent expansion valve operation can produce the following symptoms:

- Intermittent cooling
- Irregular changes in low-side gauge readings
- System operates normally on startup, but stops cooling after the initial cool down
- The evaporator outlet pipe cools and warms in response to a slight change in evaporator pressure

NOTE: Before replacing the expansion valve, eliminate any other possible cause of the symptoms. Confirm that the compressor is staying engaged, or that a variable displacement compressor is operating properly. Also make sure the controls are working correctly.

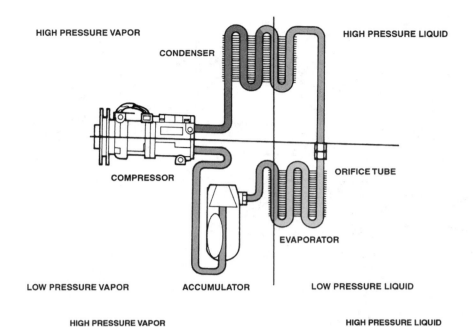

Figure 6-45. Air conditioning systems use an expansion valve or a fixed-orifice tube. (Courtesy of DaimlerChrysler Corporation.)

Expansion Valve Testing

An open expansion valve allows too much refrigerant into the evaporator, which raises the outlet pressure. A closed expansion valve restricts the refrigerant flow and lowers the evaporator pressure. With the AC system operating, the valve should be open when the capillary tube is warm and closed when it is cold. To test an installed expansion valve:

1. Confirm that the system is fully charged; correct if needed.
2. Connect a manifold gauge set. Start and run the engine at fast idle, about 1,500 rpm, with the AC system at MAX and the blower on HIGH. Operate long enough to stabilize the system.

3. Attach a thermometer to the evaporator outlet line, or, if possible, place it directly between the evaporator fins near the outlet fitting. The reading on the low-side gauge should correspond to a temperature change from 4° to 16°F (3° to 10°C) lower than the temperature reading, figure 6-46. This is a result of the superheat maintained by the expansion valve. If the measured temperature range is not within specifications, replace the expansion valve and the receiver-drier.

Expansion Valve Replacement
Keep the following tips in mind when removing or installing an expansion valve:

- Handle the capillary tube carefully, as this hollow, refrigerant-filled tube is easily damaged. Do not bend or kink the tube.
- Insert the replacement tube fully into the mounting bracket or sleeve.
- Make sure that the replacement-sensing bulb is installed in the same position as the original one.
- Replace any insulation that was removed to gain access to the bulb or tube.

An expansion valve installs in the refrigerant line between the evaporator and condenser, and the sensing bulb attaches to the evaporator suction line with a clamp, figure 6-47. Replacement procedures vary by make and model. Be sure to consult the manufacturer's service manual.

Orifice Tube Service

Ford, General Motors, and other manufacturers use an orifice tube on many of their AC systems. As the name implies, this expansion device consists of a specific diameter metering nozzle, or orifice, through which the refrigerant flows. The orifice is protected from refrigerant-borne debris by inlet and outlet screens, and an O-ring seals the assembly to the line, figure 6-48. The orifice restricts flow to control the expansion of liquid refrigerant and create a pressure differential. Replace an orifice when:

- The orifice is clogged with debris, figure 6-49.
- The inlet or outlet screens are contaminated or clogged.
- Debris has spread through the system as a result of a component failure.

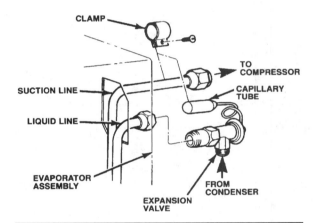

Figure 6-47. Refrigerant lines and the sensing bulb are removed when you replace the expansion valve.

R-134a EVAPORATOR TEMPERATURE-PRESSURE CHART			
FIN TEMPERATURE		VAPOR PRESSURE	
Degrees F	Degrees C	PSI	kPa
−5	−26	0	0
−10	−23	2	14
0	−18	7	48
10	−12	12	83
20	−7	18	124
25	−4	22	152
30	−1	26	179
35	2	30	207
40	4	35	241
45	7	40	276
50	10	45	310
60	16	57	393
70	21	71	490
80	27	86	593
90	32	104	717
100	38	124	855
110	43	146	1,006

Figure 6-46. A temperature-pressure chart is used to compare the evaporator fin temperature to the low-side vapor pressure.

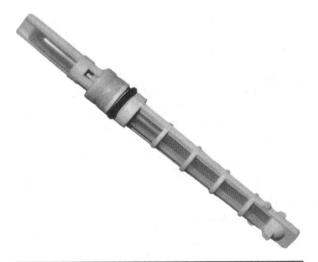

Figure 6-48. A fixed-orifice tube uses no moving parts to control the expansion of liquid refrigerant.

Figure 6-49. Always check the orifice for signs of debris.

Fixed-orifice tubes have no moving parts, so when they fail it is because they are clogged with debris or ice. The symptoms of a plugged orifice tube are similar to those of a clogged expansion valve.

- Warm or only slightly cool discharge airflow.
- Low gauge readings on both the high side and the low side.
- Sweating or frost formation on the line between the evaporator and the expansion valve.
- Evaporator outlet is warm.

Remember, these symptoms may also be caused by a low refrigerant charge. Make sure the system is fully charged before attempting to diagnose performance problems.

Orifice Tube Testing
Test for an orifice tube failure as follows:

- Connect a manifold gauge set. Start and run the engine at fast idle, about 1,500 rpm, with the AC system at MAX and the blower on HIGH. Operate long enough to stabilize the system, about 10 minutes.
- Bypass the pressure cycling switch to keep the compressor clutch constantly engaged.
- Monitor the low-side pressure gauge.

A restricted orifice is indicated if the low-side pressure drops to 5 psi or lower. Expect a low refrigerant charge if the low-side pressure does not drop below 10 psi.

Orifice Tube Replacement
The orifice tube is located in the liquid line leading to the evaporator and is held in the line by O-rings on the outside of the tube assembly, figure 6-50. An orifice tube is somewhat fragile, and the tube is prone to breaking during removal. When this happens, a special extractor tool is used to remove the remains of the orifice tube, figure 6-51. Always lubricate the O-rings on the orifice tube before installation. Some vehicles have orifice tubes that are not replaceable. These orifice tubes are an integral part of the liquid line. To replace these orifice tubes, the line assembly must be replaced.

Suction-throttling Valve

Although domestic manufacturers have not used these devices in 30 years, several late model Toyota, Lexus, and Nissan vehicles have versions of suction-throttling valves (STV). Several different suction-throttling devices are used to regulate the evaporator pressure.

Suction-throttling Valve Replacement
These devices have few moving parts and usually only fail by leaking. Most Lexus models have the STV located at the right side of the firewall area. Most Toyota STVs are midline in the evaporator suction hose. Nissan mounts its STV in the evaporator case. Removal of the case is required to access the valve.

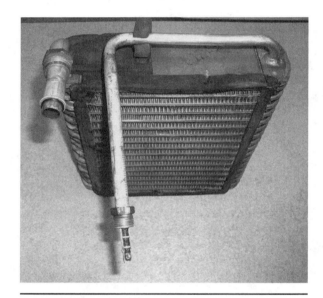

Figure 6-50. The fixed-orifice tube is at or near the evaporator on many vehicles.

Figure 6-51. This tool is used to extract the orifice tube from the line.

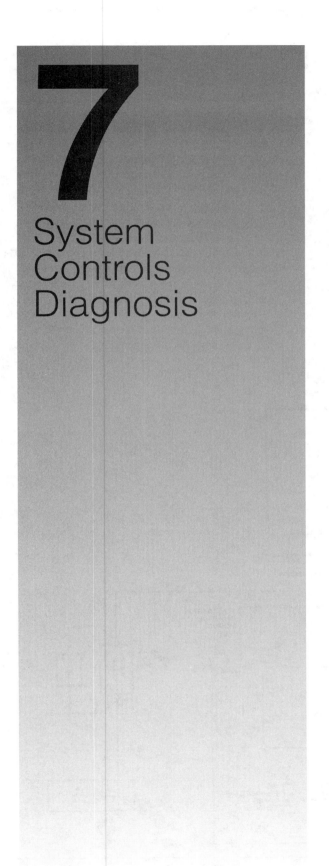

7

System Controls Diagnosis

As you learned in Chapter 7 of the *Classroom Manual,* there are a variety of electrical controls and methods of controlling the operation of the air conditioning system. Even the most basic systems use a relay, control head, and pressure switches to control the operation of the air conditioning compressor. As electronics have evolved on vehicles, so has the complexity of the air conditioning controls. Most current systems use an Electronic Control Module to engage the compressor. This module may be the Powertrain Control Module (PCM), Body Control Module (BCM), AC amplifier, electronic control head, or a unit called a programmer. In addition to controlling the compressor, these modules may also receive inputs from other sensors such as ambient sensors, sun load sensors, refrigerant pressure sensors, refrigerant temperature sensors, compressor protection switches or sensors, and the engine controller. As the complexity of these controls has grown, so has the complexity of diagnostics on these systems. To aid technicians in diagnosing these systems many manufacturers have included self-diagnostic capabilities to their systems. Scan tools have become a necessary tool to aid the technician in diagnosing air conditioning controls.

For the technician to be able to diagnose air conditioning control faults he or she must have a solid foundation in electrical troubleshooting using test lights and a DVOM. In addition, the technician must be able to read and interpret electrical schematics, diagnostic charts, and be able to use a scan tool. An understanding of how the air conditioning controls function on a particular model is necessary before the technician should begin diagnosing the system. In addition, the technician must have the required service information available, such as a manufacturer's service manual or service information from an aftermarket provider. Without this information available the technician will be very limited in his or her capability to diagnose and repair the system due to the variety and complexity of the various systems found on today's vehicles.

TESTING CONTROL MODULES

Most vehicles use an Electronic Control Module to control the AC compressor. Keep in mind that this module may be the PCM, BCM, electronic control head, AC amplifier, or a programmer. Regardless of which type of module a manufacturer uses, these modules are computers that have to receive certain inputs from various components of the air conditioning system and/or other systems. No matter what type of module is used one certainty is that there is no tester that will test these units for the technician. Your diagnosis of these units must consist of verifying that the inputs are correct and, if so, then testing the outputs to determine if they are functioning correctly. Only after the inputs to these modules have been verified and the outputs having been verified as working can a technician come to a conclusion that the module is malfunctioning. Too often technicians replace a module only to find that it is not the cause of the system malfunction. This practice not only wastes the technician's time but also creates unnecessary expense to the customer and the shop. In addition, the module could be damaged by other faults in the system.

In order to diagnose a malfunctioning module the technician must have a thorough understanding of how the system works and use a logical, systematic diagnostic approach. Failure to do this may result in a faulty diagnosis and ineffective repair. Referring to figure 7-1, let's see if we can determine how the module controls the operation of the air conditioning compressor. Keep in mind that this is only representative of one particular system. However, the PCM in this case

could just as easily be a BCM, an electronic control head, or an AC amplifier.

1. The first action that has to occur for the controller to command AC operation is that it must receive a request signal from the HVAC control head, meaning the driver must have activated a control to request that the AC is turned on. This signal could be in the form of a voltage sent to the PCM from the control head or a voltage at the PCM being grounded by the control head.

2. The PCM would next look at the input signal from the AC refrigerant pressure sensor. The PCM would want to see a voltage level between zero and five volts, indicating that there is enough pressure in the refrigeration system to enable the compressor and that the pressure is not too high.

3. After checking the refrigerant pressure, the PCM will provide a ground for the AC compressor relay coil. This will cause the relay to energize and

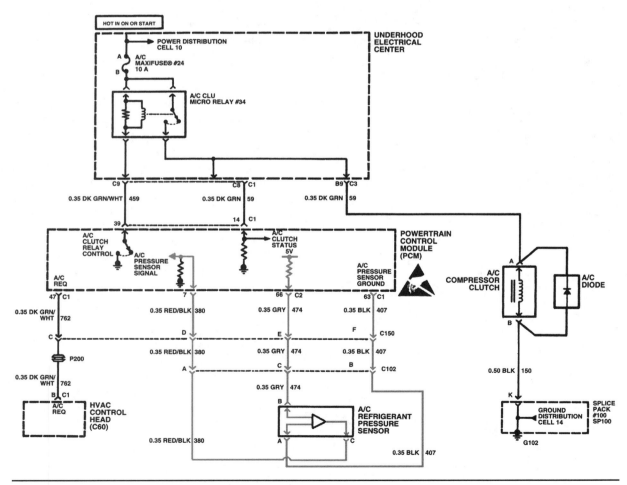

Figure 7-1. A representation of a PCM-controlled AC compressor circuit. (Reprinted with permission of General Motors Corporation.)

switch voltage to the AC compressor clutch coil. The compressor should engage.

4. The PCM will look at the AC clutch status input to determine if voltage was sent to the AC compressor clutch coil. This indicates to the PCM that the compressor should be engaged.

5. Once the compressor is engaged, the PCM will monitor the voltage from the AC refrigerant pressure sensor. This voltage will vary based on the pressure in the high side of the refrigeration system. If the pressure were too low or too high the PCM would remove the ground from the compressor relay, causing the compressor to disengage.

6. In addition to the inputs to the PCM that are part of the AC controls, there may be other inputs that the PCM may look at before deciding to engage the AC compressor. These inputs may include inputs such as the throttle position sensor (TPS), engine coolant temperature (ECT) sensor, engine rpm, and ambient temperature sensor, as well as some others. It is important to know what parameters have to be met before the PCM will engage the AC compressor. While these inputs may not be part of the AC system controls, they may influence the PCM's decision whether to engage the AC compressor or not.

This example is just a representation of the process that has to occur for AC compressor operation that is controlled by an electronic module. No matter what type of module is being used, certain inputs must be present in order for the module to enable the AC compressor. In addition to inputs that directly relate to the AC system, other inputs may play a role in determining whether the module will enable the AC compressor.

Using the same figure 7-1, we will now check each of the inputs and the outputs using a scan tool or a DVOM.

1. Checking the AC request signal with a scan tool, figure 7-2 should indicate if the module is receiving the request signal from the control head. Additionally, this signal could also be determined by measuring the voltage at the module with a DVOM, figure 7-3.

2. The signal from the AC refrigerant pressure sensor may also be checked with a scan tool on some vehicles, figure 7-4. This may be shown on the scan tool as a voltage, pressure, or both. In addition, the signal from the sensor may be measured with a DVOM to determine what pressure is in the refrigeration system, figure 7-5. This voltage may then have to be compared to a reference table to determine the pressure in the refrigeration system.

3. Testing the output from the PCM to the relay may also be confirmed with either a scan tool or a DVOM. If using a scan tool, it should indicate

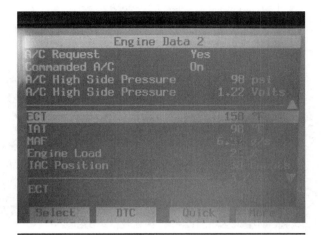

Figure 7-2. Some scan tools will show that the AC request signal is being received by the module from the control head.

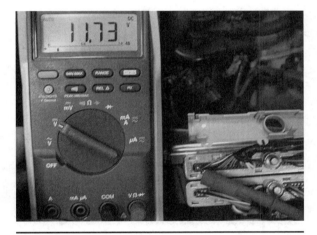

Figure 7-3. The request signal may also be verified by using a DVOM to check for voltage at the module.

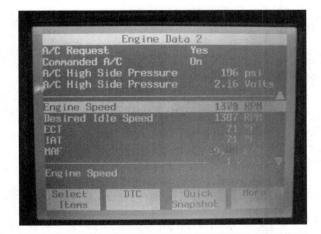

Figure 7-4. The AC refrigerant pressure sensor reading may be shown on the scan tool.

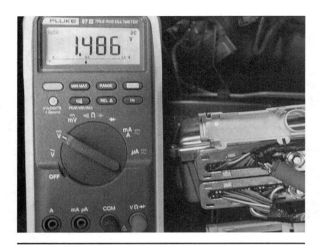

Figure 7-5. The AC pressure sensor voltage can be measured with a DVOM at the module to verify the signal is getting to the module.

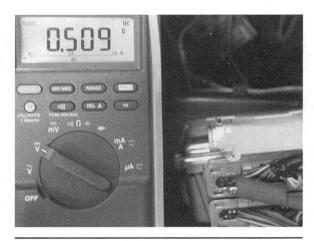

Figure 7-7. To verify that the module is actually providing the ground for the relay, use a DVOM to test for voltage at the module. If the module is grounding the relay you should measure about 0.5 volts or less.

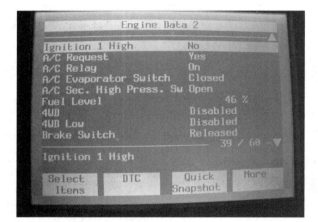

Figure 7-6. Often the scan tool will indicate that the command to enable the compressor has been given. However, this does not always indicate that the compressor is actually engaged.

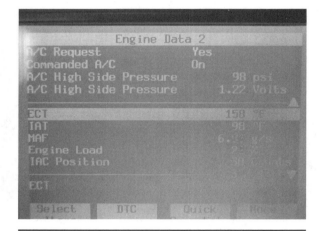

Figure 7-8. Many modules monitor the clutch circuit to determine if voltage is being supplied to the AC clutch circuit.

that the command has been given to the relay, figure 7-6. However, this may not really indicate that the ground has been provided to the relay. A DVOM would show if the ground is actually being applied by the PCM, figure 7-7.

4. The AC clutch status may be shown on the scan tool as appears in figure 7-8. It also could be determined by measuring the voltage present on the AC clutch status circuit at the PCM, figure 7-9.

5. The AC pressure sensor can also be monitored with the scan tool when the compressor is operating. A DVOM could also be used to monitor the AC refrigerant pressure sensor, figure 7-10.

6. Other inputs that are not part of the AC controls but are important to the module may also be monitored with a scan tool, figure 7-11.

Figure 7-9. You may also measure the voltage with a DVOM to confirm the AC clutch status.

VOLTAGE	CONDITION
0.0	A/C Pressure Sensor Volts Too Low (DTC)
0.150 TO 0.450	Transducer Good/Low Pressure Cut-out Condition
0.451 TO 4.519	Normal Operating Condition
4.520 TO 4.850	Transducer Good/High Pressure Cut-out Condition
5.0	A/C Pressure Sensor Volts Too High (DTC)

Figure 7-10. This AC pressure transducer voltage chart is provided by DaimlerChrysler as a reference to help the technician determine if the system's pressures are within the desired range. (Courtesy of DaimlerChrysler Corporation.)

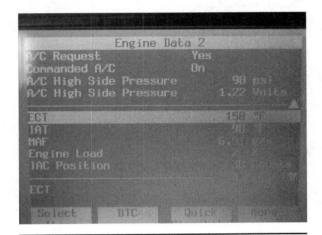

Figure 7-11. The module may also use other inputs to determine if the AC clutch should be engaged. The scan tool is useful in determining if these inputs are within the required parameters to allow AC clutch engagement.

If you followed the previous example closely, it should be apparent that to diagnose a control module you need to have a thorough understanding of how the system should work, the ability to use schematics, the ability to use a scan tool, the ability to use a DVOM, and the reference material needed. Above all, you must be able to develop a logical step-by-step diagnostic approach to determining if the module is functioning correctly. This approach will lead you to determining if the module is functioning correctly by a process of elimination, first eliminating the inputs as being the cause of the nonfunctioning AC compressor, and then eliminating the outputs as the cause for the failure. Only after you have done this can you make a decision about whether the control module is defective.

TESTING SENSORS

A variety of sensors are being used as AC system control devices. These individual sensors were discussed in Chapter 7 of the *Classroom Manual*. Sensors are usually different than switches, although sometimes the terms "sensor" and "switch" are interchanged. A sensor usually has the ability to send a varying signal to a control module. This signal may be an analog voltage, either AC or DC. In some instances the signal generated by the sensor may be digital. A switch usually only has two states, open or closed. Older AC systems relied on switches as controls, such as a low-pressure cut-off switch or a high-pressure cut-off switch. Newer systems tend to employ more sensors to signal the control modules. These sensors may include:

- AC refrigerant pressure sensor
- Ambient temperature sensor
- In-car temperature sensor
- Sun load sensor
- Evaporator fin sensor
- AC refrigerant temperature sensor

Testing the AC Refrigerant Pressure Sensor

As shown in figure 7-12, the AC pressure sensor (transducer) is supplied five volts from the control module. The transducer is basically a type of strain gauge that changes resistance as pressure changes. Thus, as the pressure inside the transducer varies, the resistance changes and causes a voltage drop. This voltage drop is monitored by the control module on the signal (sense) circuit. The transducer can be tested by measuring voltage with a DVOM, figure 7-13, or testing with a scan tool, figure 7-14.

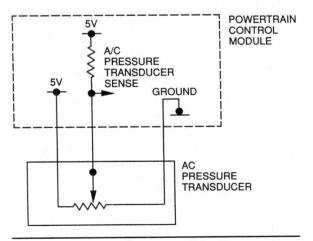

Figure 7-12. AC pressure transducer circuit. (Courtesy of DaimlerChrysler Corporation.)

Figure 7-13. The voltage at the AC pressure sensor may be checked with a DVOM by carefully backprobing the sensor.

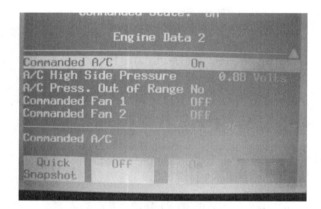

Figure 7-14. The scan tool may show the voltage from the AC pressure sensor.

Ambient Temperature Sensor

The ambient temperature sensor is a negative temperature coefficient thermistor that changes resistance with temperature. A five-volt reference voltage is sent to the thermistor from the control module. This five volts drops proportionally across an internal resistor based on the resistance of the thermistor. The control module measures this voltage drop to determine temperature. The scan tool is a good tool to quickly check the accuracy of the ambient temperature sensor by comparing it to the outside air temperature taken with a thermometer, figure 7-15. The scan tool may show the voltage reading on the temperature sensor circuit, the temperature reading in degrees, or both readings. The resistance of the sensor can be measured with a DVOM and compared to a table as illustrated in figure 7-16.

Figure 7-15. A scan tool may be used to quickly check the accuracy of the ambient sensor by comparing its reading to the actual ambient temperature.

Testing the Ambient Temperature Sensor

Many systems include an ambient temperature sensor as part of the AC control system. This sensor is a thermistor that changes resistance with changes of temperature. This sensor is used to prevent compressor operation when the outside temperatures are too low. It also may be used to display outside air temperature. It is usually mounted in front of the radiator and condenser, figure 7-17.

Test this sensor as follows:

Scan Tool Method

1. Install a scan tool and obtain the temperature reading of the outside temperature sensor.
2. Compare the scan tool value to the ambient air temperature, figure 7-18. If within ±5°F, the sensor and circuit are operating correctly. If the reading varies more than ±5°F, go to step 3.
3. If the reading varies more than ±5°F, disconnect the sensor and observe the scan tool reading. The scan tool should show −40°F (approximately) or five volts, figure 7-19.
4. Jumper the terminals together and observe the scan tool, figure 7-20. The scan tool should read 280°F (approximately) or zero volts, figure 7-21. If both the conditions in steps 3 and 4 are met, then the circuit and module are good. Replace the temperature sensor. If these conditions are not met, repair the circuit or module.

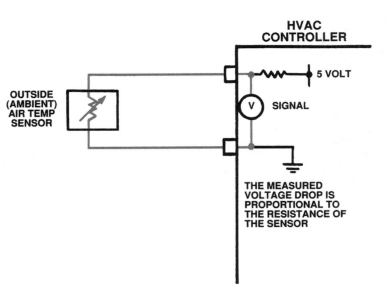

TEMPERATURE/RESISTANCE TABLE			
Resistance Ω	°C*	°F*	Analog-Digital (A/D) Counts
169,400	-40	-40	241
88,740	-30	-22	229
71,635	-27	-16	224
48,580	-20	-4	211
27,670	-10	14	187
19,315	-3	26	168
16,330	0	32	158
9,950	10	50	127
6,245	20	68	98
5,280	24	75	88
4,030	30	86	73
2,663	40	104	54
1,800	50	122	39
1,245	60	140	28
875	70	158	21
630	80	176	15
400	95	202	10

Figure 7-16. The resistance of the ambient sensor can be measured with a DVOM and compared to charts provided by the manufacturer. (Reprinted with permission of General Motors Corporation.)

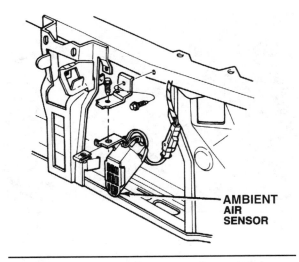

Figure 7-17. The ambient temperature switch is usually mounted near the front of the vehicle. (Reprinted with permission of General Motors Corporation.)

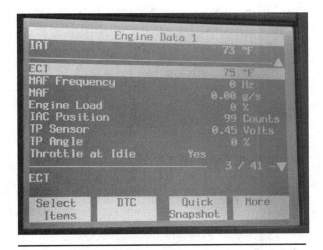

Figure 7-18. Connect a scan tool and compare the ambient sensor value to the ambient temperature. NOTE: For illustration purposes the scan tool is showing intake air temperature and engine coolant temperature.

No Scan Tool Method

1. Disconnect the sensor and measure the resistance of the sensor. Compare to a chart similar to the one shown in figure 7-22 (check the manufacturer's specifications). If the sensor is within specifications then proceed to step 2. If it is not, replace the sensor.

2. With the sensor disconnected, measure the voltage across the terminals of the connector. In most cases it should measure five volts (check the manufacturer's specifications). If it measures five volts, the circuit and module are good. If not, repair the circuit wiring or module.

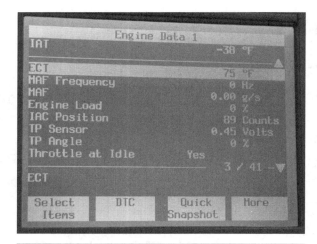

Figure 7-19. With the sensor disconnected, the reading on the scan tool will show approximately −40°F or five volts.

Figure 7-20. Jumper the sensor connector wires together.

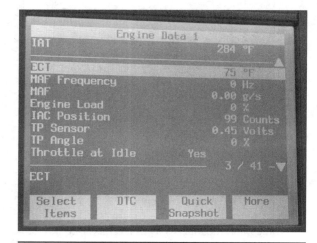

Figure 7-21. With the terminals jumped, the scan tool should display approximately 280°F or zero volts.

Resistance	°C	°F
169,400	−40	−40
88,740	−30	−22
71,635	−27	−16
48,580	−20	−4
27,670	−10	14
19,315	−3	26
16,330	0	32
9,950	10	50
6,245	20	68
5,280	24	75
4,030	30	86
2,663	40	104
1,800	50	122
1,245	60	140
875	70	158
630	80	176
400	95	202

Figure 7-22. Manufacturers often provide a resistance chart for determining the accuracy of the temperature sensor.

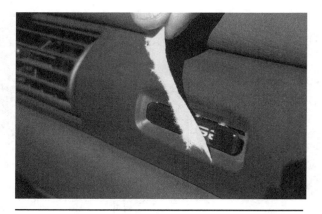

Figure 7-23. The in-car temperature sensor often has an aspirator or small fan that draws air over the sensor. Its operation may be tested by placing a small piece of tissue paper over the opening.

In-Car Temperature Sensor (Thermistor Type)

The in-car temperature sensor is the same type of device as the ambient temperature sensor. You may be able to determine the sensor reading by using a scan tool or by measuring the resistance of the sensor with a DVOM. In addition, make sure to test the aspirator by using a thin piece of tissue paper to determine if there is adequate airflow over the sensor, figure 7-23.

Figure 7-24. To test the infrared sensor, use a scan tool or a DVOM to monitor the sensor output and then place a cold object in front of the sensor.

Figure 7-25. To test the infrared sensor, use a scan tool or a DVOM to monitor the sensor output and then place a hot object in front of the sensor.

In-Car Temperature Sensor (Infrared Type)

As discussed in Chapter 11 of the *Classroom Manual*, some manufacturers are starting to use infrared-type in-car temperature sensors. These sensors detect surface temperature, such as on the seat cushion, instead of interior air temperature. They can be used to signal the control module about temperature extremes that can occur due to radiant heat entering the vehicle. A scan tool may be used to monitor the output of this infrared sensor. By passing a cold and warm object in front of the sensor you can read the change in temperature with the scan tool, figure 7-24. Another method would be to monitor the output voltage from the sensor with a DVOM while passing a cold object such as a can of soda in front of the sensor. You should see the voltage change, figure 7-25. Make sure that these in-

Figure 7-26. A scan tool may be able to display the sun load sensor readings. When the sun load is dark, the sun load sensor should have a high voltage reading.

Figure 7-27. The scan tool should show a change in voltage from the sun load sensor as it is exposed to bright light. The voltage from the sensor will decrease as the light increases.

frared sensors are not sprayed with cleaners that may cause them to send inaccurate signals to the control module.

Sun Load Sensor

As discussed in Chapter 11 of the *Classroom Manual*, the sun load sensor may be one of several different types. Most manufacturers use the photo resistor type of sun load sensor. This sensor changes resistance as light strikes it. It has five volts supplied to it from the module and causes a voltage drop across its resistance. As can be seen in figure 7-26, when the sun load is relatively dark the voltage reading should be high. As the sun load becomes brighter the voltage should decrease, figure 7-27. Monitoring a scan tool and passing a light above the sun load sensor while observing the voltage reading on the scan tool can best check the sun load sensor.

Evaporator Fin Sensor

The evaporator fin sensor is a thermistor that is inserted into the fin of the evaporator to sense evaporator temperature, figure 7-28. It is used to prevent evaporator freeze-up on some vehicles. Typically the sensor would have five volts applied to it from the control module. As the temperature of the evaporator decreases the resistance of the sensor increases. A scan tool may be used to monitor the temperature reading from the evaporator sensor, figure 7-29.

Figure 7-28. The evaporator fin sensor is a thermistor that is inserted into the evaporator fins.

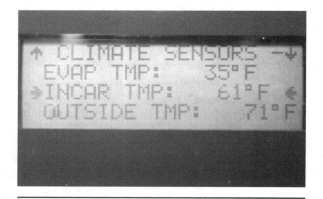

Figure 7-29. The scan tool may be used to monitor the evaporator fin sensor voltage.

Refrigerant Temperature Sensor

A few vehicles use refrigerant temperature sensors to determine high-side and low-side temperature. These sensors are thermistors that thread into the refrigerant line and are directly exposed to the refrigerant. Typically they are provided five volts from a control module. As the temperature of the refrigerant changes the resistance of the sensor changes. These values may be observed on a scan tool. A DVOM can be used to measure the resistance of the sensor and compared to a chart to check their accuracy.

TESTING PRESSURE SWITCHES

A number of different types of pressure switches have been used as controls over the years. These switches have used different names; however, they all are open or closed switches used to detect either low pressure, high pressure, or normal pressure ranges. These switches include:

- Low-pressure cut-off switch
- High-pressure cut-off switch
- Pressure cycling switch
- Evaporator fin-sensed cycling clutch switch

To test these switches you first must know what the switch is being used for and if it is normally open or normally closed; also at what pressure it opens and closes. A good schematic should show you the switches that are being used, whether they are normally open or closed, and at what pressures they open and close, figure 7-30. Some scan tools may show the state of the various switches, and you can monitor the switch using the scan tool, figure 7-31. A DVOM can also be used to check the continuity of the switch in its open and closed state. You may need to use a pressure gauge so you can determine if the switch is opening or closing at the correct pressure, figure 7-32.

Temperature Switch Testing and Replacement

There are numerous temperature switches and sensors. Some temperature switches, such as ambient or in-car sensors, are frequently used to measure conditions outside the air conditioning system. Other temperature switches, such as evaporator or cooling system sensors, are used to measure conditions within the air conditioning system. This section gives representative diagnosis and test procedures for each of these types of temperature switches and sensors. NOTE: Some confusion can result from the terms "switch" and "sensor." For the purpose of the following explanations, the term "switch" will be used when referring to a device that is either "on-off" or "open-closed." The term "sensor" will be used to refer to a component that can produce an analog signal.

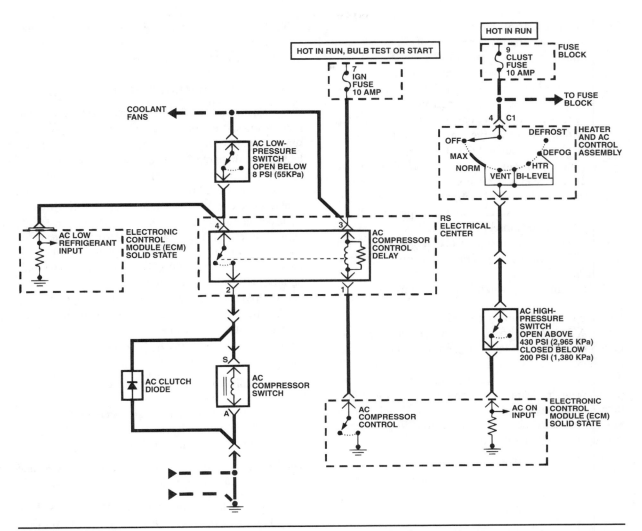

Figure 7-30. A good schematic should show the pressure switches that are used and at what pressures they are open or closed. (Reprinted with permission of General Motors Corporation.)

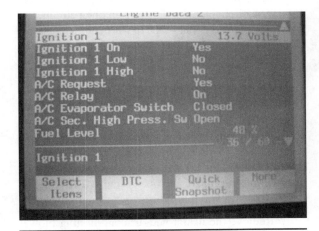

Figure 7-31. A scan tool may show the switch states.

Figure 7-32. Using a pressure gauge and a DVOM, you can determine if the switch is operating correctly.

Low-Pressure Cut-off Switch

1. Disconnect the low-pressure cut-off switch and jumper the leads together.
2. Start the engine and turn the AC on.
3. Observe the compressor operation to determine if the compressor clutch engaged.
4. If the clutch does not engage, the cycling clutch switch, fuse, or wiring may be defective. Check the clutch circuit and the clutch.
5. If the clutch engages, attach a manifold gauge set and read the evaporator suction pressure. The switch should activate the clutch at its operating pressure, which is typically 18 psi (125 kPa) or more.
6. If the evaporator pressure is below 25 psi (172 kPa), the refrigerant pressure is too low. Check for leaks.
7. Reconnect the switch if it passes this test.

Cycling Clutch Pressure Switch

Many AC systems use a pressure sensitive cycling clutch switch. It is located on the accumulator or suction hose. When the pressure reaches a factory set point, the pressure switch opens, interrupting the compressor clutch circuit. When pressure builds to a predetermined setting, the switch closes and allows voltage to reach the compressor clutch. Typical pressure settings for these switches are:

R-12	25 psi—open (compressor off)
	45 psi—closed (compressor on)
R-134a	20 psi—open (compressor off)
	40 psi—closed (compressor on)

To test this switch:

1. Remove the wires from the pressure cycling switch.
2. Check the continuity of the switch. Switch contacts are typically closed at pressures above 45 psi (311 kPa). If there is no continuity above this pressure, replace the switch (check the manufacturer's specifications for the exact opening and closing points).
3. If the switch contacts are closed within this range, verify the switch operation as follows:
   a. Reconnect the wires to the switch.
   b. Set the temperature control to MAX AC.
   c. Turn the air conditioner blower motor to LO.
   d. Operate the engine at 1,300 to 1,500 rpm for 5 to 10 minutes to stabilize the system.
   e. If the compressor cycles on and off two or three times a minute during this time, the switch operation is normal.
   f. If the compressor fails to engage, check for an open in the electrical circuit.

NOTE: On some models, the compressor clutch may be continuously engaged above 90°F (32°C) due to the high heat load. This condition is normal.

Testing Thermostatic Switches

Thermostatic switches have been used to cycle the compressor on and off on some vehicles. These switches sense evaporator temperature using a capillary tube attached to a diaphragm. The diaphragm acts on a set of switch contacts. When the temperature of the evaporator is high, the gas in the tube expands and causes the switch contacts to close. When the temperature of the evaporator is colder, the gas in the tube contracts and the switch contacts open. A DVOM can be used to check the switch contacts. In order to verify correct operation of the thermostatic switch with a DVOM, the capillary tube must be attached to the evaporator and the system must be getting cold enough to cause the contacts to open.

The thermostatic switch (also called a de-icing switch), figure 7-33, can sometimes be the source of compressor clutch failure to engage. Problems due to failure of the switch include:

- Compressor fails to engage because the switch fails to close.
- Compressor fails to cycle because the switch fails to open.
- Compressor cycles erratically.

The following procedure may be used to determine whether the switch has failed:

1. Remove the wiring from the thermostatic switch.
2. Connect an ohmmeter across the switch terminals.
3. Remove the switch capillary tube from the evaporator core.
4. Immerse the capillary tube in ice water until it is completely chilled.
5. The switch contacts should open and remain open while the capillary tube is being chilled. The ohmmeter should show an open circuit.
6. Allow the capillary tube to warm up. As it warms up, the contact points should close, and the ohmmeter should show continuity.

Evaporator Fin-Sensed Cycling Clutch Switch

Test the DaimlerChrysler fin-sensed cycling clutch switch in the same manner as described earlier for general switch testing. Switch replacement may involve a complex removal procedure, so make certain the switch is faulty before replacing it. Obtain the specific service information to remove the heater and AC housing. If the switch must be replaced, remove it as follows:

1. Remove the heater and air conditioning blower housing, if necessary.

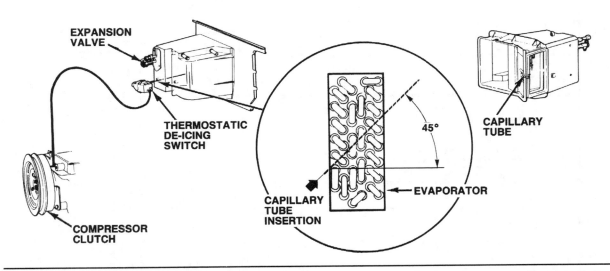

Figure 7-33. The thermostatic switch is wired in series with the compressor clutch and uses a capillary tube in the evaporator fins to sense temperature.

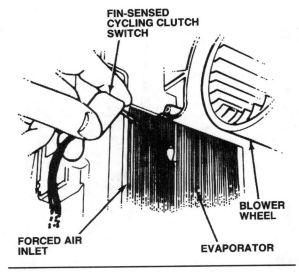

Figure 7-34. Disconnect the three-pin connector and pull the switch from the evaporator through the air inlet opening to remove this Chrysler fin-sensed cycling clutch switch. (Courtesy of DaimlerChrysler Corporation.)

2. Disconnect the three-terminal wire connector from the sensor, and push the wire grommet through the hole in the housing. Feed the connector through.

3. Pull the switch from the evaporator through the air inlet opening to the left of the blower wheel, figure 7-34.

4. Install the replacement switch. Reconnect the three-wire connector.

5. Reinstall the heater and air conditioner blower housing.

    a. Reconnect the wires to the switch.

b. Set the temperature control lever to MAX AC.

c. Turn the AC blower motor setting to LOW.

d. Operate the engine at 1,300 to 1,500 rpm for 5 to 10 minutes to stabilize the system.

e. If the compressor cycles on and off two or three times a minute during this time, the switch operation is normal.

f. If the compressor fails to engage, check for an open in the electrical circuit.

g. If the compressor fails to cycle off, install gauges and determine if the pressures fall below the opening point of the pressure switch. If they do, replace the switch.

Compressor Clutch Relay Testing

The AC compressor clutch is usually controlled by a relay. The relay switches the high current necessary for the compressor clutch. The relay in turn is usually controlled by the PCM, BCM, control head, or programmer. When the AC compressor will not engage, this relay could be at fault or the signal to the relay could be missing. The relay serves as a convenient point in the AC circuit to start your diagnosis of an inoperative AC compressor clutch. Using the diagram in figure 7-35, let's look at how the relay is controlled.

1. When the selector switch is turned to MAX, NORM, BILEVEL, BLEND, or DEFROST, voltage is supplied to the ECM as a request signal and to the relay at terminal A.

2. Fuse #9 provides voltage to the coil of the relay whenever the ignition is on.

3. The ECM provides the ground for the compressor control relay after it receives the AC request

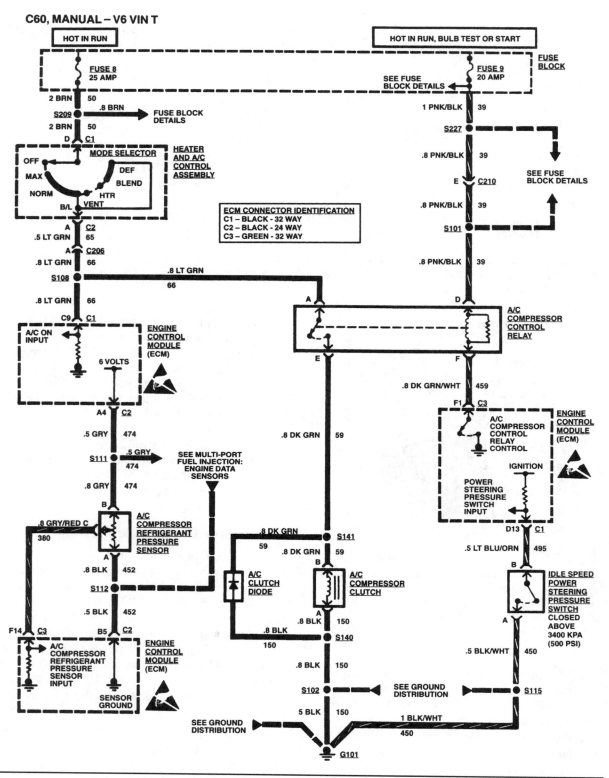

Figure 7-35. A typical compressor relay control circuit. (Reprinted with permission of ACDelco.)

at terminal C9. The ECM determines if the AC system has enough refrigerant in the system based on the input from the pressure sensor circuit at terminal F14. If these values are within the correct range, the ECM will provide a ground to the relay coil at terminal F1.

4. When the relay terminal is grounded, the relay should activate and provide voltage to the AC compressor clutch and the compressor should engage.

If the compressor does not engage, you need to verify that the appropriate voltages are present at the relay, the ECM is providing the ground for the relay coil, and that the relay is working. Test the inputs to the relay as follows:

1. Check for voltage with a test light or meter at terminals A and D of the relay (86 and 30 for ISO-numbered relays), figure 7-36. If voltage is present at both, proceed to step 2.

2. Connect a test light to battery voltage and connect to terminal F of the relay (85 for ISO relays). Switch the AC selector ON and OFF. If the ECM is providing the ground for the relay the test light should light when the ECM grounds the circuit, figure 7-37. This indicates that the ECM is providing the ground to the relay.

3. Next check for voltage at terminal E of the relay (terminal 87 for ISO relays). If voltage is present, then the relay is working correctly. If no voltage is present, then the relay needs to be replaced.

You can also remove the relay and bench test it to determine if the relay is working. This may be necessary

if you do not have a relay to substitute or if the relay terminals are not accessible due to the design or placement of the relay in the vehicle. Bench test a relay as follows:

1. Using the diagram shown on the side of the relay, determine which two terminals are the coil terminals, figure 7-38.

Figure 7-37. With the test light connected to 12 volts, connect the test light to terminal F (85 for ISO relays) and switch the AC on. If the ECM is providing a ground to the relay, the test light should light.

Figure 7-38. Using the diagram on the relay, determine the two coil terminals of the relay. In this case the coil terminals are 85 and 86.

Figure 7-36. Testing for voltage at terminals A and D (86 and 30 for ISO-standard relays). Both terminals should show voltage.

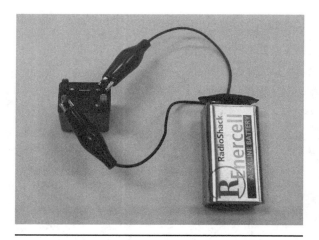

Figure 7-39. Connect a voltage source to terminals 85 and 86. A nine-volt battery can be used.

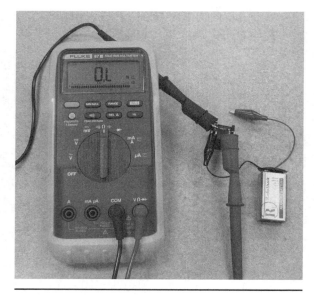

Figure 7-41. Disconnect the battery. The ohmmeter should now read OL.

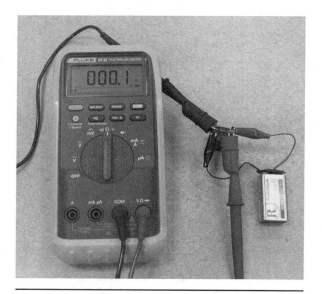

Figure 7-40. Connect an ohmmeter to the switch terminals of the relay, in this case, terminals 30 and 87. The ohmmeter should read 0.1 to 0.3 ohms.

2. Using jumper wires, connect a voltage source to the relay coil terminals (you can use the vehicle's battery or you can use a nine-volt battery), figure 7-39.
3. Connect an ohmmeter to the relay switched terminals. With the relay engaged, the ohmmeter should read 0.1 to 0.3 ohms, figure 7-40.
4. Disconnect the battery from the relay coil terminals. The ohmmeter should now show OL, figure 7-41.
5. If the relay passes these tests, then it is good.

8

Compressor Diagnosis and Service

This chapter details the causes of compressor failure, how to recognize the problem, how to maintain and test the compressor, and how to repair several typical compressors.

In most automotive repair shops, a faulty compressor is usually replaced with a new or rebuilt unit. The old, defective compressor is then repaired or rebuilt at a specialty shop. These rebuilders have the parts and special tools required for compressor service.

However, it is a good idea to have an understanding of the internal workings of compressors and how to repair them. This fundamental knowledge will help you diagnose compressor problems.

GENERAL COMPRESSOR DIAGNOSIS

Compressor diagnosis can be divided into the following areas:

- Drive problems—belt, pulley, or clutch operation
- Compressor control problems
- Refrigerant leakage and contamination
- Internal compressor problems

Inspect the Components

Begin your inspection with the compressor. Confirm that the compressor is properly mounted, and that its mounting bolts are securely in place. Make sure that the brackets are in good condition. Check the compressor connections to confirm that the electrical contacts are clean and tight. Look for damage to the compressor housing or indications of a leak. Look for a dirty, oily patch near a seam, joint, or hose connection on the compressor.

Next, inspect the condition of the belts. Look for cracks, splits, or glazing. Check the belt tension. Make sure the belts are riding in the pulley properly and confirm that there is no slippage.

Inspect the refrigerant lines. Check the line connections at the compressor. Check the lines and hoses throughout the system for damage and leaks.

Inspect the condition of the fuses. They are usually located in the instrument panel or the underhood fuse panel. Also, check inline fuses, fusible links, resistors, and relays. Use a wiring diagram to locate these components.

Next, use a manifold gauge set to test the operating condition of the system. With the manifold gauge set attached, operate the system until all normal operating pressures are reached. While the system is operating, listen for unusual or excessive noise from the compressor, hoses, lines, and belts. Set the system to MAX, the blower on HIGH, and the temperature to its coldest setting. Use a thermometer to check the vent outlet temperature. Confirm that the system operating pressures are neither too high nor too low under these conditions.

Next, test the compressor cycling operation if it is a cycling clutch system. Observe the changes in pressure as the compressor cycles on and off. Check the on/off ratio and cycling times against the vehicle specifications. If the cycle on and off points are different from the specifications, the problem is more likely a problem with the pressure switch or refrigerant level, rather than the compressor. If you discover a problem, proceed to your service manual for troubleshooting charts and diagnostic information to further pinpoint the cause of the problem.

COMPRESSOR FAILURES

Compressors have many internal components, figure 8-1, which makes compressor damage one of the most severe and expensive failures of the air conditioning system. In addition to the cost of overhauling or replacing the compressor, debris from a failed compressor may spread throughout the system. This can clog or damage other components, which may have to be cleaned, repaired, or replaced. Common problems include:

- Defective clutch assembly
- Leaking front seal
- Worn bearings
- Damaged reed valve(s)
- Mechanically damaged pistons and cylinders
- Compressor contamination due to a failure elsewhere in the system

Inadequate lubrication is the most common cause of compressor damage. Many compressors do not have compressor oil reservoirs or positive displacement lubrication systems. These compressors are lubricated by splash circulation of refrigerant oil. Failure to keep the required amount of oil circulating will lead to compressor failure.

It is important to remember that after determining which compressor parts are faulty, you must also determine why the parts failed. Correcting the problem that damaged the compressor in the first place is the only way to ensure that the problem will not reoccur.

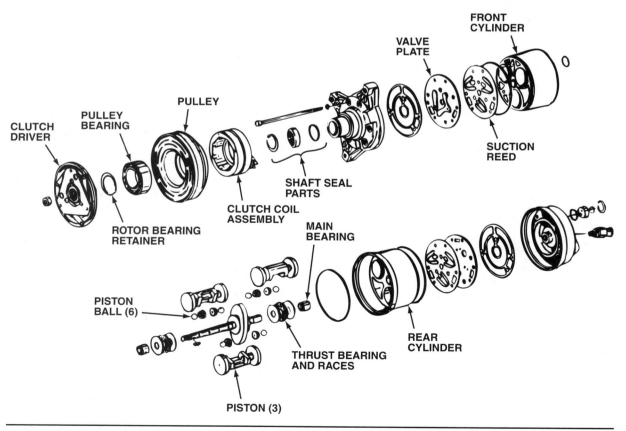

Figure 8-1. Compressors contain many moving parts. Most of these parts are in metal-to-metal contact with one another and fail if they are not properly lubricated.

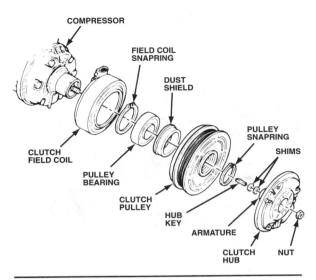

Figure 8-2. Energizing the field engages the clutch by coupling the hub to the rotating pulley, which transfers crankshaft torque to the compressor.

Clutch Failures

The stationary field electromagnetic clutch is used in all modern compressors. The field coil and its housing are bolted or pressed onto the compressor and remain stationary during clutch operation. When the field windings are energized, the field coil pulls the clutch hub toward the compressor drive plate, figure 8-2.

The clutch hub is at the outer end of the assembly and has an extension, which is keyed to the compressor shaft. When the field coil pulls the clutch hub toward it, the pulley engages with the clutch hub.

The pulley and its bearing ride on an extension of the compressor case, and the pulley is usually held in place with a snapring. The pulley is driven by a belt and is always turning when the engine is running. When the clutch hub engages with the pulley, the force from the turning pulley is transferred to the compressor shaft through the clutch hub, rotating the compressor shaft.

When the field coil is deenergized, the clutch disengages from the pulley, the compressor shaft stops turning, and the pulley freewheels. Common clutch failures include:

- Open field windings
- Slippage due to clutch circuit problems
- A jammed or warped hub assembly
- A damaged or bent pulley
- A defective bearing
- Wear from excessive cycling or contamination

Begin troubleshooting clutch problems at the field windings by checking the power and ground wire con-

nections leading to the field coil. With the engine running and the air conditioner on, check for a voltage drop on the clutch circuit. Connect a voltmeter in parallel to take voltage drop readings. On a typical 12-volt system there should be a minimum of 11 volts on the supply side and a maximum of 0.5 volts on the ground side of the circuit. If supply side readings are low, check the supply side for excessive resistance. If the ground side readings are high, check for corrosion or bad connections. If the field coil is receiving a low voltage supply or has a poor ground, it will not engage the clutch properly. This results in slippage and exposes the clutch to excessive and deteriorating heat.

The clutch assembly may jam if the hub or pulley is physically damaged, warped, or if the clutch plate surface is dirty or oily. Check the pulley, as it may be bent or damaged. Damage to the clutch hub or pulley will lead to problems such as slippage, failure to engage, or failure to disengage.

The clutch bearing is permanently lubricated and is not likely to fail if the pulley drive belt tension is properly adjusted and the bearing seal is intact. If the bearing is worn due to incorrect belt tension or dirt contamination, replace it. A defective bearing produces a growling sound, which changes with the load placed on the bearing. Most clutch bearings that are noisy will be louder when the clutch is not engaged and will get somewhat quieter when the clutch is engaged. Disassembly or discharging of the refrigeration system is usually not required when replacing the bearing in the clutch assembly.

Seal Failures

The front seal, located behind the clutch, is the hardest working seal in the compressor, figure 8-3. It must hold system pressure while allowing the compressor

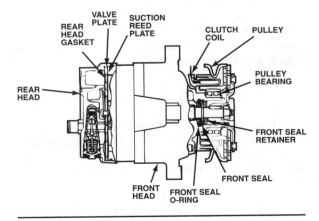

Figure 8-3. The front seal maintains compressor pressure while allowing the crankshaft to rotate.

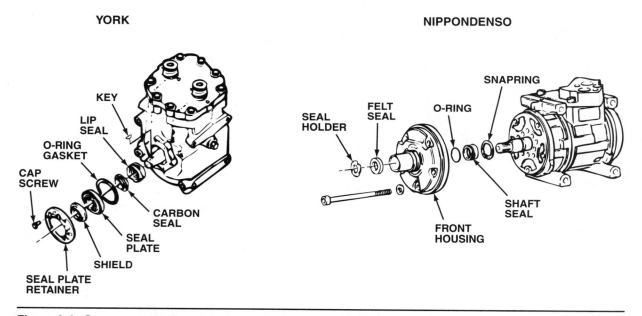

Figure 8-4. Compressor shaft seal design varies by manufacturer and model.

shaft to rotate. The front seal may consist of a steel ring or plate, O-rings, sleeves and/or bushings, as well as other components. Different types of seal and component assemblies are shown in figure 8-4. Front seal failures are caused by:

- Wear, which prevents adequate sealing against the compressor shaft.
- Running surface contamination, which again prevents adequate sealing.

- Physical seal damage resulting from corrosion.
- Front compressor bearing damage, which leads to seal failure.

Seal damage occurs in a number of ways. A cracked, split, or pinched O-ring or loose mounting bolts can cause seepage, figure 8-5. The bellows area of the seal can be distorted by heat. Damage to the bellows causes refrigerant to leak from the compressor seal. Older compressors are designed to allow the compressor seal

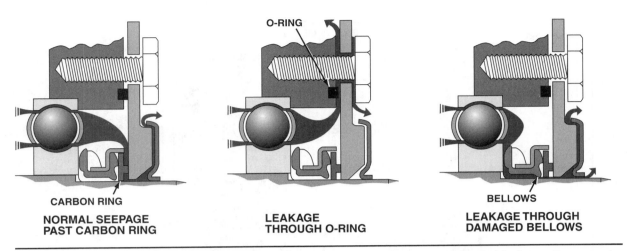

O-RING

CARBON RING

**NORMAL SEEPAGE
PAST CARBON RING**

**LEAKAGE
THROUGH O-RING**

BELLOWS

**LEAKAGE THROUGH
DAMAGED BELLOWS**

Figure 8-5. Some seepage is normal on an older compressor, but a damaged O-ring or bellows allows excess seepage.

to seep slightly. Approximately 1/2 to 1 ounce (15 ml to 30 ml) of refrigerant seeping past the seal per year is enough to lubricate the seal, yet not damage the system. Some leak detectors have sensitivity controls that allow them to ignore normal levels of refrigerant seepage from the front seal.

Normal refrigerant seepage may result in an oily smear in the area immediately behind the seal. However, the oil seepage should not be heavy enough to spread to the compressor body or beyond the immediate area of the clutch. If the oil spreads, the system has a leak and must be repaired. Recover the refrigerant, replace the seal, check the amount of oil in the system, and replace the oil as needed.

When you replace a front seal, the magnetic clutch, and sometimes the front head mounting to the compressor, must be removed. Many manufacturers have designed the compressor so that the seal can be serviced with the compressor still mounted on the vehicle. Other compressors must be removed for seal service. Your service manual should provide the information you need to decide whether this is an off-vehicle service or not.

Replacing the seal while the compressor is in the vehicle may not always be practical. The mounting position of the compressor or other accessories, such as the radiator, fan, and power steering pump and hoses, often limits access to the compressor. Special tools designed for servicing compressors, such as pullers, seal removers, and seal installers, are often needed to replace the seal. Consult the appropriate service manual for any special tools needed for servicing the compressor.

Bearing Failures

The front compressor shaft bearing withstands the weight of the clutch hub. The front and rear shaft

bearings, called the main support bearings, carry the weight of the compressor shaft and associated reciprocating forces, figure 8-6. These are usually ball or roller bearings.

In addition to the main support bearings, some compressors use thrust bearings to provide endplay control. This is especially true of compressors with swash plates, figure 8-7. Compressor bearings are lubricated with refrigerant oil, either from a sump in the compressor, or by constant circulation of refrigerant, which contains refrigerant oil. Compressor shaft bearing failure results from:

- Inadequate lubrication due to a low refrigerant and/or oil charge.
- Damage due to a collision.
- Damage due to heat and oil contamination.
- Damage due to a faulty or out-of-balance compressor clutch.

Replacing the compressor's main bearings is a major service that requires complete disassembly of the compressor. This procedure is normally done by specialty compressor rebuild shops and is not likely to be done in a general repair facility. Replace the compressor if the main bearings fail.

Reed Valve Failure

The suction and discharge reed valves control vapor flow through the compressor, figure 8-8. These valves are made of thin steel that bends under the force of pressure or suction. When the compressor piston begins its intake stroke, the suction created in the cylinder pulls the suction reed valve open to allow refrigerant vapor in, and holds the discharge reed valve closed. When the piston begins its discharge stroke, the discharge reed valve opens and the suction reed valve is

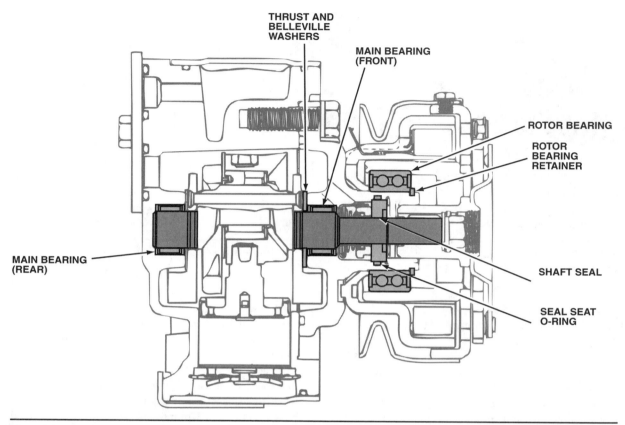

Figure 8-6. The support bearings, located at the front and rear of the compressor shaft, bear the turning force of the compressor crankshaft and the torque from the pulley.

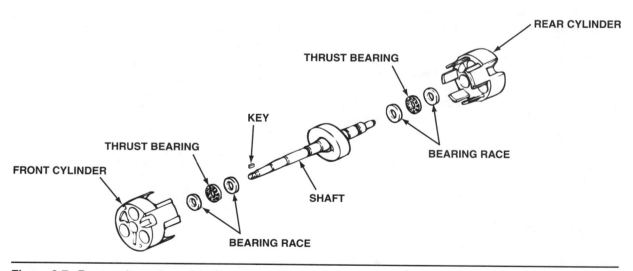

Figure 8-7. Front and rear thrust bearing assemblies control endplay on a swash plate compressor.

held closed. Some discharge reed valves use an over-travel limiter to prevent fatigue cracking.

Damaged reed valves are easily detected with the gauges connected to the system, the engine running, and the compressor engaged. A rapidly oscillating high-pressure and/or low-pressure gauge needle is an indication of damaged reed valves. Damaged reed valves may be caused by:

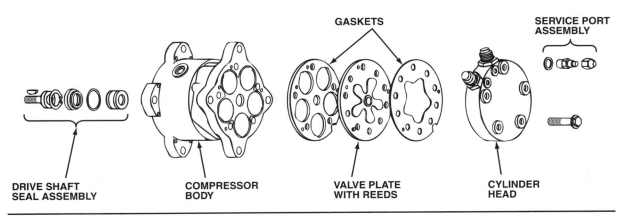

Figure 8-8. The inlet and outlet reed valves on this Sankyo/Sanden SD-series compressor are located under the cylinder head.

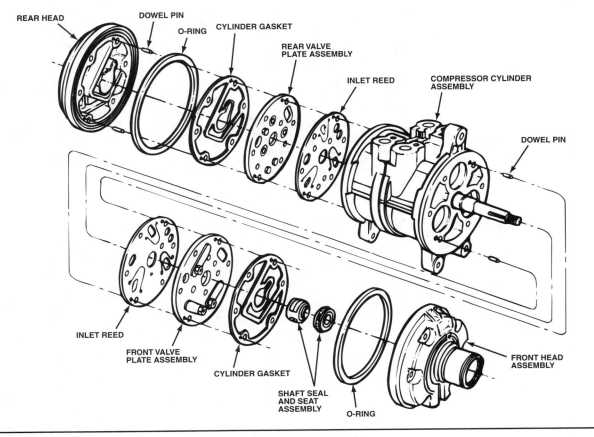

Figure 8-9. Reed valves may be located on one end or both ends of the compressor.

- Liquid refrigerant, rather than vapor, entering the suction side of the compressor.
- Debris in the system that plugs or holds the reed valve open.
- Excessively high system pressure.
- Internal compressor failure.

Reed valves can be replaced in some compressors by removing the compressor head. Replacement on other models requires completely disassembling the compressor. Some compressors have reed valves on one end of the compressor; others have reed valve sets at both ends of the compressor, figure 8-9.

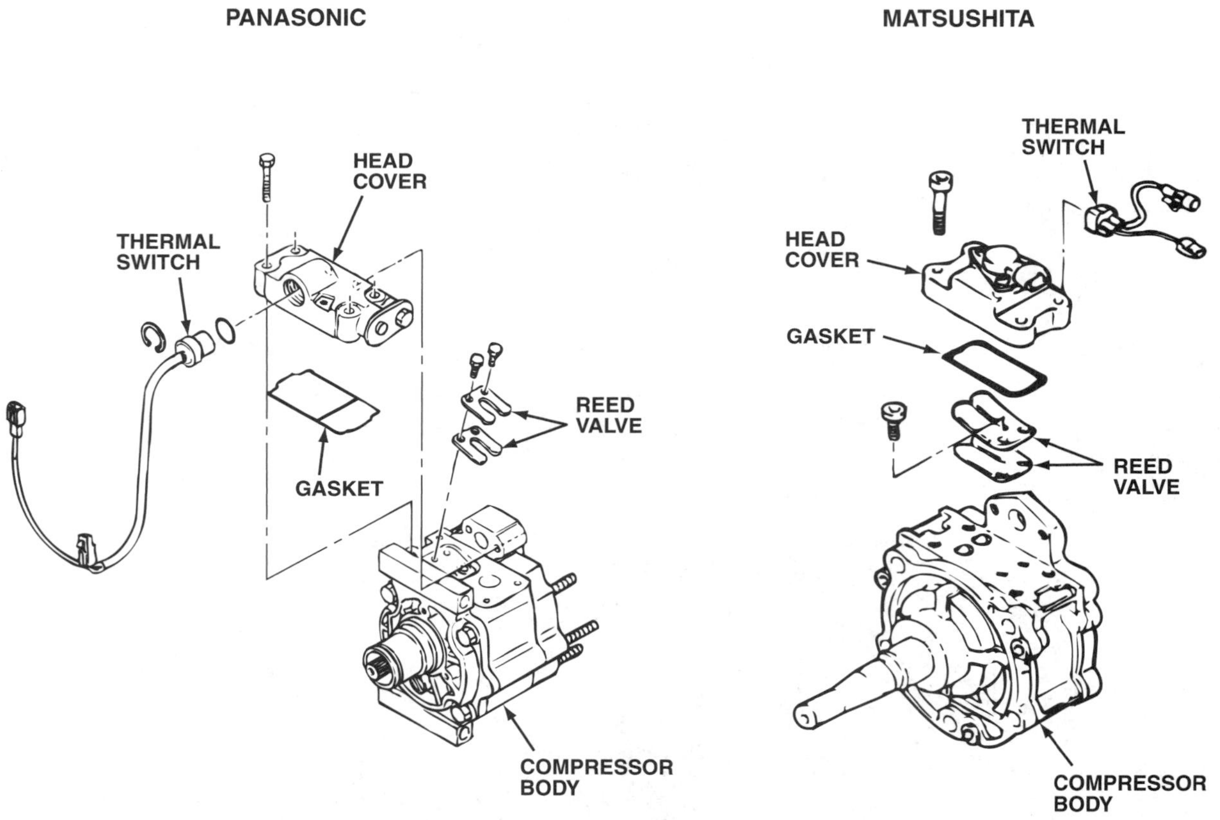

PANASONIC   **MATSUSHITA**

Figure 8-10. Rotary vane compressor valve plates are a variation of the typical reed valve plate design.

Even on rotary vane compressors, such as Matsushita and Panasonic, the valve plates are a variation of the typical reed valve plate design, figure 8-10. Scroll compressors are the only designs that do not use some form of reed assembly.

Mechanical Failure

Damage to the pistons, cylinder walls, swash plates, and other parts may be caused by:

- Insufficient refrigerant or lubricant in the system.
- Damage due to collision.
- Contamination from damaged internal parts elsewhere in the system.
- Debris, such as broken reed valves or piston rings, in the cylinder.
- Incorrect assembly or disassembly.

As mentioned earlier, inadequate lubrication is the most common cause of compressor mechanical failure. A lack of lubrication results in excessive friction, overheating, and seizure of the compressor's moving parts. If this happens, the compressor will have to be rebuilt or replaced.

Contamination

As mentioned previously, major damage to other components in the air conditioning system will likely contaminate the compressor. Also, improper recovery, evacuation, flushing, and charging procedures leave moisture or contaminates in the system. This moisture forms corrosive acids that will damage compressor parts. Assemblies such as the condenser and evaporator can be flushed to remove debris, as mentioned in earlier chapters. However, the compressor cannot be flushed while assembled and on the vehicle. If badly contaminated, you must disassemble and clean or replace it.

Removing and Replacing Compressors

Correct removal and replacement procedures for the compressor are very important to minimize system contamination and prevent damage to hoses, connections, and other components.

The exact procedures to remove and replace a compressor vary, depending on the type of vehicle. Many vehicles need to be raised on a lift or supported on jack stands. The following procedure is a general guideline. Refer to your service manual for specific procedures:

1. Disconnect the negative battery cable.
2. Identify and disconnect the electrical connector at the compressor.
3. Use approved recovery/recycling equipment to discharge the air conditioning system.
4. Disconnect the refrigerant hoses from the compressor. Immediately cap or tape off hose openings to prevent moisture and dirt from entering the system.
5. Loosen and remove the compressor and accessory drive belts as needed. In some cases, loosening the engine idler pulley is necessary to remove the drive belt.
6. Remove the mounting bracket bolts as necessary. Note the location of any bolts that are of a different size or length.
7. Remove the compressor. On some vehicles, the compressor is removed from the top of the engine compartment. On other vehicles, it is removed from the bottom.
8. Drain and measure the oil from the old compressor. Record this amount.
9. Check the new compressor for oil. Some compressors come with a full charge of oil and other compressors are shipped dry. If the compressor is shipped with a full oil charge you must drain this from the compressor and add the amount of oil that was drained from the old compressor.

NOTE: Be sure to consult the manufacturer's service information regarding the amount of oil to add when changing the compressor. Make sure that you use the type of oil specified by the manufacturer of the compressor. Failure to use the correct type of oil may void the warranty on the compressor and cause premature failure.

Compressor Testing

Troubleshooting a compressor problem involves diagnosing the entire air conditioning system. To prepare, review the instructions on how to use a manifold gauge set included in Chapter 3 and the air conditioning system troubleshooting procedures, including the section on abnormal gauge readings, in Chapter 5 of this *Shop Manual*.

Checking Compressor Operating Pressures

Although operating pressures vary by system and ambient conditions, typical pressure readings for a good compressor in an automotive air conditioning system that is fully charged are as follows:

- Low-side readings are high if above about 45 psi.
- High-side readings are low if below about 150 psi.

The key to efficient compressor operation is the pressure differential between the two sides. It is possible to have low-side pressure above 40 psi (275 kPa) on a hot day, and have high-side pressure below 150 psi (1,035 kPa) when testing with a low heat load. However, these two conditions should not exist at the same time.

The two primary indicators of a defective compressor are improper pressure readings and noise. Below are six common compressor faults.

1. Defective reed valves, if equipped. Symptoms include rapid oscillations of the needle on the high-pressure gauge, the low-pressure gauge, or both, figure 8-11.
2. Worn or scored pistons, rings, or cylinders on piston-type compressors. This causes a reduction in the amount of refrigerant that is pumped, and therefore, a reduced pressure differential between the high side and the low side.
3. Worn swash plate on piston compressors. This creates noise.
4. Worn scroll mechanism on scroll-type compressors. This causes a reduction in the amount of refrigerant pumped, and, therefore, a reduced pressure differential between the high side and the low side.
5. Worn vanes on a rotary vane compressor. This causes a reduction in the amount of refrigerant pumped and, therefore, a reduced pressure differential between the high side and the low side.
6. Stuck or malfunctioning control valve on a variable displacement compressor. This can cause a reduction or increase in the amount of refrigerant pumped, creating either too much of a pressure differential or too little of a pressure differential.

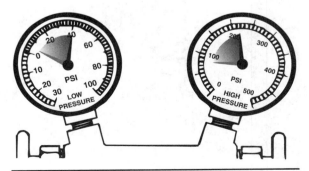

Figure 8-11. Rapid oscillations on either or both manifold gauges may be caused by a defective reed valve.

Compressor Noise and Vibration

Grinding or banging noises from the compressor while it is running may indicate mechanical failure. If the fuses for the clutch blow frequently, the electrical system should be checked for heat problems caused by clutch slippage. To check for seizure:

1. Make sure that the magnetic clutch is not engaged, then turn the engine off. If necessary, disconnect the wire from the compressor.
2. Try to turn the compressor shaft by hand.
3. If you hear grinding or feel a great deal of resistance, the compressor is probably seized or the bearings are worn, figure 8-12. If the compressor turns easily, the piston rings may be worn.

When a customer complains of compressor-related noise or vibration, perform the following checks:

- Verify the complaint by operating the system. Some system noise is normal. Rhythmic noises are not a cause for alarm. If in doubt, compare the noise and vibration levels to a system that is known to be operating correctly.
- Look for missing or damaged compressor mounting bolts and brackets. Tighten and replace them as necessary.

- Look for damaged or worn idler pulleys, magnetic clutches, and hub pulley bearings.
- Look for foreign material that may be blocking the condenser and causing abnormally high system pressures.
- Check cooling fan operation. If the fan is not operating properly, it may cause abnormally high systems pressure.
- Inspect the refrigerant line routing and clamps. Make certain the lines are in place and do not contact other engine compartment components while the system is running, figure 8-13.
- If the noise seems to be coming from the front of the compressor, engage and disengage the clutch by turning the system on and off with the engine running. If the noise level changes, check the clutch pulley bearing for wear or damage.
- Perform a refrigerant system pressure test. If the system pressures are abnormally high or low, troubleshoot the cause.
- Run the engine at 1,500 rpms. Listen for excessive rumble or knock that disappears when the compressor clutch is engaged and disengaged. After making all the previous checks, replace the compressor as needed.

Checking for Seal Leaks

Evidence of some oil at the compressor seal may or may not indicate a problem. Note the following when checking the seal for a suspected leak:

- Verify the type of compressor on which you are working.
- Consult the service manual for recommendations regarding seal leaks, refrigerant oil type, and whether the seal is serviceable.

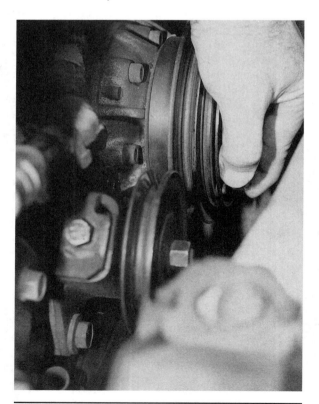

Figure 8-12. Most compressors can be turned by hand to check for worn bearings.

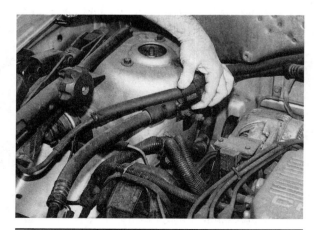

Figure 8-13. Noise and vibration are often caused by unsecured or incorrectly routed refrigerant lines and hoses.

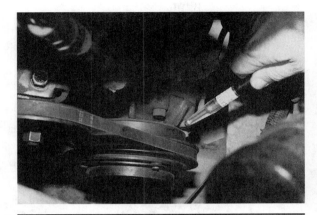

Figure 8-14. Use a refrigerant leak detector to check for compressor seal leakage.

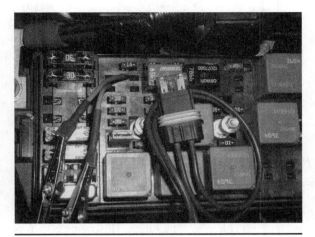

Figure 8-15. It may be necessary to force the compressor clutch to engage during troubleshooting. Remove the compressor relay and use a fused jumper to engage the clutch.

- Inspect around the shaft seal and adjacent surfaces for signs of refrigerant oil spray. On some older compressors, oil traces may be normal and do not require changing the seal. These compressors and seals are designed to seep a small amount of oil for lubrication purposes. Change a shaft seal if you find a large amount of sprayed oil or if you find a refrigerant leak during a leak test, figure 8-14. Be aware that evidence of oily spray may be the result of engine oil being spilled on the compressor drive belt. Always check for leaks with an electronic tester before you condemn the compressor seal.

Checking the Compressor Clutch Operation

When the electromagnetic compressor clutch is operating properly, force is applied to the compressor shaft only when current is flowing in the clutch field winding. If the clutch remains engaged when current is not applied to the field windings, the clutch is faulty. Conversely, if the clutch does not engage when the system is turned on or when normal cycling occurs, a fault in the electrical circuit to the clutch or the clutch coil is at fault.

If the clutch will not engage, the clutch circuit needs to be tested. To test the clutch, perform the following:

1. Disconnect the electrical connector from the compressor clutch.
2. Using a jumper wire, ground one side of the clutch coil connector. Then, using a fused jumper, apply 12 volts from the battery to the other side of the clutch coil, figure 8-15.
3. If the clutch engages, then the problem is in the clutch electrical circuit and not the clutch coil itself.
4. Follow the manufacturer's diagnostics for troubleshooting the reasons of no clutch engagement.

If the clutch engages when the vehicle is running and the air conditioning is turned on, but shows evidence of slipping, perform the following checks:

- Inadequate amount of voltage applied to the clutch coil.
- An excessive air gap between the clutch plate and the pulley.
- Excess friction or bindings that prevents the clutch plate from seating firmly to the pulley.
- Oily or worn clutch plate surfaces.
- A binding, seized, or partially seized compressor.
- A clutch coil that has excessive resistance in the windings. Measure the resistance with a DVOM and compare to the specifications, figure 8-16.

Figure 8-16. If the compressor clutch will not engage when jumping with a fused jumper wire, measure the resistance of the clutch coil with a DVOM.

Compressor Protection Devices

Almost all modern compressors are equipped with at least one kind of protection device. Most compressor protection devices fall into one of the following categories:

- High-pressure cut-off switches
- High-pressure relief valves
- Low-pressure cut-off switches
- Thermal protection devices
- Lock-up protection devices

High-Pressure Cut-off Switches

Almost all modern air conditioning systems have a preset high-side operating range. This range is different for each type of vehicle or system. However, when the high pressure rises beyond a preset shut-off, the high-pressure cut-off switches stop compressor operation. This prevents excessive high-side pressure and protects the system components against further possible damage. This high-pressure cut-off switch may be in the compressor, figure 8-17, or installed in a high-pressure refrigerant line, figure 8-18.

Common reasons for excessive high pressure include compressor malfunction, air in the system, inadequate airflow across the condenser, and restrictions in the system.

High-Pressure Relief Valves

Many compressors are equipped with a safety valve mounted in the head of the compressor on the high or discharge side, figure 8-19. If the system is not equip-ped with a high-pressure cut-off switch, or if the high-side pressures spike beyond the cut-off point of the switch, the safety valve vents the refrigerant from the compressor. Such extreme pressure is usually caused by a blockage in the condenser or a restriction

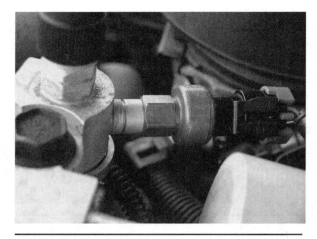

Figure 8-18. The high-pressure cut-off switch may be mounted on a high-pressure line or the receiver-drier.

Figure 8-19. The pressure-relief valve is mounted in the compressor and serves as a safety valve if the high-side pressure goes too high and the compressor does not shut down.

in the high-side line. Excessively high pressure could damage the compressor seals, rupture refrigerant lines, and cause other damage.

Venting the refrigerant is potentially damaging to the ozone layer. Therefore, virtually all late-model applications use a high-pressure cut-off switch to avoid this potential. Only if the high-pressure cut-off switch should fail would the pressure-relief valve vent refrigerant to the atmosphere.

When the high-pressure relief valve bleeds off the excess refrigerant pressure, look for restricted airflow through the condenser due to leaves, debris, or an inoperative cooling fan. Also check for system restrictions, especially on the discharge side of the compressor, and other signs of damage. If the system is still operational, the system may have a refrigerant overcharge, which

Figure 8-17. The high-pressure cut-off switch may be mounted in the compressor.

can be checked with the manifold gauge set, or by recovering the refrigerant from the system.

Low-Pressure Cut-off Switches

If the system loses its refrigerant charge, the low-pressure cut-off switch disables the compressor and stops air conditioning operation. Since the compressor is partially or fully lubricated by the refrigerant oil circulated with the refrigerant, compressor damage would result if the system continued to operate with extremely low refrigerant levels. Low-pressure conditions are generally associated with refrigerant loss. Check for signs of leakage or frost, which could indicate a restriction in the system.

Thermal Protection Devices

As with the high-pressure protection devices mentioned previously, thermal protection devices, figure 8-20, measure compressor or system temperature, which of course is related to pressure. Should any extremely high temperature be sensed in the system, the thermal protection device shuts the compressor off. When a thermal protection device shuts down the compressor, check for compressor malfunction, system blockage, hose restrictions, condenser damage, or restriction to determine the cause of the temperature buildup.

Lock-up Protection Devices

In the event of compressor lock-up, the lock-up protection device prevents the compressor from burning up the drive belt when the speed of the compressor no longer matches the speed of the engine. If the electronic module senses compressor lock-up, it disengages the compressor clutch. This protection system is used by Toyota and Mitsubishi, and is also found on some Chrysler systems with Mitsubishi compressors, figure 8-21.

If the compressor appears locked up, check for problems within the compressor itself. Then inspect the drive belt and pulleys to confirm that they are functioning correctly. If the compressor is not locked up, check for a correct compressor speed signal to the Electronic Control Module from the compressor rpm sensor. The best way to check the rpm sensor, which mounts on the compressor, generally with a two-wire connector, is to monitor the signal with a lab scope or graphing multimeter, figure 8-22.

COMPRESSOR SERVICE PROCEDURES

The techniques for lubricating the compressor, servicing the clutch, and replacing front seals are different for each brand and model of compressor. Review a service manual for the particular compressor you are working on before you begin your service.

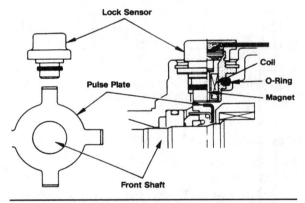

Figure 8-21. Toyota's belt protection sensor. (Reprinted with permission of Toyota Motor Corporation.)

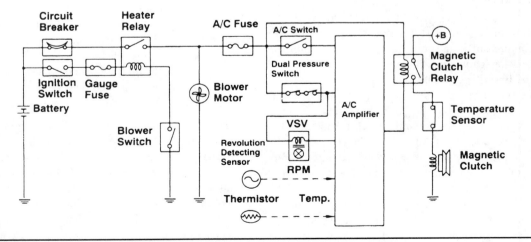

Figure 8-20. As can be seen from this schematic, the compressor thermal protection device (temperature sensor) is wired in series with the magnetic clutch. (Reprinted with permission of Toyota Motor Corporation.)

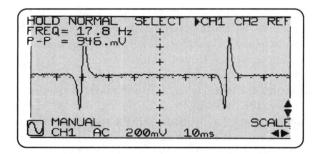

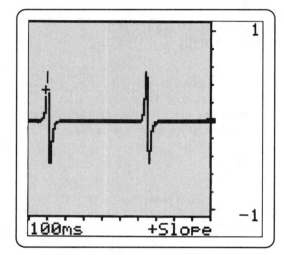

Figure 8-22. Lab scope (upper) and GMM (lower) patterns of a good compressor rpm sensor signal.

Checking the Oil Level

Inadequate oil is the leading cause of compressor failure. Always make certain that the correct amount of oil is in the system. This is particularly true with late-model compressors that do not have an oil reservoir and rely on the oil being carried by the refrigerant as the sole source of lubrication. These systems generally contain about six to eight ounces (190 to 210 ml) of oil. Keep in mind that the oil capacity stamped on the compressor is the total system capacity, not the compressor capacity. Always check your service manual for oil specifications.

The type of refrigerant oil is critical, as R-12 systems use different oil than R-134a systems. An R-12 system generally uses mineral oil, while most R-134a systems use a PAG oil. A few R-134a systems use Ester oil. Other alternative refrigerants may have different lubrication oil requirements. Different refrigerant oil types cannot be mixed.

Earlier Harrison, or Delco, compressors store excess oil in a sump. Some compressors have pumps that circulate the oil under pressure. These systems have as much as 10 to 11 ounces (300 to 325 ml) of refrigerant

oil. Again, always check the manufacturer's specifications for the correct oil capacity.

Too much oil causes excessive high-side pressures or poor cooling. This is because the excess oil coats the inner walls of the condenser tubes and prevents proper cooling of the refrigerant. Too little oil will damage the bearings and seals, as well as the piston and cylinder surfaces of the compressor.

Keep in mind that the oil circulates with the refrigerant. Anytime that you work with the refrigerant, you are working with the lubrication as well. Refrigerant oil can be lost from the system when:

- An air conditioning component is replaced, but the oil it contained is not added back to the system.
- Oil that is recovered with the refrigerant is not replaced.
- A system leak removes refrigerant and its oil.

Refrigerant oil is highly refined, wax-free oil that is dried to remove almost all moisture. The purity and dryness of the oil are crucial for proper system operation. You must take precautions to prevent oil contamination from dirt and moisture. When working with refrigerant oil:

- Keep refrigerant oil containers sealed when not in use. If a container is left open, the oil will absorb moisture from the atmosphere and become contaminated.
- Keep all fittings and surrounding areas clean.
- Always cap all system connection openings during the removal and installation of any system components.
- Do not return used oil to the system. Always replace oil with the specified amount, type, and grade of fresh, clean oil.

Use the following tips to maintain the correct amount of oil in the system.

- Measure the amount of oil lost during system recovery, and replace that amount with fresh oil.
- Drain and measure the oil from the replaced components if possible. In many cases it is impossible to drain the oil from the components. In that case follow the manufacturer's recommendations on adding oil to each component replaced.

Checking the compressor oil level is not a routine service procedure. However, you should check the oil level if you suspect oil has been lost from the system, if you are replacing the compressor, or if you are not sure how much oil you should add after replacing a major component. Some manufacturers include a chart, figure 8-23, in their service manuals to help determine when to check and add oil to a compressor. Many compressors are shipped with the full system oil charge in them.

COMPRESSOR OIL LEVELS

AC SYSTEM OIL LEVEL REQUIREMENTS

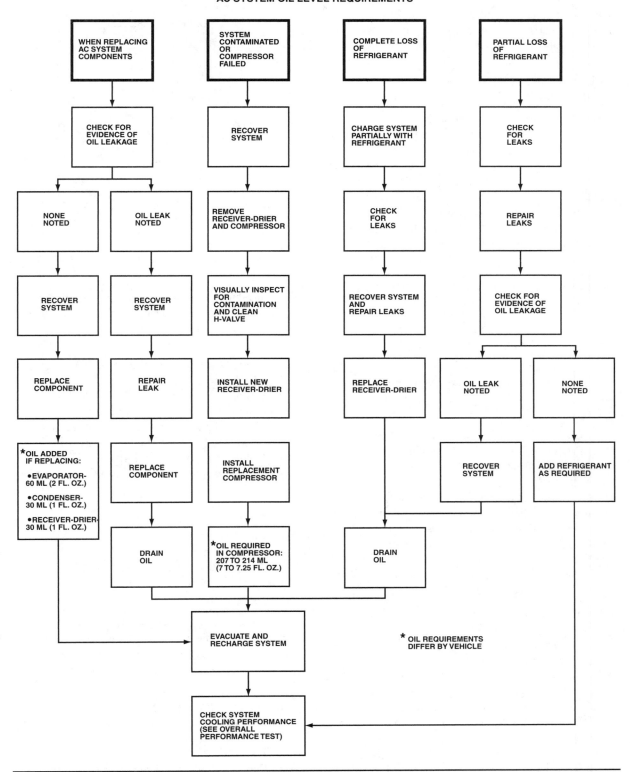

Figure 8-23. Some manufacturers provide a chart to help determine when to check or add refrigerant oil.

However, do not assume that you should install the compressor with this oil charge in the compressor. Usually the manufacturer will require that you drain this oil from the compressor and add fresh oil based on the amount of oil that you drained from the old compressor. Be sure to follow the manufacturer's recommendations.

Stabilizing the Compressor

Stabilizing the compressor is the process of fully circulating the refrigerant oil through the system. You must stabilize the compressor before you measure the amount of oil to ensure an accurate measurement.

The oil level in the compressor is ideally checked if the compressor is operational, and the air conditioning system does not have any notable faults, such as leaks or failed components. When the system first starts, refrigerant oil begins to move through the system. After about 10 minutes, the oil is fully distributed to all parts of the system.

Checking the Oil Level with a Dipstick

A dipstick is used to check the oil level in the sump of a compressor with low- and high-side service valves. Included in this group of compressors are the:

- York Rotary
- Sanden (Sankyo) five and seven cylinder

When you check the oil level, check the quality of the oil as well. If the oil contains metal particles or other debris, flush the system. Always replace the receiver-drier or accumulator and clean any filter screens at the expansion device whenever the oil is replaced due to contamination.

The oil sump is located on the discharge side, so a pressure differential forces refrigerant oil around the vanes to the low-pressure side. The compressor pump needs an ample oil supply or the compressor will be severely damaged. As a precaution, the pump is designed so that the clutch will disengage if the system pressure drops too low. Check the oil as follows.

1. With the vehicle parked on a level surface, start and run the engine for 10 to 15 minutes to stabilize the system. Shut the engine off.
2. Recover the refrigerant.
3. Remove the refrigerant lines from the compressor.
4. Rotate the compressor 10 times in a counterclockwise direction.
5. Remove the drive belt and tilt the compressor so the suction and discharge ports are level.
6. Insert the dipstick to measure the oil, figure 8-24.
7. There should be two to four ounces (60 to 120 ml) of oil in the compressor. Add new oil through the discharge port until the oil level is within the specified range.

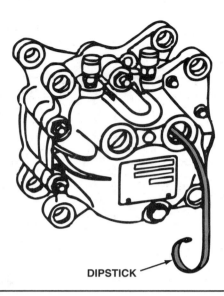

Figure 8-24. Insert the dipstick to the bottom of the sump, then remove it to read the oil level.

If you need to remove the compressor from the vehicle to check the oil after you have recovered the refrigerant, proceed as follows:

1. Remove the oil drain plug.
2. Drain the oil in a calibrated container to measure the amount of oil.
3. If less than two ounces (60 ml) of oil is drained, replace it with two ounces of new oil.
4. If more than two ounces (60 ml) is drained, replace it with the same amount of new oil.
5. Install new O-rings on the suction and discharge fittings, and then install the fittings on the compressor.
6. Install the compressor.
7. Evacuate and recharge the system.
8. Check for leaks.

Checking the Oil Level of a Sanden (Sankyo) Five- or Seven-Cylinder Compressor

If the compressor oil plug is readily accessible, you do not need to remove the compressor from the vehicle. Otherwise, remove the compressor from the vehicle and perform this service on the workbench. To check the oil level:

1. With the vehicle parked on a level surface, run the air conditioning 10 to 15 minutes to stabilize the system.
2. Recover the refrigerant.
3. Place an angle gauge across the mounting tabs, then measure and record the mounting angle of the compressor.
4. Remove the compressor and place it on the bench.

5. Clean the area around the oil fill plug.
6. Slowly remove the oil fill plug, as there may be some residual pressure.
7. Look through the oil fill hole, and rotate the clutch front plate to position the piston so the dipstick can be inserted, figure 8-25.
8. Insert the dipstick to its stop position. The stop is the point where the dipstick bends, figure 8-26.
9. The point in the bend of the dipstick must be to the left if the mounting angle is to the right, whereas the point of the bend in the dipstick must be to the right if the mounting angle is to the left.
10. Remove the dipstick. Count the increments of oil, figure 8-26.
11. Use the mounting angle table, figure 8-27, to determine the correct oil level for the compressor.
12. If the oil level is not within correct specifications, add or remove oil until you reach the midrange specification.
13. Make certain that the oil fill plug O-ring is clean and properly positioned. Install the oil fill plug and check for leaks.
14. Remount the compressor to its original position. Tighten the drive belt and mounting bolts.
15. Evacuate and recharge the system.

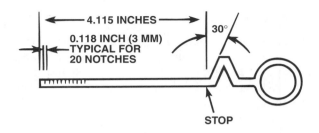

Figure 8-26. Insert the dipstick for the compressor to the stop.

MOUNTING ANGLE (DEGREES)	ACCEPTABLE OIL LEVEL IN INCREMENTS					
	505	507	508	510	708	709
0	4-6	3-5	4-6	2-4	4-6	3-5
10	6-8	5-7	6-8	4-5	5-7	4-6
20	8-10	6-8	7-9	5-6	6-8	5-7
30	10-11	7-9	8-10	6-7	7-9	6-8
40	11-12	8-10	9-11	7-9	8-10	7-9
50	12-13	8-10	9-11	9-10	9-11	8-10
60	12-13	9-11	9-12	10-12	10-12	9-11
90	15-16	9-11	9-12	12-13	11-13	10-12

Figure 8-27. Some manufacturers provide a compressor mounting angle chart to determine the correct oil level.

Checking the Compressor Oil Level without a Dipstick

On many compressors, you cannot check the oil with a dipstick. Compressors of this type include:

- Calsonic V5 and V6 variable displacement (Nissan, Infiniti, and Subaru)
- Ford (FS-10, FX –15) 10 cylinder
- G-Ladder scroll (Honda and VW)
- Harrison (Delco or Delphi) four, five, and six cylinder (GM)
- Nippondenso six cylinder (Ford FS-6 and Chrysler C-171)
- Nippondenso six cylinder variable displacement
- Nippondenso 10 cylinder (10PA15, 10PA17, and 10PA20)
- Sanden (Sankyo) scroll

Since these compressors have no oil reservoir, they are lubricated internally only by the refrigerant oil as it circulates through the compressor with the refrigerant. Normally, the oil level does not need to be checked. However, if there is a system malfunction that is caused by a failed component or there has been a large leak that has caused a loss of oil, check the oil level after making repairs. Keep in mind that usually these compressors do not retain much oil in them. Make sure you follow the manufacturer's guidelines for oil replacement.

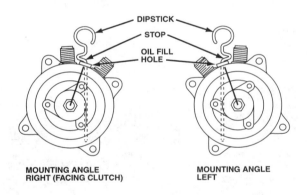

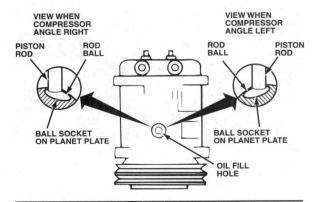

Figure 8-25. Compressor manufacturers may recommend checking compressor oil level with the compressor vertical or at some other specific angle.

Servicing Compressor Clutches

Clutch mating surfaces will scar over time during normal operation. If the clutch slips a great deal, it may be badly scarred. When you remove the clutch, inspect it for cracking, heat checking, and scarring deeper than 0.050 inch (1.3 mm). Replace the clutch assembly if any of these conditions are present. Typical compressor clutch service procedures include:

- Clutch removal
- Bearing replacement
- Field coil replacement
- Clutch installation

You must remove the clutch for normal repairs, such as bearing or field coil replacement. Replace the entire clutch in the event of mechanical damage, when replacement parts are not available, or the manufacturer does not recommend repair.

You need special tools and pullers to remove the compressor clutch. Often, these tools are unique to the compressor being serviced. Failure to use the proper tools and seal removers may result in serious damage to the compressor or clutch. The following procedure is typical for servicing the clutch, bearing, or seal. Individual compressor service may vary. Be sure to consult the manufacturer specifications before attempting any of these compressor services. Many manufacturers may only allow certain of these items to be serviced.

1. Recover the refrigerant and remove the compressor from the vehicle.
2. Using the proper clutch holding tool, remove the compressor shaft nut, figure 8-28.

Figure 8-28. Using a clutch holding tool, remove the compressor shaft nut.

3. Use the specified puller to remove the clutch from the compressor shaft, figure 8-29. This is usually a press fit that requires a special puller. DO NOT PRY ON THE CLUTCH PLATE.
4. After removing the clutch, if the hub and bearing need to be serviced, remove the snapring holding the pulley and bearing assembly to the compressor front head, figure 8-30.
5. A compressor shaft protector tool may be required in order to prevent damage to the compressor shaft, figure 8-31.

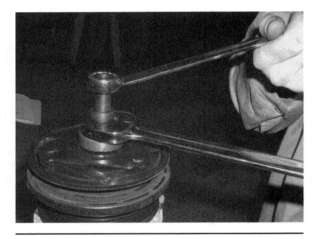

Figure 8-29. Use the correct puller to remove the clutch plate from the compressor shaft.

Figure 8-30. If the pulley and bearing is being serviced, remove the snapring that retains the bearing and hub onto the compressor body.

6. Using the appropriate puller, remove the pulley and bearing assembly, figure 8-32.
7. If the compressor seal needs to be replaced it is often retained with a snapring, figure 8-33.
8. Remove the snapring that retains the compressor shaft seal in place, figure 8-34.
9. Using the proper tool, remove the front compressor shaft seal and discard, figure 8-35. Be careful not to nick the seal seating area or the shaft during this procedure.

Figure 8-33. If the compressor seal is going to be replaced, the snapring that retains the seal must be removed.

Figure 8-31. A special tool protects the compressor shaft from damage when removing the pulley and bearing assembly.

Figure 8-34. Remove the snapring, being careful not to nick the seal seating area.

Figure 8-32. A special puller is used to remove the pulley and bearing assembly.

Figure 8-35. A special tool is needed to remove the old seal from the compressor.

10. Before installing the new seal, a seal protector must be used to protect the new seal during installation, figure 8-36.
11. Lubricate the new seal with refrigerant oil before installing, figure 8-37. Be careful not to handle the seal as the acid from your skin can damage the seal.
12. Install the new seal and snapring. Make sure that the snapring is fully seated, figure 8-38.
13. If the pulley bearing needs to be replaced it must be driven out with a driver, figure 8-39.
14. After installing the new bearing it may need to be staked with a punch or staking tool, figure 8-40.
15. Install the pulley and bearing assembly onto the compressor front housing, figure 8-41.

16. Position the woodruff key in the clutch, slight-ly protruding, so that it may be fully engaged into the compressor shaft slot before the clutch is pressed onto the compressor shaft, figure 8-42.
17. Using the proper installer, press the clutch onto the compressor shaft. Check the air gap with a feeler gauge to ensure that the air gap setting meets manufacturer specifications, figure 8-43. **NOTE:** Some manufacturers control the clutch air gap with shims.
18. Install the shaft nut and torque to specifications, figure 8-44.
19. Install the compressor on the vehicle, evacuate, recharge, and leak test the system.

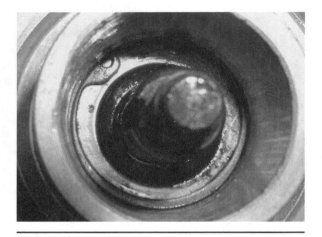

Figure 8-38. Install the new snapring provided, ensuring that it is fully seating in the groove.

Figure 8-36. A seal shaft protector must be used to prevent damaging the new seal during installation.

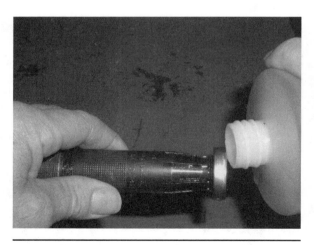

Figure 8-37. Lubricate the new seal with refrigerant oil before installing it. Be careful not to touch the seal with your hands.

Figure 8-39. If the pulley bearing needs to be replaced, it must be driven out with a hammer and a special driver.

Figure 8-40. After installing the new bearing in the pulley and hub, it must be staked to retain it in the hub.

Figure 8-41. Gently tap the pulley and hub assembly onto the compressor body and install the snapring.

Figure 8-42. The woodruff key must be carefully positioned in the groove of the clutch to ensure proper alignment with the compressor shaft.

Figure 8-43. Using the proper installer, press the clutch onto the compressor shaft. You must measure the air gap with a feeler gauge and set the air gap to specifications.

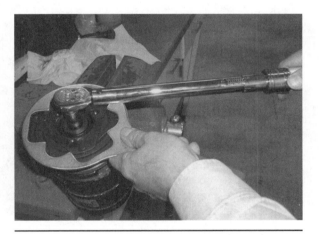

Figure 8-44. Install the shaft nut and torque to specifications.

Compressor Suction Screens

When a compressor fails often, it spreads debris in the refrigeration system. As discussed in previous chapters, manufacturers have different recommendations on dealing with this debris. Some manufacturers recommend component replacement, installation of inline filters, or flushing the system. Another method of preventing this debris from reaching the compressor is the suction inlet screen, figure 8-45. It has been found that often this debris gets pushed into the suction-side hose from high pressure in the system. This debris can then be sucked into the replacement compressor, causing it to fail. Some manufacturers recommend the installation of a suction screen in the suction line after compressor replacement. The suction inlet screen is installed as follows:

Figure 8-45. This suction screen kit made by Airsept® includes suction inlet screens, installation tools, and removal tools. (Courtesy of Airsept.®)

1. Remove the line assembly from the compressor, figure 8-46.
2. Use the sizing tool to determine the appropriate screen to use, figure 8-47.
3. Install the correct mandrel onto the installation tool, figure 8-48, and lubricate the screen.
4. Align the installation tool onto the refrigerant line fitting so the screen will go in straight, figure 8-49.
5. Press the suction screen into the bore until it is flush or slightly below the surface, figure 8-50.
6. Reattach the line assembly onto the compressor and torque to bolt to specifications.
7. Install a label onto the line to indicate to technicians that a suction screen has been added, figure 8-51.
8. A special tool is needed if the suction screen needs to be removed, figure 8-52.

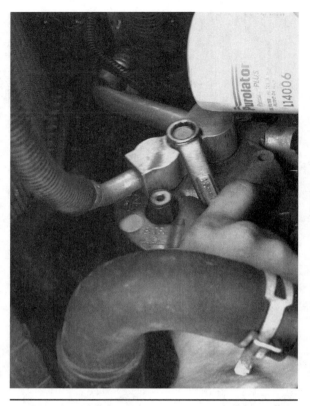

Figure 8-46. Remove the line assembly from the compressor. (Courtesy of Airsept.®)

Figure 8-47. Use the sizing tool to determine the proper size screen to install. (Courtesy of Airsept.®)

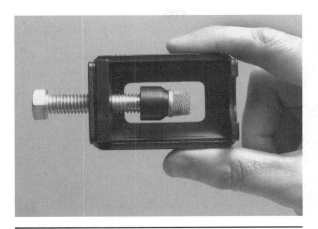

Figure 8-48. Install the correct mandrel onto the installation tool and lubricate the screen. (Courtesy of Airsept.®)

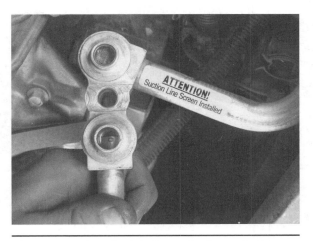

Figure 8-51. Install a label onto the line to indicate to technicians that the vehicle is equipped with a suction inlet screen filter. (Courtesy of Airsept.®)

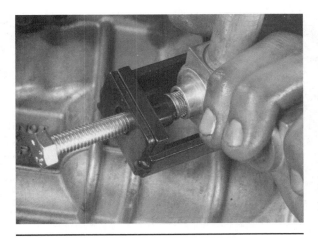

Figure 8-49. Align the installation tool onto the refrigerant line fitting so that the screen is square to the fitting. (Courtesy of Airsept.®)

Figure 8-52. Should the suction screen need to be replaced, a removal tool is provided to remove the screen. (Courtesy of Airsept.®)

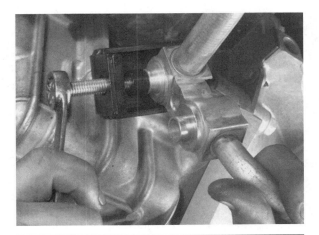

Figure 8-50. Press the suction screen into the line until it is flush or slightly below the surface of the fitting. (Courtesy of Airsept.®)

PART THREE

Diagnosing Cooling Systems, Air Delivery Systems, and Retrofitting

9

Cooling System Diagnosis and Service

Most of the energy produced by the internal combustion engine is converted to friction and heat rather than mechanical motion. This heat must be controlled because too little or too much heat causes the engine to run inefficiently, and may cause engine damage as well. Controlling engine heat is the primary function of the engine cooling system.

COOLING SYSTEM MAINTENANCE

Many cooling system problems are the result of poor maintenance. Old coolant, rust and deposits in the radiator and engine block, low coolant level, and damaged or worn hoses and belts are just a few factors that can cause a significant loss of cooling system efficiency. Regular maintenance helps prevent these failures. In general, cooling system maintenance involves system inspection, replacement of worn out or defective parts, coolant replacement, system flushing at recommended intervals, and adjusting coolant level and concentration.

Cooling systems are pressurized and extremely hot during operation. Allow the engine to cool down so there is no pressure in the system before performing any service. Always wear suitable protection and follow safety precautions when working on or around cooling systems.

Drive Belts

Accessory drive belts are an important part of the cooling system. These belts must be in good condition, properly tensioned, and aligned. Drive belt condition must be checked periodically, as belts wear and stretch with age. Most manufacturers recommend checking and adjusting drive belts every 6 to 12 months. Replace the belt, if needed. Locate and inspect all belts for:

- Glazing, deterioration, cracking, or fraying, figure 9-1.
- Replacement interval. Most vehicle manufacturers recommend service intervals for belt replacement. If the manufacturer does not specify a belt replacement interval, replace belts at 48,000 miles or four years, regardless of appearance.
- Proper belt and pulley alignment. An accessory drive belt is designed to run straight, so the pulleys must be straight, not at an angle to each other. If a pulley is even slightly out of alignment, belt damage occurs.
- Proper tension. A tension gauge is the best method of checking belt tension, figure 9-2. Automatic belt tensioners should be checked to ensure proper operation of the tensioning spring. Belt tension adjustment varies; refer to the service manual for the correct procedure.

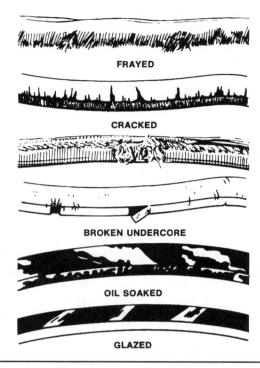

Figure 9-1. Replace the drive belts if you detect any type of damage.

Most late-model vehicles use a multi-groove drive belt to power the engine-driven accessories. This design is commonly known as a serpentine belt because of the way the belt is routed around the various pulleys, figure 9-3. Older vehicles typically use a number of V-belts, one to drive each of the engine accessories, figure 9-4. On some late-model engines, the water pump is driven by the camshaft-timing belt or gears, figure 9-5.

The top of a V-belt does not exhibit wear, so twist the belt to inspect the underside and sides. Turn the en-

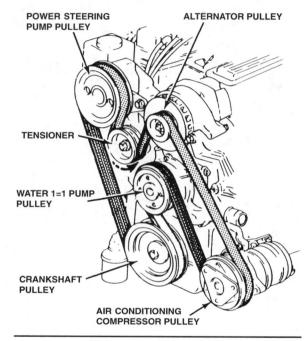

Figure 9-3. A serpentine belt uses a single belt to drive all accessories.

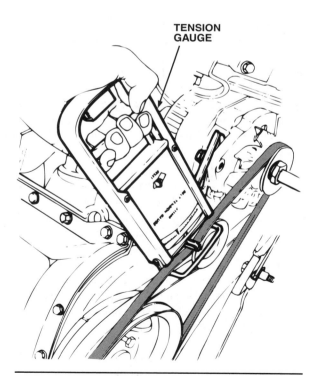

Figure 9-2. A tension gauge measures accessory drive-belt tension.

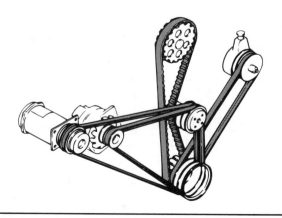

Figure 9-4. On V-belt systems, most accessories have separate drive belts.

Figure 9-5. Some water pumps are gear driven or driven by the timing belt or chain.

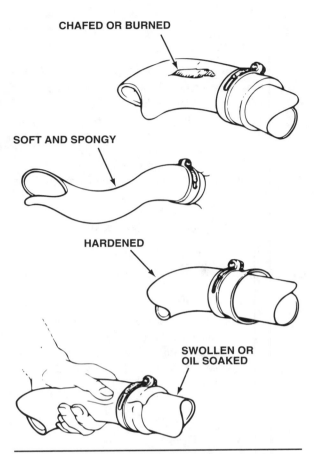

CHAFED OR BURNED

SOFT AND SPONGY

HARDENED

SWOLLEN OR OIL SOAKED

Figure 9-6. Replace damaged cooling system hoses and hose clamps.

gine over a few times to examine the full length of the belt. If the sides are shiny and hard, the belt is glazed, which can cause the belt to slip. Check both V-belts and serpentine belts for oil and engine coolant contamination, which breaks down rubber, causing it to crumble. Replace oily or wet belts, and repair the source of the leak.

Never twist a serpentine belt more than 90 degrees when checking for wear, as this can damage the belt. Inspect a serpentine belt as you would a V-belt, and check the ribs for cracking. A few random cracks across the belt are normal, but a series of cracks is not. Replace a serpentine belt if there are a series of cracks within one inch (25 mm) of each other.

Inspect the accessory and crankshaft pulleys for signs of wear and damage. A worn pulley allows the belt to ride too low in the pulley groove, which causes overheating and premature wear. The top edges of a V-belt should be even with or slightly above the top of the pulley, while serpentine belts generally ride below the outer edges of the pulleys. Also, check pulleys for nicks, burrs, and cracks that may accelerate belt wear.

System Hoses

Inspect all system hoses, including heater hoses, for:

- Hardness, cracks, cuts, or other damage, figure 9-6.
- Sponginess or other interior damage. To check, squeeze the hoses by hand.
- Loose connections or leakage. Make certain that all hoses fit securely, the hose clamps are the correct size, the hoses are fully positioned on their connections, and the clamps are properly tightened, figure 9-7. Do not use hoses or hose clamps that fit poorly.

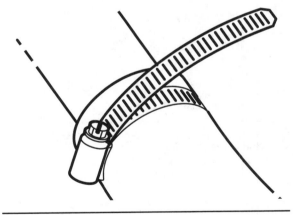

Figure 9-7. This hose clamp is too large for the hose and may interfere with other hoses or components.

- Age. Check the OEM service manual for hose replacement intervals. If the manufacturer does not specify a hose replacement interval, replace the hoses at 48,000 miles or four years, regardless of appearance.

Leaks

Check for leaks or corrosion at the:

- Core plugs, figure 9-8. These plugs are a machined, press fit. They must be in good condition and show no signs of deterioration.
- Water pump shaft seal, figure 9-9. While a slight amount of seepage from the water pump weep hole is considered normal, a significant amount of coolant accumulation indicates that the shaft seal is failing. A cooling system pressure test may indicate a leak.
- Water pump and thermostat gaskets. Clean these areas with a shop rag while checking for signs of leakage.

Radiator

Inspect the radiator for:

- Leaks or corrosion at the tank seams, or on the outside of the radiator tubes.
- Clogged or bent radiator core fins. If the damage is not too severe, a fin comb, or straightener, restores bent fins.

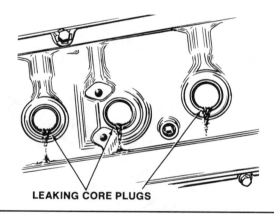

LEAKING CORE PLUGS

Figure 9-8. Trails of rust around the core plugs and down the engine block indicate that the plugs are leaking and should be replaced.

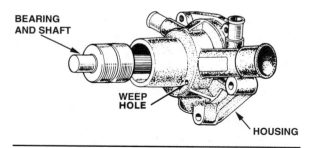

BEARING AND SHAFT

WEEP HOLE

HOUSING

Figure 9-9. Coolant leaking from the weep hole in the water pump indicates the internal seal has failed.

- Blocked air intake paths. Check the radiator fins, deflectors, shrouds, and air intake openings for any damage, foreign material, or disconnected parts.
- Loose or missing mounting bolts. The radiator must be securely mounted in place to avoid unnecessary movement and vibration.
- Proper connections to the coolant recovery tank. Make certain that the overflow outlet located under the radiator cap is in good condition, the hose to the overflow tank is properly connected, and that the hose is in good condition.
- Correct coolant level in the recovery tank. Check the coolant level when the engine is cold, and again when the engine is hot.
- Coolant concentration. Test the coolant for the specified ratio. Too low a concentration does not provide adequate freeze protection, while too high a concentration reduces heat transfer and cooling efficiency.
- Coolant age. As coolant ages, it loses its ability to provide adequate corrosion protection and heat transfer. Coolants that contain silicates, which most do, should be replaced every two years regardless of mileage.
- Rust, oil, or other contamination in the coolant.

Radiator Cap or Pressure Cap

Inspect the radiator cap or pressure cap for:

- A secure fit at the filler neck. If the cap does not fit snugly, the cap may be damaged or the wrong cap may be installed.
- Correct pressure rating. Pressure test the radiator and cap any time you suspect cooling system problems.
- Effectiveness. If the upper radiator hose collapses as the system cools, the radiator cap vacuum valve is not working. This can be accurately checked with a cooling system pressure tester.
- Brittle or damaged seal, figure 9-10.
- Sufficient spring action, figure 9-11.

Heater Assembly

The heater assembly consists of the heater core, heater control, hoses, and housing. Inspect the heater assembly for:

- Signs of rust or green corrosion, indicating heater core leakage. One symptom of a heater core leak is that the windshield fogs up when the defroster is in operation. This fog may be coolant leaking from the heater core. An oily film on the inside of the windshield is an indication of leaking coolant.
- Loose hose connections, allowing leaks.

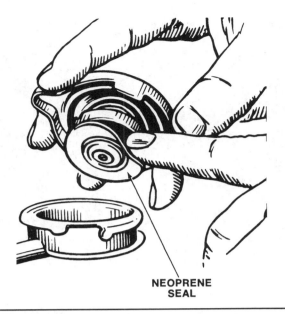

Figure 9-10. The rubber seal on the radiator cap should not be dry or cracked.

Figure 9-11. The spring on the radiator cap should move freely and not bind when pressure is applied to it.

- Condition of the heater hoses. Check for cracks, areas that have been overheated by engine components, and indications of rubbing on other components.
- Condition of heater control valve. Check for proper movement of the heater control valve as the heater controls are operated. Inspect for signs of leakage.

- Coolant leaks inside the passenger compartment. Check the carpet and areas around the heater housing. Dampness may indicate a leak from the heater core or attaching hoses.

Water Pump

Inspect the water pump for:

- Leakage around the pump housing, shaft seal, hose connections, and gasket sealing surfaces.
- Drive pulley and belt alignment. Check the condition of all of the pulleys and drive belts.
- Excessive play. Due to bearing clearance, some play is normal. However, too much side-play or endplay in the water pump shaft bearing results in bearing noise and water pump seal failure.

Radiator Fan

Inspect the radiator fan for:

- Bent or cracked fan blades.
- Binding between the fan and its shaft.
- Proper operation of the fan clutch or electric fan. The fan clutch is designed to "slip" during certain operating conditions to reduce drag on the engine. Electrically operated fans are thermostatically controlled and can come on at any time, even when the engine is off in some instances.

NOTE: Inline engines generally have a crankshaft-driven fan, while transverse-mounted engines in front-wheel-drive vehicles use electric cooling fans. On either type, a separate electric fan may be used to circulate air through the condenser. Some vehicles have two cooling fans.

Fan Shrouds and Air Deflectors

Inspect the shrouds and air deflectors for:

- Location and mounting. Inspect the radiator fan shroud and air deflector, if used, to make sure that they are in place and secure.
- Check the fan shroud and air deflector for cracked, broken, or missing parts.
- Check the fan blade rotation within the shroud. Make certain the fan blades have adequate clearance and do not touch the shroud.

Coolant Disposal and Recycling

Used coolant is a toxic waste that must be disposed of or recycled according to EPA or local guidelines. There are two ways to dispose of used coolant. Recycling coolant offsite requires your shop to provide a

Figure 9-12. A coolant recycling machine attaches to the engine and recycles the coolant while it performs a cooling system flush.

Figure 9-13. This is an example of deposits formed in the heater core due to poor cooling system maintenance.

dedicated storage container for used coolant. A contracted hazardous waste disposal company regularly collects and recycles the coolant that is collected. Some shops have a coolant recycling and flushing machine that recycles used coolant onsite, figure 9-12. These machines attach to a vehicle and flush the cooling system. The contaminates are filtered out, and additives are mixed back into the glycol base. The coolant purity is restored, and the coolant can be reused in the vehicle.

Cleaning the Cooling System

Contaminates such as fuel, lead, copper, zinc, and grit interfere with heat transfer from the engine to the coolant and from the coolant to the radiator. Additionally, ethylene glycol breaks down over time to form organic acids, which may corrode a cooling system. Corrosion, contaminates, and hard water minerals all work together to form hard deposits which interfere with the cooling system heat transfer, figure 9-13. The system must be serviced at regular intervals as specified by the manufacturer to maintain efficient operation.

In some cases, radiators and heater cores become so clogged that normal flushing techniques cannot adequately restore coolant flow. This typically occurs if the system has been poorly maintained or severely contaminated. It may be necessary to either have components cleaned or repaired by a radiator repair shop, or simply replace them with new ones.

Cooling System Flushing

Until recently, most manufacturers recommended periodically cleaning the cooling system by flushing. However, current recommendations often require a coolant recycling station to service the system. It is extremely difficult to bleed the air out of the cooling sys-

tem on some newer models, and using a recycling station or coolant exchanger is the only way to avoid air intrusion into the system during service.

On older vehicles, occasionally clean the cooling system by flushing with water or backflushing. If the system is severely contaminated, a chemical cleaning may be performed. General procedures for each type of flushing follow. Always refer to the vehicle service manual for specific requirements of the system being worked on. With any method of flushing, be sure to observe all federal, state, and local regulations concerning used coolant disposal and handling.

Flushing with Plain Water

Flushing the cooling system with plain, cold water only dissolves contaminates that are water soluble. A plain water flush will not remove oil, scale, or sediment. Perform this procedure only on cooling systems in good repair that do not have heavy buildup. To flush with water:

1. Drain the old coolant and dispose of it properly. Some engines do not have drain plugs on the radiator or engine. Drain these systems by disconnecting the lower radiator hose. Automatic flush and fill equipment is especially suited for these systems.
2. Remove the thermostat and reinstall the thermostat housing.
3. With the radiator and engine drain plugs open, place a hose in the radiator filler neck and adjust the water flow rate to keep the water level at the top of the radiator, matching the water flowing out of the drains. Be aware that all of the water draining from the system must be handled as used coolant.
4. Flush the system with clean water for about 10 minutes. You may want to run the engine at idle

while flushing to get complete circulation. Be
sure to keep the water level full in the radiator
while running the engine to avoid the possibility
of overheating.

5. When finished, reinstall the thermostat, with a
   new gasket, and close all the drains.
6. Fill the system with the recommended amount
   and type of coolant, and adjust the coolant concentration as necessary.
7. Make certain to follow the OEM service manual
   instructions when refilling the cooling system.
   Many late-model cooling systems require bleeding.
8. Run the engine until normal operating temperature is reached. Recheck the coolant level and
   adjust as needed.

Backflushing

The backflushing, or reverse flushing, method is used
when heavy deposits of rust and scale are found in the
system. A backflush attachment shoots high-pressure
water through the cooling system in the opposite direction of normal coolant flow. This reverse pressure
washing breaks up the sediment so the plain water can
flush it away. Prepare for backflushing by first performing the plain water flushing procedure previously
explained. Then backflush the radiator as follows:

1. With the radiator cap in place, remove both radiator hoses and attach flushing hoses to the upper
   and lower radiator tanks.
2. Attach the flushing unit to the lower hose, turn
   on the water, and allow the radiator to fill,
   figure 9-14.
3. Apply air from the flushing unit in short spurts.
   Water will rush from the upper hose.

4. Allow the radiator to fill between blasts. Continue this action until the water runs clean from
   the upper hose.

To backflush the engine, use the same equipment and
the following procedure.

1. Make certain the thermostat is out of the engine.
   Remove the flushing hoses from the radiator
   and attach them to the engine water openings,
   figure 9-15.
2. With the flushing unit attached to the upper hose,
   turn on the water and allow it to run until it flows
   clean from the lower hose.
3. Apply air pressure in short spurts. **CAUTION:**
   Too much air pressure can damage the water
   pump seal.
4. Remove the flushing hoses, replace the thermostat, and reconnect the radiator hoses.
5. Fill the system with the recommended amount
   and type of coolant, and adjust the coolant concentrations as necessary. Run the engine to normal operating temperature and check for leaks.
   Recheck the coolant level and correct as needed.

Chemical Cleaning

Chemical cleaning is performed on a severely contaminated system. The system is backflushed with plain
water, followed by a chemical cleaning solution. There
are a wide variety of chemical cleaning agents available
for cooling system service. Oxalic acid is one common
flushing solution. Make certain to follow the instructions from the manufacturer for the correct use of flushing compounds. In general, the procedure is as follows:

1. Fill the cooling system with plain water.
2. Add the acid granules or flushing solution.
3. Bring the engine to operating temperature.

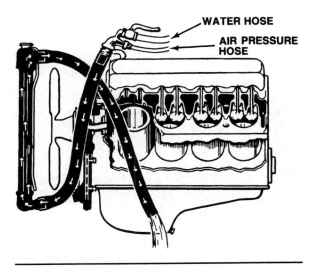

Figure 9-14. A backflush attachment uses air pressure to force water through the radiator in the opposite
direction of its normal flow.

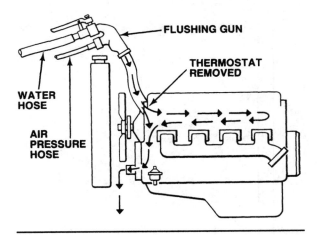

Figure 9-15. Backflush the engine to remove heavy
deposits from the block.

4. Allow the hot solution to circulate for 30 minutes.
5. Switch the engine off, and drain the mixture.
6. Refill the system with plain water and an acid neutralizer. The neutralizer ensures that no acid is left in the system. Start the engine and allow the neutralizer solution to circulate for several minutes.
7. Turn off the engine.
8. Drain the cooling system.
9. Refill the system with the recommended amount and type of coolant. Adjust the coolant concentration as necessary.

Be aware that leaks often appear after a cooling system has been flushed. Inspect and pressure test to make sure the system is sealed after flushing.

Cooling System Bleeding

In late-model vehicles with low hood lines, the radiator filler neck is often below the level of the cylinder head and heater core. This makes it necessary to purge air from the cooling system when refilling it. Many vehicle manufacturers install air bleed valves in the system, figure 9-16. Some engines overheat, which can lead to damage if the trapped air is not bled out of the cooling system.

When servicing a cooling system, look for a valve or plug that is designed to relieve trapped air. These valves are located at a high point in the cooling system such as the engine outlet flange or thermostat housing. Refer to OEM service manual information to determine the correct bleeding procedure on any vehicle. The following are general guidelines for bleeding a cooling system.

1. Remove the vent plug or open the bleeder and fill the radiator.

2. Close the vent when a clear coolant stream flows from the vent.
3. Top off the radiator, replace the cap, and fill the overflow tank.
4. Start and run the engine until the thermostat fully opens.
5. Top off the radiator with the engine running at idle.
6. Check the coolant level and top off the overflow tank, if necessary.

Belt Replacement

Accessory drive belts on most older vehicles were simple V-belts. A V-belt system uses multiple belts to drive different pulleys, such as the water pump, radiator fan, alternator, AC compressor, and power steering pump. Most engines produced since the mid-1980s use a single multiple-groove, or serpentine, belt to power all the engine-driven accessories. A serpentine belt is a single wide belt with several V-shaped ribs that ride in corresponding grooves on the pulleys. Some engines may use a single V-belt to drive one accessory and a serpentine belt to drive the other accessories.

An automatic, spring-loaded tension pulley is used to maintain proper belt tension on most serpentine belts, figure 9-17. This automatic tensioning device eliminates the need for serpentine belt adjustment and simplifies replacement. However, belt tension should still be periodically checked with a gauge to make sure the automatic tensioner is applying adequate force.

Serpentine belt routing can be complex. Many vehicles have an underhood decal that shows the correct routing of the belt on the accessory pulleys, figure 9-18. If a diagram is not available, sketch one

Figure 9-16. Many vehicles have bleed screws to bleed trapped air from the cooling system. Many times they are located on or near the thermostat housing.

Figure 9-17. Automatic belt tensioners are generally used with serpentine belts.

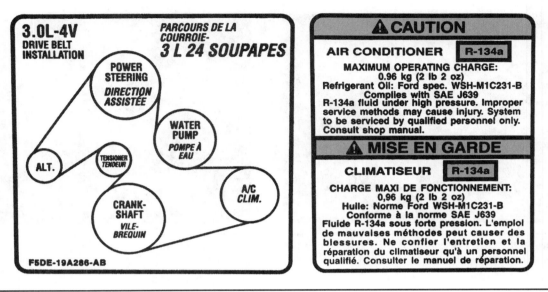

Figure 9-18. When installing a serpentine belt, follow the belt installation diagram found on the underhood decal or in the service manual.

before removing the belt to ensure proper routing on installation. Incorrectly installing a serpentine belt may result in driving pulleys in the wrong direction, which causes damage.

Serpentine Belt Removal and Installation

Inspect serpentine drive belts as previously described in this chapter. If the belt needs replacement, locate or make a routing diagram before removing the old belt. To replace a serpentine belt:

1. Most older engines with serpentine belts use a tensioner that is levered out of the way to release the belt. Typically, the tensioner has a half-inch square bore machined into it so that a breaker bar can be used as a lever. Many later engines have a ratchet in the tensioner assembly and a stationary bolt on the idler pulley that releases tension, figure 9-19. Turning the bolt moves the tension pulley.
2. On engines with a tensioner, push the lever downward and hold it in that position to force the tensioner pulley up to relieve tension on the belt. On engines with a bolt, turn the ratchet to move the pulley until the tension is relieved, figure 9-20.
3. Slip the old belt off the pulleys to remove it. If using leverage, allow the tensioner or idler pulley to return to its original position, figure 9-21.
4. Inspect the pulleys, as previously described in this chapter, and clean any dirt, debris, or other buildup from the grooves.

IDLER PULLEY

Figure 9-19. A ratchet moves the idler pulley to apply and release tension on a serpentine belt.

Figure 9-20. Use a ratchet or a wrench to relieve the tension from the belt.

Figure 9-22. Route the replacement belt around the pulleys following the belt routing diagram.

Figure 9-21. After the tension is relieved, you can slip the old belt off.

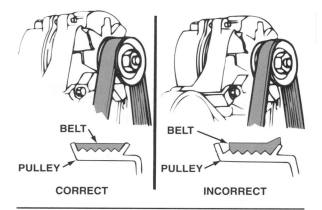

Figure 9-23. Serpentine belt ribs fit into the grooves on the pulleys.

5. Route the new belt around all the accessories. With a lever-type tensioner, fit the belt onto the tensioner pulley last by applying force to move the pulley as needed to slip the new belt onto the tensioner, figure 9-22.
6. After the belt is in place, remove the lever or release the bolt, which allows the pulley to return to its original position and apply tension to the belt.
7. Start the vehicle and observe the serpentine belt to ensure that it runs true and is installed on all the pulleys correctly.

When installing a serpentine belt, make certain that all its grooves contact all the pulleys correctly, figure 9-23. Some serpentine belts have arrows to indicate the direction of rotation. Inspect the belt and make certain to install the belt in its proper position.

Water Pump Service

Defective water pumps are replaced, rather than rebuilt in the field. Rebuilt water pumps are available for most models; actually rebuilding the pump requires tools and equipment not found in a typical repair shop. Although exact water pump removal and installation are unique for each engine and model, most are similar. The following procedure describes a typical water pump replacement. Always consult the OEM service manual for the vehicle being serviced for specific requirements and specifications. To replace the water pump:

1. Drain the coolant from the radiator and the engine.
2. Remove the radiator fan and clutch assembly, if it is driven by the water pump shaft.
3. Remove belts and any other accessories and brackets that interfere with water pump removal.

4. Remove the water pump attachment bolts and nuts. Pump bolts tend to corrode and seize on some models, so be careful when loosening. Never force a bolt to loosen it, as it may break off. If a bolt cannot be loosened with moderate pressure, apply penetrating oil, allow it to soak, and try again. Sometimes a few light taps on the head with a hammer breaks up the corrosion enough to free it.

5. After all the fasteners are removed, remove the pump from the engine. Lightly tap the pump body with a hammer to break the gasket seal, if needed.

6. Carefully scrape all traces of the old gasket off of the engine block mounting surface. Gasket material left on the block can cause leaks and warp or crack the new pump housing when the bolts are tightened.

7. Coat the new gasket with gasket sealer (if recommended by the manufacturer), and then position it on the new pump or on the engine block. Use only the type of gasket sealant recommended by the manufacturer.

8. Install the new water pump carefully. *Never* hit the end of the shaft while trying to seat the pump onto the engine block.

9. Install the bolts and tighten them evenly in a star pattern. Use a torque wrench to tighten the bolts as specified by the manufacturer.

10. Check the pump shaft after installation. It should rotate freely and smoothly.

11. Install the fan and other parts and accessories removed to access the water pump.

12. Replace the drive belt. Use a tension gauge to measure drive-belt tension.

CAUTION: Belt tension must be properly adjusted to prevent bearing failure of the new pump. An overtightened drive belt, whether it is a V-belt, serpentine belt, or timing belt, causes side-loading of the water pump shaft bearing, which can cause premature bearing failure.

13. Fill and bleed the cooling system as previously described in this chapter. Avoid spilling coolant on belts and hoses, as it causes rubber deterioration.

14. Run the engine to operating temperature and bleed the cooling system, if necessary. Check for leaks. Recheck the coolant level before releasing the vehicle to the customer.

COOLING SYSTEM DIAGNOSIS

There are several ways to determine the cause of a cooling system problem. The following procedures are typical troubleshooting methods.

Figure 9-24. A coolant hydrometer measures the ratio of antifreeze to water in the coolant mixture.

Coolant Concentration Testing

As detailed in Chapter 9 of the *Classroom Manual,* the most widely specified coolant mixture is a 50 percent blend of coolant and water. Automotive coolant is typically a base of ethylene glycol with additional chemicals to prevent rust, foaming, and wear. The ratio of coolant to water can be measured with a hydrometer, figure 9-24. A hydrometer measures the specific gravity of a liquid. Specific gravity is used to determine chemical composition, or in this case, the percentage of coolant to water. There may be slight differences in how to use each hydrometer, so refer to the tool instructions for specific details of the instrument being used.

Before attempting any work on the cooling system, allow the engine to cool so there is not any pressure in the cooling system. After circulating through the engine, the coolant may be heated to above its boiling point when there is no pressure applied. Severe burns may result if the pressure cap is released.

A common type of cooling system hydrometer is the ball or float design. To test coolant concentration with a ball or float hydrometer:

1. Remove the radiator cap.
2. Hold the hydrometer vertically and submerge the tip of the tool into the coolant.
3. Squeeze and release the bulb to draw a sample of coolant into the hydrometer. If the hydrometer has a thermometer, draw the coolant in and out of the tool a few times to stabilize the internal temperature. Then, draw the sample into the hydrometer.
4. Count the number of floating balls, or note the position of the float on the scale.
5. Compare the reading to the chart that is included with the hydrometer, which lists the coolant to water ratio. Use the temperature correction scale if there is one.
6. Add water or coolant as needed to adjust the mixture to specified concentrations.

Another type of cooling system tester is the optical refractometer, figure 9-25. It is an optical device that uses a light beam to measure chemical composition. To test the coolant concentration with an optical refractometer:

1. Remove the radiator cap.
2. Draw a small sample of coolant into the eyedropper provided with the tool.
3. Pull the refractometer stage cover up and put a few drops of coolant on the stage, figure 9-26.
4. Close the stage cover, figure 9-27.
5. Look through the eyepiece and read the position of the refracted shadow against the coolant scale. The refractometer may also have a battery electrolyte scale; make certain you read the correct scale, figure 9-28.
6. Add water or antifreeze as needed to adjust the mixture to the specified concentration.

Despite the term "permanent antifreeze" that appears on most automotive coolant labels, coolant should be

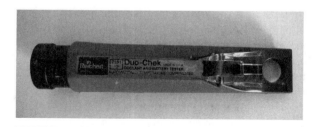

Figure 9-25. The optical refractometer can be used to test the coolant concentration.

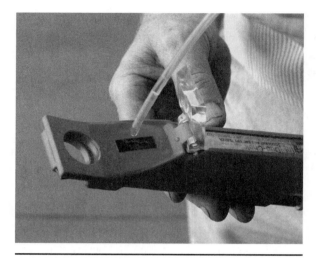

Figure 9-26. Open the refractometer cover and place a drop of the coolant sample on the stage.

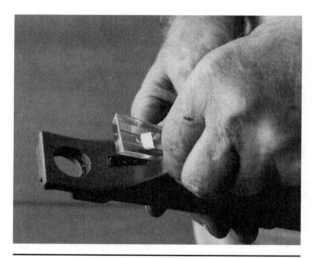

Figure 9-27. Close the stage cover and hold the refractometer toward the bright light while looking through the eyepiece.

replaced as often as recommended by the manufacturer. For many years coolant was replaced at 30,000-mile intervals. As advances in coolant formulation occur, manufacturers recommend longer coolant service intervals, and also specify different types of coolant. Always follow the manufacturer's recommendations. Also, make sure to use the correct type of coolant when performing cooling system maintenance. Some additives in the coolant, such as rust inhibitors, lose their effectiveness over time. This leads to a buildup of rust particles in the coolant that act as an abrasive on parts of the cooling system such as the water pump impeller, figure 9-29. Replacing the coolant and properly flushing the system are good preventative

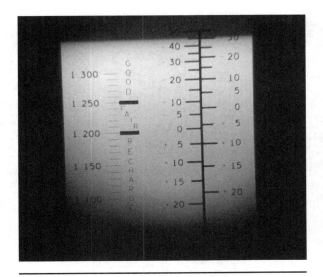

Figure 9-30. Pressure test the cooling system by installing a cooling system pressure tester. Pump up the tester to the manufacturer's specifications.

Figure 9-28. Looking through the refractometer, you should see a scale. The line that separates the light area from the dark area indicates the concentration level of the coolant.

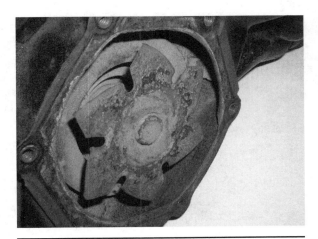

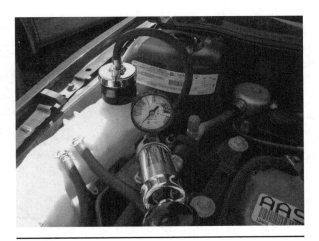

Figure 9-31. Some vehicles do not have a radiator cap. Pressure testing of this system with a surge tank must be done with a special adapter at the surge tank.

Figure 9-29. The impellor blades of this water pump are worn away from abrasives in the coolant.

maintenance practices, which reduce the possibility of costly repairs in the future.

Pressure Testing

The engine cooling system is designed to operate at up to 18 psi (124 kPa) of pressure. Increasing cooling system pressure with a pressure cap rated at 15 psi (103 kPa) raises the boiling point of a 50/50 coolant mixture to about 265°F (130°C). This increased pressure allows a more efficient exchange of heat between the coolant and the radiator fins. A decrease in pressure reduces system efficiency. The cooling system is pressure tested to verify that there

are no leaks. The pressure cap is pressure tested to verify that it can hold the specified system pressure, and can open to relieve pressure during an overpressure condition.

A simple hand pump with a pressure gauge, hose, and adapters is used to pressure test both the cooling system and the pressure cap. How much pressure a particular system operates at is specified in the service manual. Check the service manual specifications before conducting a pressure test. Always test on a cool engine to avoid being burned by hot coolant. To pressure test:

1. Remove the pressure cap, and attach the pressure tester to the radiator neck or the pressure cap opening, figure 9-30 or figure 9-31.
2. Pump the tester until the gauge reads the pressure recommended by the manufacturer. The

Figure 9-32. The pressure cap is also tested with the coolant system pressure tester. Make sure that it holds the specified pressure and vents pressure above that reading.

system should hold this pressure for at least five minutes.

3. If the pressure drops or falls away gradually, have an assistant maintain system pressure by pumping the tester, while you inspect the vehicle to locate the source of the leak. Tighten, repair, or replace leaking components and repeat the test.

4. Remove the tester from the filler neck or pressure cap opening and use the adapter to attach the pressure cap, figure 9-32. Be sure the cap seal is wet and clean.

5. Pump the tester to the specified system pressure.

6. The cap should hold pressure for at least 10 seconds before gradually beginning to fall off.

7. If the pressure gauge drops rapidly and excessively, replace the pressure cap.

8. Pump the tester to exceed the specified system pressure and observe the gauge. The vent should open and release the excess pressure. If not, replace the cap.

Testing the Thermostat

Thermostats are subject to contamination, corrosion, and other forms of damage. The thermostat must open and close smoothly to regulate engine temperature and maintain operating efficiency. Test the thermostat by simply checking the temperature before and after the thermostat. This can be done using a:

• Noncontact thermometer
• Pyrometer

Figure 9-33. A noncontact infrared thermometer senses infrared radiation from an object and electronically calculates its temperature.

• Temperature-sensitive labels
• Temperature-sensitive markers

A noncontact infrared thermometer is an electronic thermometer that measures temperature by simply aiming an infrared light source at the area to be measured, figure 9-33. A pyrometer is an electronic thermometer that records temperature with a probe that attaches to specific points in the system to take measurements. Temperature-sensitive labels usually have dots marked with different temperatures, and the dots turn black to indicate the temperature reading, figure 9-34. A temperature-sensitive marker is made of wax that melts when the specified temperature is reached.

In addition, engine coolant temperature readings are available on the serial datastream on many vehicles with onboard diagnostics (OBD) systems. Use a scan tool to access the OBD data and read the engine coolant temperature, figure 9-35.

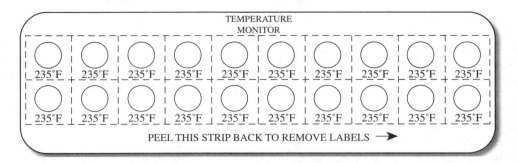

Figure 9-34. The dots on temperature-sensitive labels turn black to indicate the coolant temperature.

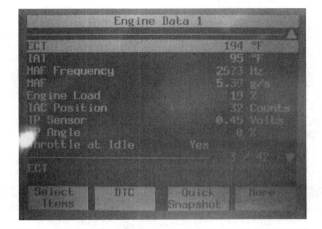

Figure 9-35. The scan tool can be useful in testing the operation of the thermostat.

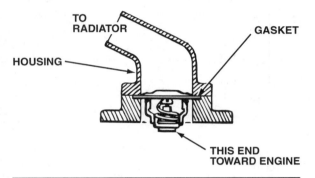

Figure 9-36. Install the thermostat with the sensing end toward the engine.

The thermostat is tested with the engine cold. Prior to testing, remove the pressure cap, and top off the coolant as necessary. If using a temperature-sensitive label, place it on the radiator inlet header tank. For a temperature-sensitive marker, draw a mark on or near the thermostat housing. With an OBD system, attach a scan tool to the data link connector (DLC), access the datastream, and monitor the engine coolant temperature.

Infrared thermometer and pyrometer readings are taken at the radiator header tank or thermostat housing. Use only one location for consistent comparison of readings taken at different times. With an infrared thermometer, aim it at the test spot and pull the trigger to obtain readings. With either device, take an initial reading on the cold engine, then repeatedly take readings at regular intervals as the engine warms up.

To test the thermostat, start and run the engine to bring it up to normal operating temperature. Watch the coolant through the radiator filler neck as the engine warms up. When the thermostat opens, the coolant should begin to swirl. Note the temperature when this happens. If the coolant circulates immediately after starting the engine and the temperature rises slowly, re-place the thermostat. This indicates the thermostat is stuck open or missing from the system.

In general, temperature readings on the discharge side of a good thermostat rise slightly as the engine warms up, then quickly jump to the temperature rating when the thermostat fully opens. If the thermostat opening temperature is above or below specifications, replace the thermostat.

If the thermostat shows signs of rust or damage, or does not open or close completely, replace it. Before installing a new thermostat, scrape all traces of the old gasket and sealer from the mating surfaces. Install the thermostat using a new gasket. Be sure that the thermostat seats firmly and the gasket seals in the housing.

Check the thermostat for proper installation. The sensing end must always be installed toward the engine, figure 9-36. Some thermostats have a small arrow that must point toward the front of the engine. Check the service manual if you are not sure. If the thermostat is installed backwards, it will not open at the proper temperature and the engine is likely to overheat.

Testing the Radiator Fan

There are two types of radiator fans: engine driven and electric. Longitudinally mounted engines often use a belt-driven fan mounted to the water pump shaft, while transverse-mounted engines usually have an electric fan mounted to the radiator. Some vehicles have a second electric fan that provides additional airflow when the AC is turned on or operating temperatures are higher than normal.

Inspect the fan itself before beginning the inspection of the fan system. The blades must be straight and securely attached to the fan hub. If a fan blade appears to be bent, remove the fan and lay it on a flat surface. If there is more than a 3/32-inch (2-mm) difference between any blade, the fan must be replaced. Check for blade looseness or cracked blade rivets. A loose fan is out-of-balance when it rotates, which damages the water pump shaft bearings. Do not attempt to straighten fan blades.

Testing Clutch Fans

Use the following procedure to determine if a fan clutch is working properly.

1. Attach a thermometer to the engine side of the radiator.
2. Connect a timing light and tachometer to the engine, then start and run the engine.
3. Note the thermometer reading when the engine is cold. Aim the timing light at the fan blades; they should appear to move slowly.
4. Block the airflow through the radiator and continue watching the thermometer and timing light. Do not allow the engine to overheat.
5. When the thermometer indicates the specified fan engagement temperature, unblock the radiator. At this point, the fan clutch should actuate, which causes the fan speed to increase. If not, replace the fan clutch.

Following are some quick checks that are used to determine if the fan clutch needs further testing.

- Water pump bearing failures often cause fan clutch failures, and vice versa.
- Check the fan clutch bearing. With the engine off, grasp the fan at the outermost edge of the blade and push it back and forth. If the fan moves from side to side by more than 1/4 inch (6 mm), the fan clutch bearing is defective and should be replaced.
- Use a finger to spin the fan. If the fan rotates more than twice, the clutch is freewheeling and should be replaced.
- The clutch oil used in some clutches is a silicone-based fluid that does not evaporate. If it is leaking, oil will spin off the fan and leave oily lines that radiate from the bearing seal. If you detect leaks, replace the fan clutch.

Testing Electric Fans

All electric fan systems have a fan and electric motor mounted on a shroud behind or in front of the radiator. Some systems use two-fan motor assemblies. Fan operation is controlled in one of the following ways:

- A fan switch that closes when the engine temperature reaches a predetermined value. Usually this switch completes a ground circuit to the fan relay and causes the relay to engage.
- A fan relay that is activated by the PCM based on a signal from the engine coolant temperature sensor.

When the engine coolant reaches a specified temperature, the coolant temperature switch closes to either energize the fan relay or complete the circuit to the fan motor (least common method). Generally fan motor operation can quickly be checked by bypassing the coolant temperature switch and watching for fan operation. This verifies the integrity of the fan motor and circuit but not the switch. The switch can be verified by allowing the engine to warm up until the switch temperature is such that the switch should close. A DVOM can be used to check the switch when this happens.

Electric fan systems that are PCM controlled have specific diagnostic procedures for each vehicle. However, often fan operation can be verified by using a scan tool to command fan operation, figure 9-37. Be sure to follow the manufacturer's procedures when diagnosing PCM-controlled fans. Using a schematic, the fan circuit can be diagnosed with the aid of the scan tool and DVOM. The fan relay(s) can be tested as described in Chapter 7 of this manual. Follow figure 9-38 for the description of a PCM-controlled two-speed fan system.

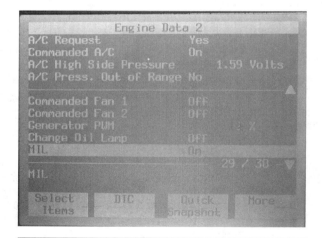

Figure 9-37. Many coolant fans that are PCM controlled can be commanded on using a scan tool.

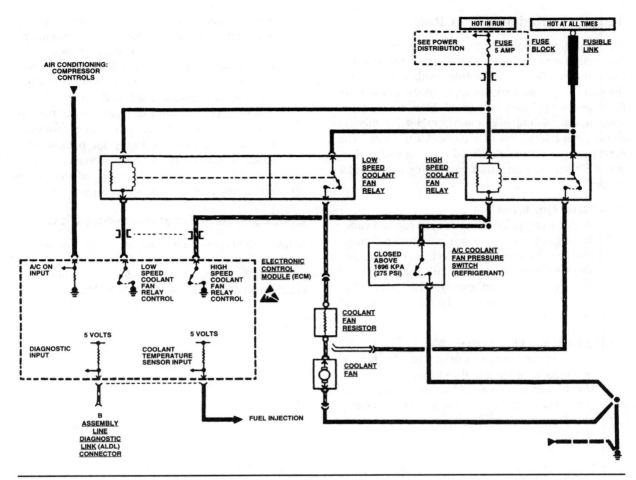

Figure 9-38. Electric coolant fan (two speed). (Reprinted with permission of General Motors Corporation.)

The PCM controls the operation of the cooling fans based on engine temperature or air conditioning operation. When the AC on input is received by the PCM, the low speed coolant fan relay control is grounded. This will cause the low speed coolant fan relay to energize. B+ from the fusible link is fed to the relay. When the relay is energized, the B+ is switched at the relay and sent to the coolant fan motor through the coolant fan resistor. This causes a voltage drop, which means that the fan will not receive full voltage from the relay. The fan motor should operate at a reduced speed. The fan would also be activated in the same manner based on the input to the PCM of the engine coolant temperature sensor. When the engine operating temperature reaches a predetermined level, the PCM would ground the low speed coolant fan relay control and cause the coolant fan to operate on low speed.

High-speed fan operation is controlled in one of two ways. If the AC is operating and the high-side pressure rises above 275 psi (1,896 kPa), the AC coolant fan pressure switch will close and provide a path to ground for the high speed coolant relay. This relay would energize and direct voltage from the fusible link to the coolant fan motor, bypassing the coolant fan resistor. This would cause the coolant fan to operate at high speed because it is now receiving a higher voltage. The other method of obtaining high speed is for the PCM to ground the high speed coolant fan relay control. This grounds the high speed coolant fan relay and causes the coolant fan to operate at high speed. The PCM would command the fan on high when the operating temperatures are high and there is a need for more radiator cooling.

This illustrated fan circuit is just one of many variations that manufacturers use. You must be familiar with the particular fan circuit that you are working on. Refer to the service manual to determine how a particular fan circuit operates.

Testing the Radiator Flow Rate

The flow rate of coolant through the radiator indicates the condition of the interior of the radiator. If it has become partially clogged or filled with sediment, the flow rate drops and the capacity to conduct heat away from the engine block is reduced. Flow testing measures the rate of fluid, in gallons per minute, that the radiator is able to accept at a particular pressure. The most accurate way to check flow rate is with a flow meter. Check flow rate after completing any radiator repairs.

Flow Meter Quick Test

1. With the engine cool, remove the radiator cap.
2. Fill the radiator completely with water, then remove the lower radiator hose from the radiator.
3. The water should flow at full outlet capacity with the radiator cap removed. Less than a full capacity rate indicates that the radiator is blocked by deposits.

Testing without a Flow Meter

1. Start and run the engine until it reaches normal operating temperature, then turn the engine off.
2. Use a noncontact infrared thermometer, or run your hand along the core fins, to measure temperature at different points. The infrared thermometer accurately measures and displays the temperature of the radiator at any point, making it easier to isolate clogged sections. With a downflow radiator, start at the top and work down. With a sideflow radiator, move from one side to the other.
3. The downflow radiator should be hot at the top and warm at the bottom, with an even temperature decrease from the top to the bottom. The sideflow radiator should have an even temperature change from one side of the radiator to the other. Any cool spots indicate clogged sections.

Cooling System Troubleshooting Chart

Using a troubleshooting chart assists in diagnosing some of the more common engine cooling system problems. Nearly all shop manuals have troubleshooting charts for this purpose, figure 9-39.

Symptom	Possible Cause	Repair
Engine overheats at regular intervals	Low coolant level, coolant leak Defective or incorrect pressure cap	Repair leak, add coolant, bleed system Replace pressure cap
Engine overheats at random intervals	Defective thermostat Low coolant level, coolant leak	Replace thermostat Repair leak, add coolant, bleed system
Engine overheats at idle and low speed only	Slipping fan clutch Electric fan not operating	Replace fan clutch Test and repair fan system
Engine overheats at high speed only	Collapsed lower radiator hose	Replace hose
Poor airflow through radiator	Reversed fan blade Broken or missing fan shroud Lean air/fuel mixture	Repair fan blade Repair or replace shroud Test and repair engine
Poor coolant circulation	Plugged or restricted radiator tubes Corrosion or rust in system Damaged or missing air dam	Repair radiator Flush cooling system Repair or replace air dam
Engine overheats at all times May get hot at high speed and not cool down at low speed	Water pump blades loose on shaft Radiator too small	Replace water pump Check for accessory items adding heat to the system
Too much heat being added, not enough being removed	Retarded ignition timing Thermostat not fully opening Slipping fan belt Exhaust gas in cooling system Air in cooling system Lean air/fuel mixture Air cleaner heat valve inoperative EFE heater grid staying on	Adjust timing to specification Replace thermostat Adjust or replace belt Repair engine Bleed system Test and repair engine Repair or replace valve Repair electrical system
Engine does not reach operating temperature	Thermostat stuck open or missing	Replace thermostat
Engine temperature gauge reading incorrect, or warning lamp on in error	Defective temperature sending unit Open or short temperature sending unit circuit Defective gauge unit	Replace sending unit Repair circuitry Replace gauge
Coolant loss	External system leak Internal system leak Defective or incorrect pressure cap Coolant concentration too low	Repair leak Repair engine Replace pressure cap Test and adjust concentration

Figure 9-39. A typical cooling system troubleshooting chart.

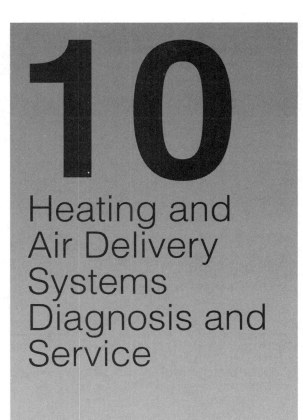

10

Heating and Air Delivery Systems Diagnosis and Service

The heating system can be divided into two subsections: the liquid side and the air delivery side. The liquid side includes the coolant, heater hoses, the heater core, and sometimes the heater control valve. The air side includes the heater core, blower motor and its controls, plenum chamber, blend door, and ducting. This chapter details how to diagnose, test, and repair the major components of the heating and air delivery systems.

HEATING SYSTEMS

Organized troubleshooting includes correctly identifying the type of system that you are servicing. There are three basic systems used for heating the passenger compartment. The primary difference between these systems is how they regulate the temperature of the air entering the passenger compartment. These basic systems are:

1. The heater control system
2. The blend door system
3. A combination of the two

The Heater Control System

The heater control valve, figure 10-1, regulates the amount of coolant that passes through the heater core. The valve opening is controlled by a cable, a vacuum motor, or by electric motor. A given amount of engine-heated coolant heats a given amount of air. Increasing or decreasing the amount of coolant flow through the heater core alters the amount of heat transferred to the air passing through the core.

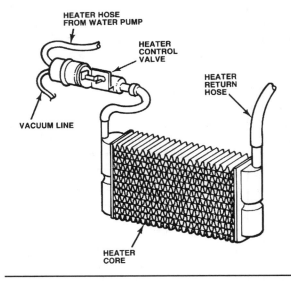

Figure 10-1. The heater control valve is located by following the hoses from the heater core.

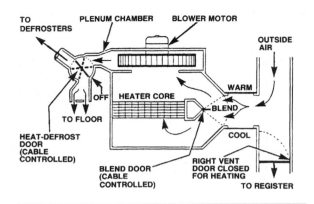

Figure 10-2. The blend door system uses airflow regulation to control the air temperature. The door position determines if air flows through the heater core, or bypasses it.

The Blend Door System

The blend door system is the most common system in use today. In the blend door system, figure 10-2, air passes through the evaporator to dry the air and then to the blend air door. This multi-position door controls the amount of air that passes through the heater core versus the amount that bypasses the heater core. Increasing the amount of air channeled through the heater core increases the discharge temperature while decreasing the amount of air through the heater core decreases the discharge air temperature.

Combination System

The combination system, figure 10-3, uses both a heater control valve and a blend door to regulate the discharge air temperature. The primary control is the blend door because this method is far more sensitive and responsive than the heater control valve method. The heater control valve supplies supplementary control.

Heating Problems

There are some common customer complaints about the heating system. Generally, your customers will notice coolant leaks, insufficient heat, excessive heat, or heat being delivered out the wrong vents.

Begin your heating system diagnosis by starting and running the engine until it reaches normal operating temperature. The upper radiator hose should be warm and pressurized, indicating that the thermostat has opened. Turn the heater temperature control to full heat, select the HEAT mode, and turn the blower to HIGH. Use a test thermometer to check the air temperature discharging from the floor vents. Use a manufacturer's temperature test chart, figure 10-4, to

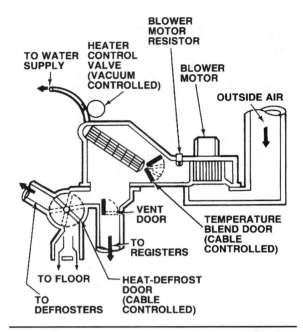

Figure 10-3. This example of a combination heater system uses a vacuum-operated heater control valve to regulate coolant flow, and two cable-actuated blend doors to direct airflow.

Ambient Temperature		Minimum Heater System Floor Outlet Temperature	
Celsius	Fahrenheit	Celsius	Fahrenheit
15.5°	60°	62.2°	144°
21.1°	70°	63.8°	147°
26.6°	80°	65.5°	150°
32.2°	90°	67.2°	153°

Figure 10-4. Manufacturers' service manuals have charts to determine if the heater is operating within its temperature range specification.

determine the proper heater output. If a temperature test chart is not available, you will have to judge the air temperature by touch. The air should be uncomfortable as it blows on a bare hand at about 150°F (65.56°C).

Testing No-Heat Conditions

1. Determine if the coolant flow through the heater core is blocked by feeling the heater hoses. If one or both hoses are cool while the prewarmed engine is running, the problem could be a plugged heater core, faulty heater control valve, or blocked hoses.
   a. Inspect the hoses and fittings. Look for evidence of kinking or pinching.

b. The use of radiator sealants can often result in a blocked or restricted heater core. Put on safety glasses and disconnect both heater hoses from the heater core. Determine the direction of coolant flow. Place the end of the inlet heater hose in a drain pan and use a water hose to try to flush out the blockage. If the blockage does not free immediately, note the amount of water passing out of the hose into the drain pan. If less than it should be, remove the heater core and send out for repairs or simply replace it.

c. If the heater core is not restricted, use the water hose to test the flow rate through the heater control valve. Use the cable or hand vacuum pump to alter the valve opening.

2. If the heater hoses are warm yet there is no heat being delivered to the heater vents of the passenger compartment, then the blend door or other air doors may be in the wrong position. The airflow is either prevented from passing through the heater core or being diverted around the heater core. Refer to the manufacturer's service manuals for tables or diagrams that show the correct position of the blend doors for different modes of the heating system, figure 10-5. Check the doors to make certain that they are not stuck. Check the control cables, electrical wiring, or vacuum hoses to be sure they are not disconnected or broken. Refer to the manufacturer's testing procedures for these systems.

3. Blocked air inlet ducts may cause poor airflow through the heating system. To test for blocked ducts, change the mode selector to the RECIRCULATION setting. If the airflow improves markedly, check for blockage in the ductwork or the cowl air intake at the front of the windshield. This vent is usually covered with a screen to keep leaves and debris out of the system. Remove any debris and check the airflow again.

4. Reduced airflow is sometimes due to a defective blower or reduced current to the blower. If the blower is running slowly or not at all, refer to the instructions later in this chapter.

Insufficient Heat

1. If the heater does not supply a sufficient amount of heat, confirm that the engine is warmed up properly. Also, make certain that the coolant is filled to the proper level. If the coolant is low, usually the first symptom is insufficient heat.

2. If heated air does reach the passenger compartment, but its temperature is too low, inspect the heater control valve for proper operation. If the

heater control valve is faulty, coolant flow to the heater core may be reduced. Ensure that the valve opens and closes smoothly. Look for a faulty electrical connection, and check the valve controls, figure 10-6, for incorrect adjustment, defective control cables, or a leak in the vacuum system.

3. Some vehicles use an auxiliary pump to provide coolant flow to the heater core. If the vehicle is equipped with an auxiliary electric coolant pump, check to see if it is operating correctly.

4. A heater hose may be kinked or partially clogged, especially at the fittings. Sometimes, when old heater hoses are removed for replacement, these fittings are crimped. Check for kinks or restrictions in the hose that may reduce coolant flow to the heater core. Also check the service history or talk to the vehicle's owner to determine if radiator sealants have been used. Sealants may be clogging the heater core.

5. A badly contaminated cooling system or a low coolant level can result in reduced flow to the heater core. Look inside the radiator for signs of rust or scale around the filler neck, which can indicate cooling system problems.

6. A low heat problem may also be due to an improperly adjusted blend door or cable. Check the movement of the door and its linkage, figure 10-7.

7. A defective thermostat, one with the wrong temperature range, or an incorrectly installed thermostat makes the engine run too hot or cold. If the engine coolant does not warm up because the thermostat is stuck open or has an insufficient temperature rating, there will not be enough heat available at the heater core. Confirm the type and operation of the thermostat, figure 10-8.

8. The heater core may be partially blocked. Perform the heater core test discussed later in this chapter to confirm heater core operation.

Excessive Heat

1. Check the blend door position and movement. If the door is stuck open, air will be warmed even if the heater setting is on LOW HEAT. Make certain the door linkage moves freely and does not bind. Keep in mind that this problem can cause the perception of an inefficient air conditioning system.

2. Check the position of the heater control valve. It may be stuck open due to a misadjusted controller or stuck open because of a broken valve. Check all valve controls for defective control cables, a leak in the vacuum system, or faulty electrical system.

MODE SELECTOR VALVE POSITIONS	
1	OFF
2	MAX
3	VENT
4	BI-LEVEL
5	HTR
6	BLEND
7	DEF

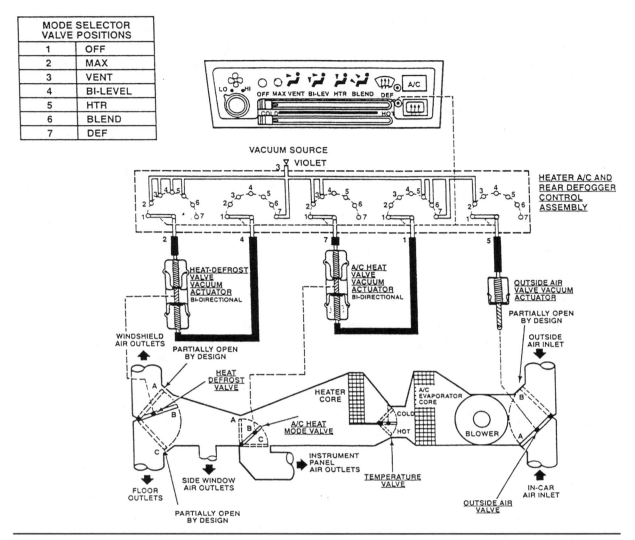

Figure 10-5. Manufacturers' service manuals have a table or diagram that shows the location and position of blend doors for each heating, ventilation, and air conditioning mode of operation. (Courtesy of General Motors.)

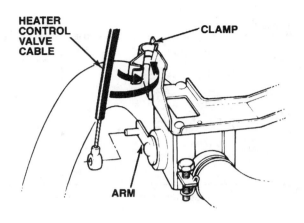

Figure 10-6. Check the cable, vacuum line, or electrical connection that actuates the heater control valve. If the valve does not open fully, coolant flow to the heater core will be reduced.

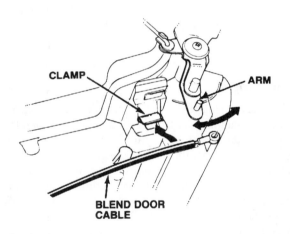

Figure 10-7. Make sure the blend doors and cables move freely. Inspect clamps and linkages for corrosion, damage, or bent parts that may hamper movement of the door.

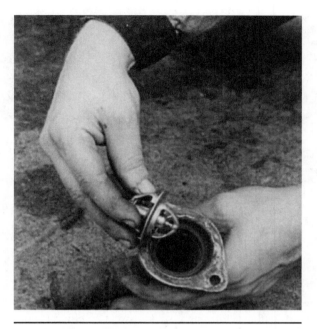

Figure 10-8. Check the thermostat for the correct installation and temperature rating.

Figure 10-9. A clogged heater core can reduce the overall capacity of the cooling system.

HEATING SYSTEM SERVICE

Many problems with the heating system are caused by a heater core failure. These failures disrupt proper heater operation and cause other problems such as fogging of the windshield and dripping coolant onto the passenger compartment floor. An undetected leak from the heater core can rapidly reduce the amount of coolant in the engine cooling system. A clogged heater core can reduce the overall cooling capacity of the cooling system, figure 10-9. Inspect the heater core if the coolant level drops and you cannot detect a leak in the cooling system. Service procedures for testing the heater core include:

- Pressure testing
- Bench testing
- Flushing

Pressure Testing

Pinholes in the heater core allow coolant to leak in the form of steam. The steam can enter the passenger compartment along with the heated air. When this air

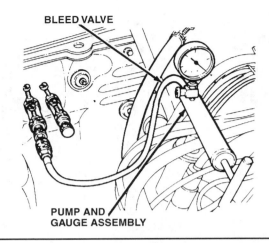

Figure 10-10. Use adapters to connect the pressure tester to the heater core tubes after removing the hoses.

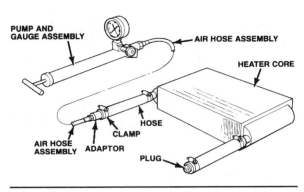

Figure 10-11. After plugging one end, use a hand or air pump to pressurize the heater core.

condenses against the cold windows, the coolant deposits there, forming a sticky, sweet-smelling residue on the windows that does not evaporate. Refer to Chapter 9 in this *Shop Manual* for the procedures to pressure test the entire cooling system, or perform an on-vehicle pressure test of the heater core as follows.

1. Drain the coolant from the system.
2. Disconnect the hose clamps, and then disconnect the heater hoses from the heater core tubes. **CAUTION:** The heater core inlet and outlet tubes can be easily damaged or deformed when removing heater hoses. Be careful when you remove heater hoses from the heater core. You may have to cut the hoses instead of pulling them off of the heater core tubes.
3. Attach a cooling system pressure tester to the tubes, figure 10-10. Use adapters, which are often sold with the pressure tester, to connect the tester to one heater core tube and block the other tube.
4. Apply pressure with the pump and watch the pressure gauge for at least three minutes. If there is a pressure drop, then the heater core is leaking.

Bench Testing

Remove the heater core from the vehicle. This may require considerable disassembly of the heating and ventilation system. Remove the heater core from the plenum assembly. Perform these additional bench tests to locate the leak.

1. Empty the coolant and plug one of the heater core tubes with a suitable stopper.
2. With a suitable piece of hose, connect a hand or air pump to the other tube, figure 10-11.
3. Apply the manufacturer's recommended pressure to the heater core. Most manufacturers rec-

ommend no more than 20 psi (104 kPa). Exact pressure specifications vary, so consult your factory service manual for the system you are servicing.
4. Submerge the pressurized heater core in a tank of water. Look for a stream of bubbles, which indicate the location of the leak.
5. If you see bubbles, repair the leak or replace the heater core.

Flushing

A heater core may collect sediment or scale that can act as an insulating layer between the hot coolant and the metal of the heater core. This reduces the amount of available heat that the heater core can radiate into the airstream passing into the passenger compartment.

Backflushing can remove this sediment, and is the best method to avoid having to remove the heater core from the vehicle. As with flushing the cooling system, backflushing means that the water flow is opposite to the normal direction of the coolant flow. Backflush the heater core as follows.

1. Remove the heater hoses.
2. Connect a drain hose to the inlet tube.
3. Use a backflush gun to spray pressurized water into the outlet of the heater core.

Chemicals, such as oxalic acid, can be used to remove deposits as well. Chemical cleaning is better than using plain water because the acid breaks up oily, scaly deposits in the system that cannot be dissolved by water. Chemically clean the heater core when you clean the engine cooling system. However, some manufacturers prohibit chemical flushing. Check your factory service manual to be sure.

Heater Control Valve

Many heating systems use a heater control valve to regulate the flow of coolant into the heater core. These

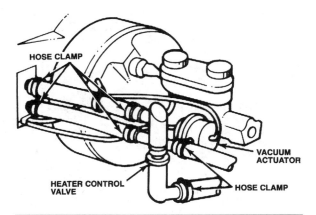

Figure 10-12. This DaimlerChrysler heater control valve is actuated by vacuum. (Courtesy of DaimlerChrysler Corporation.)

valves are actuated by cables, servomotors, vacuum motors, figure 10-12, or electric solenoids. To check a heater control valve:

1. Determine if the valve is normally opened or closed.
2. Check the valve position when it is not actuated. Then check the valve operation. A correctly operating valve should open and close smoothly and completely.

A vacuum-operated heater control valve that is used on a blend door system is usually open until a vacuum is applied to close it. Use a hand-held vacuum pump to confirm that the valve opens smoothly and evenly when the correct amount of vacuum is applied.

VENTILATION SYSTEMS

The ventilation system allows the driver to select the direction from which fresh air will come. Ducts are commonly located in the center of the dash, beneath the dash on the right and left sides, and beneath the center of the dash at foot level. Most late-model vehicles allow the driver to select the source of the air that will be brought into the heating, ventilation, and air conditioning system. Ventilation systems on late-model vehicles can be quite complex. Cables, vacuum diaphragms, or motors control the air door positions. Given the complexity of late-model systems, accurate technical service information is a must.

Ventilation System Problems

Many ventilation system problems involve fogged windows, incorrect airflow, or poor air circulation in the vehicle. The following are ventilation system troubleshooting procedures.

No Airflow

1. If the complaint is there is no airflow, determine if there is no airflow at all in the passenger compartment, or if there is no airflow only through a certain vent. If only one vent is working improperly, check the duct leading to that vent. Also inspect the condition of the vent door and cables.
2. If there is no or very little airflow from all vents, inspect the blower. Turn on the blower while the system is in the VENT mode. Operate the fan at each setting. If there is no airflow, or if the airflow rate is less than expected, refer to the procedures on the blower motor circuit later in this chapter.

Insufficient Airflow

A frequent complaint is that the airflow is inadequate. Check the items below if the airflow is insufficient.

1. Ensure that the vent grilles are open. If most of the vent grilles are blocked, total ventilation of the vehicle is reduced.
2. Check the screen covering the cowl intake vent for partial blockage.
3. Check the air ducts for partial or total blockage. Both the inlet and outlet ducts must be clear. (Air can enter the vehicle only if there is an outlet for the stale air.) On some vehicles, air flows out at the pressure relief grilles located in the rear door pillars, figure 10-13. Another common outlet

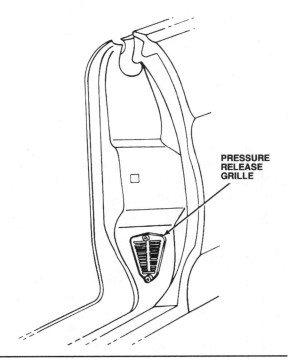

Figure 10-13. The pressure release grilles must be clear in order for air to circulate back out of the car.

Figure 10-14. Inlet air filters can become restricted if they are not serviced at regular intervals. This can result in reduced airflow into the passenger compartment.

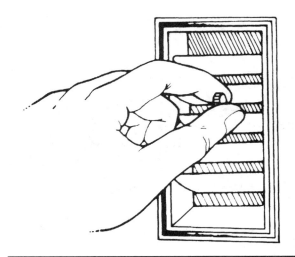

Figure 10-15. Most vents have adjustable slats to direct airflow in the passenger compartment.

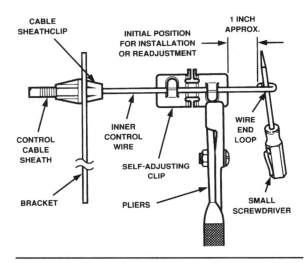

Figure 10-16. Although this control cable is self-adjusting, it must be preadjusted before installation.

system vents stale air under the rear seat, into the trunk, and out of the vehicle. If these vents are blocked, ventilation is reduced.

4. A restricted inlet air filter, figure 10-14, can cause insufficient airflow. Many newer vehicles are equipped with inlet air filters. These filters remove dust and pollen before it enters the vehicle. It is not always clear as to which vehicles are equipped with these filters; therefore, they are not always serviced as recommended by the manufacturer. Make sure that you check this filter if the vehicle is equipped with one.

5. Confirm the blower operation, as described later in this chapter.

Other Ventilation Problems

The driver or the passenger can control the direction of the air coming through the ventilation system by adjusting slats in the vents, figure 10-15. Be sure these slats open and close easily, and are not the cause of the ventilation complaint. Inside the plenum, air doors control the amount of air that goes to the center dash grilles, the floor outlets, and the defroster outlets. Incorrect adjustment or operation of these doors may cause air to flow in the wrong direction. Correct this problem by checking the doors and adjusting cables, if necessary.

Control Cable Service

The most common complaint with control or Bowden cables is incorrect adjustment and kinking. Adjusting the cable is a matter of changing the position of the bracket that holds the cable sheath. Here is a typical adjustment procedure for a heater control cable on a blend door system.

1. Make certain the control cables are properly attached to the levers on the control panel.

2. Move the temperature control to the fully closed or COOL position.

3. Be sure that the cable is attached to the heater valve lever. Loosen the cable bracket and slide the cable until the temperature door is fully closed. Tighten the cable screw.

4. Check for proper cable operation and readjust if needed.

Late-model heater control cables have a self-adjusting clip feature. However, these cables have a limited range of self-adjustment, and must be preadjusted before installation. Failure to preadjust may result in a kinked cable. For self-adjusting cables, figure 10-16, use the preadjustment procedure as follows.

1. Insert a small pocket screwdriver into the temperature control cable wire loop at the end of the temperature crank arm.

2. Slide the self-adjusting clip down the control wire (away from the end loop) by about one inch.
3. Place the temperature control lever in the maximum cool position, then snap the temperature cable housing into the mounting bracket.
4. Attach the self-adjusting clip to the temperature door crank arm.
5. Move the temperature control lever to the opposite end of the control lever assembly. Position the self-adjusting clip and check for proper operation of the cable.

Blower Motor Service

The blower motor circuit includes the blower switch, resistor block, blower motor, and control panel. Setting the control to any air delivery mode may cause the blower to come on, or there may be a separate blower control switch that has to be turned on to operate the blower motor. Blower control circuits use ground-side switching, figure 10-17A, or positive-side switching, figure 10-17B. Blower motor operation is identical in these two circuits.

Blower motor failures are more common as the vehicle ages. Bushings that support the blower motor shaft are usually made of permanently lubricated brass or nylon. If these bushings fail, they either apply a drag on the motor shaft or allow unguided rotation of the motor. If a motor shaft is tight, the motor will overheat and seize as the shaft turns, often causing the blower circuit to blow a fuse. If a bushing is loose, the blower motor will often be noisy, because this same bushing usually supports the fan.

The blower motor switch is cycled on and off many times during the life of the vehicle. If these switches fail it is usually a result of arching across the contacts caused by repeated on and off cycles.

The resistor or resistor block is another item to check when the blower motor does not work correctly. These resistors are prone to failure due to overheating when they are not mounted in the airstream. Overheating may also occur at various connectors between the control panel and the blower motor due to the high current that flows in the blower circuit, especially when the blower motor is run on HIGH speed.

Blower Motor Does Not Operate at Any Speed
Blower motor troubleshooting procedures vary depending on the manufacturer. Always refer to a factory service manual for the manufacturer's procedure of the system that you are servicing. Following is the blower motor operation troubleshooting for a 1992 General Motors B platform vehicle.

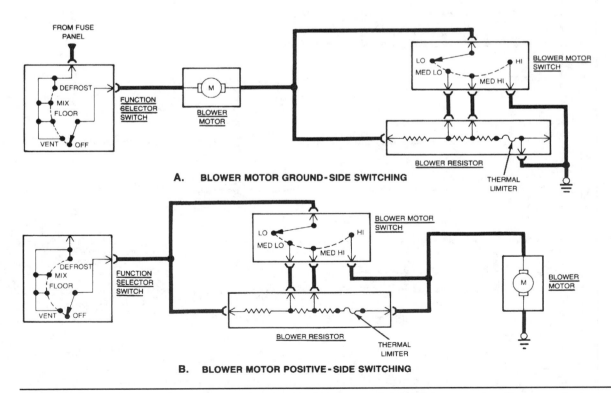

A. BLOWER MOTOR GROUND-SIDE SWITCHING

B. BLOWER MOTOR POSITIVE-SIDE SWITCHING

Figure 10-17. A blower motor with ground-side switching is actuated when the control setting grounds the motor and completes the circuit. The positive-side switching method supplies power to the motor when the control setting is turned on.

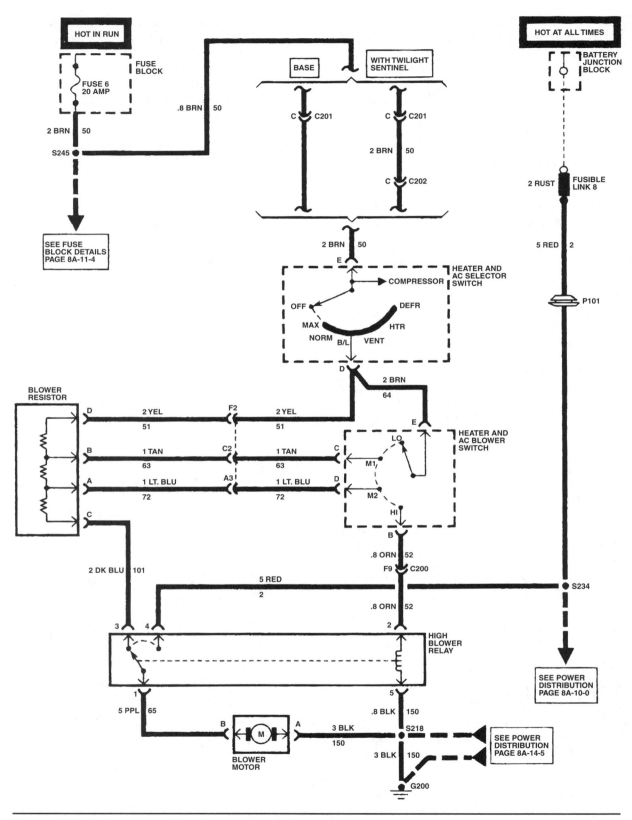

Figure 10-18. Inspect your wiring diagram to see what components you are working with before you begin your diagnosis. (Reprinted with permission of General Motors Corporation.)

Before you begin blower operation testing, confirm what the symptoms are by performing a functional test.

These symptoms may be:

- Blower does not operate at all.
- Blower operates on HI, but not all or some of the lower speeds.
- Blower operates on lower speeds, but not HI.

Once you have confirmed the symptoms, trace the circuits on a wiring diagram to see which components are affected, figure 10-18. Follow the current flow for the involved circuit. When testing, always have the settings with the problem existing at that time. When testing, backprobe the connectors.

Blower Motor Does Not Operate at All

1. Check the circuit fuse.
   a. If the fuse is blown, replace it. If the motor does not run with a new fuse, continue to step 2.
   b. If the fuse does not appear to be blown, test for battery voltage at both sides of the fuse with a 12-volt test light. Replace the fuse if there is voltage only on the battery side.
2. Test for voltage at the blower motor connector. If there is not voltage, proceed to step 3. If voltage is present, check for voltage on the ground circuit.
   a. If there is voltage to the motor, and no voltage on the ground circuit, replace the motor.
   b. If there is voltage on the ground, repair the ground circuit.
3. Test for voltage at the heater and AC selector switch. There should be voltage at both terminals in all positions except OFF.

Blower Motor Operates on HI, But Not on All or Some Lower Speeds

1. Test for voltage at the "B" terminal at the resistor block. If there is no voltage, test the circuit to the heater and AC selector switch. If there is no voltage, test for voltage at the "C" terminal. If there is no voltage at "C," replace the blower resistor block. If there is voltage, proceed to step 2.
   a. If the blower stays on LO, or drops to LO when another setting is made, test the heater and AC blower switch. Test for voltage on both "A" and "B" terminals when the switch is in the MED settings.
2. Test for voltage at the "3" terminal at the high blower relay. If there is no voltage, repair the circuit from the blower resistor. If there is voltage, test the "1" blower motor. If there is no voltage, replace the relay.

Blower Motor Operates on Lower Speeds, But Not on HI

1. With the blower speed on HI, test the "2" terminal at the high blower relay. It should have voltage. If there is voltage at "2," test "5" for voltage. If there is voltage on "5," repair the ground. This involves testing the circuit that energizes the relay. If this circuit tests OK, proceed to step 2.
2. Test for voltage at terminal "4" at the relay. If there is no voltage, repair the open in the battery circuit. If there is voltage, test the "1" terminal. If there is no voltage, replace the relay.

Blower Motor Circuit Test

Use the following test procedures while troubleshooting the blower motor circuit.

Blower Switch Continuity Test

The blower switch may be tested with a DVOM, figure 10-19. The DVOM indicates internal resistance of the switch and shows the actual resistance between the terminals that should have continuity. Blower motor switches have multiple terminals and more than one position. Use a wiring diagram from the manufacturer when conducting these tests.

1. Disconnect the switch connector and check the terminals for each switch position.
2. When several terminals are involved in one switch position, hold the ohmmeter lead on one terminal. Use the other lead to probe each of the remaining terminals used in that position, one at a time. Note the ohmmeter reading at each terminal. The reading

Figure 10-19. Testing the blower switch out of the vehicle with a DVOM.

should be zero or nearly zero for each test point that requires continuity in the position tested.

3. Before moving to the next switch position, check all the other terminals to make sure they read infinite resistance (no continuity).

4. Repeat this procedure for all remaining switch positions. Replace the switch if it fails any part of the test.

Blower Motor Draw Test

The amount of current that a motor draws is directly related to the load on the motor. Blower motors are fused to allow enough current to rotate the blower, plus a margin to permit normal, temporary load increases. Any additional current draw will blow the fuse. Common causes for extra current draw in blower motors include:

• Defective motor
• Defective motor bushings or bearings
• Defective wiring

If a blower motor has blown a fuse, use the current draw test to determine the cause. If the problem is intermittent, be sure to monitor the current long enough for the blower motor to fully warm up. Some motor bushings will operate fine at room temperature, but will tighten when hot. This motor current draw test is especially important for motors that use an electronic module instead of resistors to control blower motor speed. If the blower motor draws too much current it can cause the blower module to fail. Make sure that you test all blower motors for excessive current draw before you replace a defective blower module.

1. Attach an inductive ammeter on the blower motor positive lead, figure 10-20.

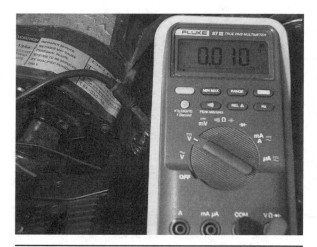

Figure 10-20. An inductive amp probe should be used to test the blower motor current draw. Remember when using an inductive amp probe with a DVOM that amperage is measured on the voltage scale. This reading would be equal to 10 amps.

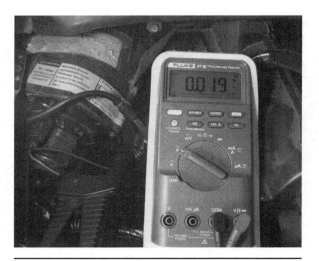

Figure 10-21. With the blower motor on HI, measure the current draw and compare it to manufacturer specifications.

2. Measure the current draw of the motor at each speed range, figure 10-21.

3. Compare these readings to manufacturer specifications.

4. As a rule, the ammeter should not read more than about two-thirds of the rating of the fuse that protects the circuit. This is a general guideline that can be used when there are no specifications listed by the manufacturer for the motor draw.

Resistor Block Testing

A resistor block is connected in series with the blower motor. The resistors are made of coiled nickel chromium wire, which cannot be soldered, so the resistor ends are mechanically clinched in place. Over time, these connections can loosen due to repeated heating and cooling, resulting in open or intermittent open connections to the resistor.

A resistor can also overheat and burn out. This is more likely to happen in cases where the resistor is mounted in a place where it receives poor ventilation. In either case, the test for a bad resistor or resistor connection is the same.

1. Use an ohmmeter to measure the resistance of the resistor.

2. Compare the actual resistance with the rated resistance, which is usually stamped on the bracket that mounts to the resistor end, or as shown in the manufacturer's specifications, figure 10-22.

3. If you suspect an intermittent open, wiggle the resistor gently as you observe the ohmmeter, figure 10-23. If the measured value fluctuates rather than remaining steady, replace the resistor block.

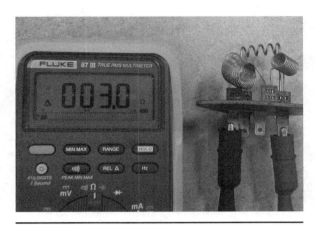

Figure 10-22. The blower resistor block can be tested with an ohmmeter.

Figure 10-23. If you suspect an intermittent open, gently wiggle the resistor while observing the ohmmeter.

4. If individual resistors are open or loose, the resistor block is defective and must be replaced.

Some systems use a thermal limiter that is mounted on the resistor block, figure 10-24. The thermal limiter is built into the circuit to protect the wiring if the blower motor overheats. Like a fuse, the thermal limiter must be replaced if it blows.

Blower Motor Relay Testing

Most blower motor circuits contain at least one relay, usually to provide HI blower motor operation. Some systems may use more than one blower relay to control how much resistance is in the blower motor circuit, figure 10-25. Regardless of how many relays are used, you will need to use a schematic to help you diagnose a relay problem. You may test the relay in the circuit as previously described in this chapter or you may remove the relay and bench test it as described in Chapter 7 of this *Shop Manual*.

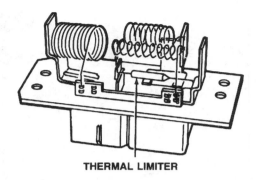

THERMAL LIMITER

Figure 10-24. The thermal limiter, located on the resistor block, protects the circuit if the motor overheats.

VACUUM SYSTEM SERVICE

Intake manifold vacuum operates the controls and actuators in vacuum-controlled ventilation systems. Vacuum-controlled systems can easily be as complex as the vehicle's electrical system. Obtain the manufacturer's vacuum diagram for the specific make and model of the vehicle that you are testing.

Most vacuum readings are taken with the engine at idle. A vacuum gauge or small hand-operated vacuum pump can be used for vacuum testing. The gauge is graduated in inches of mercury (in-Hg) or millimeters of mercury (mm-Hg). In many cases, you can test a component without removing it from the vehicle.

Vacuum Control System Diagnosis

Some vacuum system faults may require reference to the manufacturer's service information for proper diagnostic steps. Performing the diagnostic steps may require disassembly of ventilation ducts, dashboard components, or other items. However, some vacuum system problems are simple and can be diagnosed and repaired without a complex diagnostic procedure. Perform the following checks before you disassemble the ventilation system.

1. Perform a visual inspection. Many vacuum system faults are easily identified by a visual inspection. Disconnected or broken vacuum lines, broken vacuum connectors, misrouted vacuum lines, or loose or disconnected electrical connections on vacuum switches can all be visually identified and repaired. Vacuum system failures may also be audible. A vacuum leak can frequently be heard as a hissing noise.
2. Check the source vacuum. The vacuum system may have one or more sources of vacuum. Use a vacuum gauge to check for vacuum at the source, figure 10-26. If there is vacuum at the source, check the vacuum circuit for vacuum at other places that are convenient.

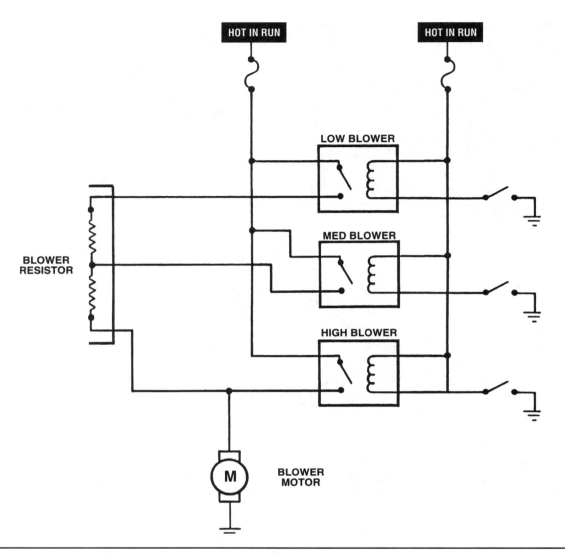

Figure 10-25. Some blowers use relays to control blower fan speed. (Reprinted with permission of General Motors Corporation.)

Figure 10-26. Always make checking the source vacuum one of your preliminary steps when diagnosing air delivery complaints on vacuum-operated systems.

3. Check the individual components. Some components, such as vacuum check valves, vacuum reserve tanks, and vacuum motors may be easily accessible. If the component is part of the malfunctioning vacuum circuit, and is easily accessible, test the component individually.

If the previous checks do not locate a problem, follow the manufacturer's diagnostic procedure to isolate the vacuum system failure.

Vacuum Component Service and Replacement

To test a vacuum actuator, such as a vacuum motor:

1. Connect a vacuum pump to the diaphragm inlet port and apply about 15 to 20 in-Hg (350 to 500 mm-Hg) of vacuum, figure 10-27.

Figure 10-27. Use a hand-held vacuum pump to test a vacuum actuator.

Figure 10-29. With vacuum applied, observe the door and make sure that it moves to the full open position and that the diaphragm holds vacuum.

Figure 10-28. Check the operation of the diaphragm in all positions and make sure the linkage is not binding.

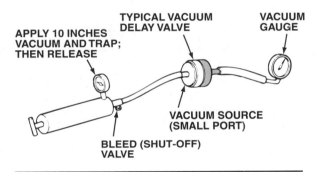

Figure 10-30. Check the time required for vacuum to stabilize on both sides of a vacuum delay valve.

2. Check the operation of the diaphragm plunger or linkage in all positions, figure 10-28.
3. Observe the vacuum pump gauge to determine if the diaphragm is leaking.
4. Repeat for each inlet port of the vacuum motor.
5. Be sure that the door moves when vacuum is applied, figure 10-29.

To test a vacuum delay valve:

1. Attach a second vacuum gauge to the outlet port, figure 10-30.
2. Apply vacuum to the valve inlet port.
3. Note the time required for the two gauge readings to stabilize and compare this to the manufacturer's specifications.

Testing a Vacuum Solenoid

Some ventilation systems use vacuum solenoids to apply vacuum to the vacuum diaphragms. These solenoids are electrically operated to either allow vacuum flow through them when they are energized, or block vacuum through them when they are energized. Test these solenoids as follows:

1. Apply battery voltage to energize the solenoid, figure 10-31. In some cases you may need to complete the ground circuit to the solenoid.
   a. If you feel the valve housing click, the solenoid is probably functioning correctly. Go to step 2.
   b. If the housing does not click, the solenoid does not work. Replace the solenoid valve.
2. Determine whether the vacuum solenoid is normally open or normally closed. Use a vacuum pump and apply vacuum to the solenoid.
   a. If the passage is open, the valve is either normally open or the solenoid is defective. Go to step 3.

Figure 10-31. Electric solenoids can be tested by applying vacuum with a hand-held vacuum pump, then energize the solenoid to determine if it releases the vacuum.

Figure 10-32. There are a wide variety of electric actuators used to move mode and blend doors.

    b. If the passage is closed, the valve is either normally closed or the solenoid is defective. Go to step 4.
3. While applying vacuum with the vacuum pump, energize the solenoid. It should now hold vacuum. If it does not, replace the solenoid.
4. While applying vacuum with the vacuum pump, energize the solenoid. It should now vent the vacuum. If it does not, replace the solenoid.

Testing Electric Blend or Mode Door Actuators

Many air delivery systems have moved away from using cables or vacuum control actuators in favor of electric or electronic actuators. Some systems use electric actuators exclusively while other systems use a combination of cable or vacuum actuators along with electric actuators. For a review of the various electric actuators used, refer to Chapter 11 of your *Classroom Manual*.

Electric actuators may be a variety of different types, figure 10-32. Basically they can be divided into several different categories: dual-position, three-position, and variable position actuators. In addition, they may be two-wire, three-wire, or five-wire actuators. Some actuators have a feedback sensor incorporated into them to signal their position to a control module, while other actuators are "smart" actuators that contain their own microprocessor used to determine their position. Make sure that you refer to the manufacturer's service information to determine which type of actuator is being used on the vehicle that you are servicing.

Two-wire actuators are typically used for doors that can have only two positions such as the outside/recirculation mode door. This door is either in the outside air position or the inside air position and gen-

erally there is no need for the control module to know its position. This type of actuator is moved by the control module, which supplies a voltage and a ground to each of its leads. This voltage might be 8 volts or 12 volts depending on the system. To reverse the direction that the actuator moves, the ground and voltage is switched between terminals to obtain bidirectional capabilities. These actuators are relatively straightforward to diagnose using a DVOM. Simply check for voltage to either lead as the control is switched to command the actuator to operate. Then reverse the leads and check for voltage at the other terminal when the actuator is commanded to the opposite position.

Testing Three-Wire Variable Position Actuators

The three-wire variable position actuator is typically used as the blend door actuator. It can be commanded to any position from full cold to full hot and any position in between. Referring to figure 10-33, you can test the actuator as follows.

1. Check for power and ground to the actuator, figures 10-34 and 10-35. If there is no power, test the circuit to the fuse as well as the fuse itself. If there is no ground, verify the integrity of the ground circuit.
2. If power and ground are both present, test for a signal coming from the control head to the actuator, figure 10-36. This voltage should vary as the temperature lever is moved from cold to hot. The actual range of this voltage may vary between manufacturers; however, what is important is that you see a significant voltage change on your DVOM as the temperature lever is moved from one extreme to the other. These voltages may range from zero volts to 12 volts, or some lesser value. Refer to the manufacturer's service information for the correct range. If voltage is present and it varies as the temperature lever is moved, then replace the actuator.

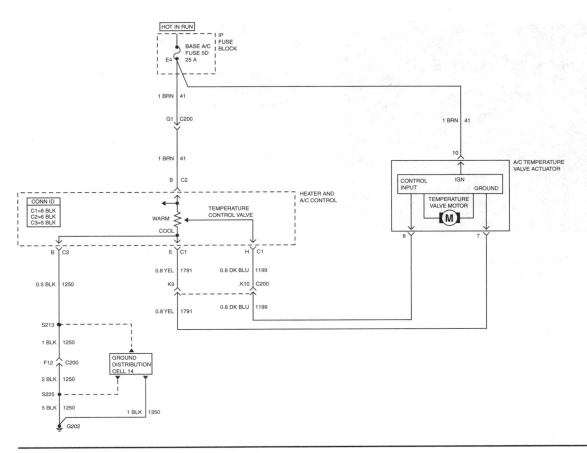

Figure 10-33. A typical three-wire actuator circuit.

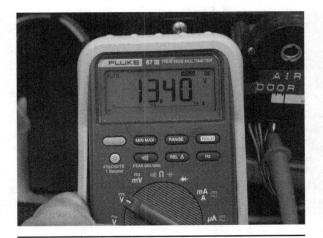

Figure 10-34. Test for power to the actuator using a DVOM.

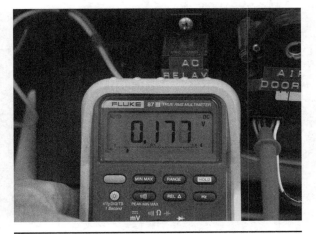

Figure 10-35. Test the ground for the actuator by measuring the voltage on the ground circuit.

3. If the voltage does not change as the temperature lever is moved, then test and repair the circuit between the actuator and the control head, or the control head itself.

Testing Five-Wire Actuators

A five-wire actuator has five wires to the actuator, figure 10-37. These wires usually consist of B+ feeding the actuator, a control circuit from the control head, a five-volt

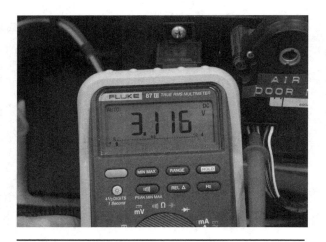

Figure 10-36. After verifying power and ground to the actuator, measure the signal voltage to the actuator. It should vary as the temperature is changed on the control panel.

reference from the control head to the actuator, a feedback circuit from the actuator to the control head, and ground. This actuator uses a feedback position sensor to indicate to the control module the position of the actuator. This is common on actuators that have the capability of three different positions. Test this actuator as follows.

1. Check for power and ground to the actuator. If both power and ground are present, proceed to step 2. If not, repair the power or ground to the actuator and test for proper operation.

2. Using your DVOM, test for voltage on the control circuit. Check this voltage and watch for a change at the actuator, figure 10-38, as the control head functions are changed. The voltage measured on the control circuit should vary between 0 V, 2.5 V, and 5 V, depending on the position of the control head mode switch. If these voltages are present, then replace the actuator. If these voltages are not

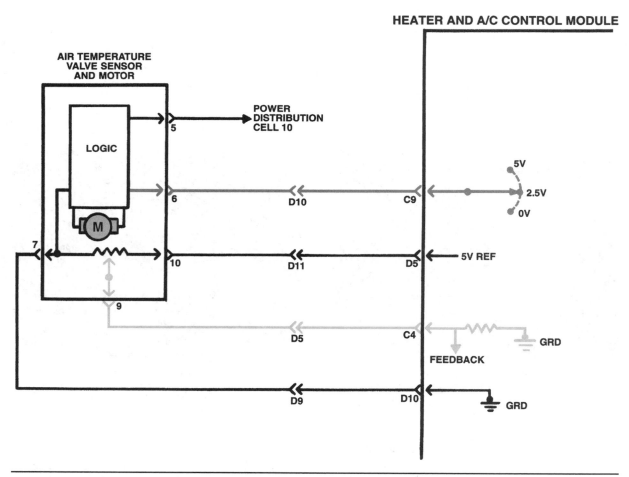

Figure 10-37. A five-wire actuator incorporates a feedback sensor into the actuator. (Reprinted with permission of General Motors Corporation.)

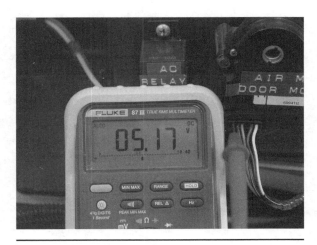

Figure 10-38. The control voltage should change as the actuator is signaled to move.

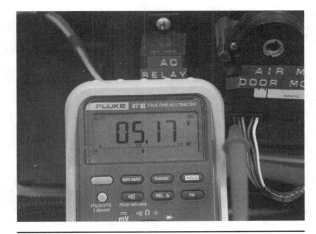

Figure 10-39. The actuator should also have a five-volt reference used for the feedback sensor.

correct, test and repair the circuit between the actuator and the control head or the control head itself.

3. Check for five volts on the reference circuit. This voltage is required for the actuator to generate a feedback signal, figure 10-39. If this is missing the actuator may not work correctly.

4. Test the feedback signal from the actuator. It should show a variable five volts as the actuator moves. If no voltage is present or it does not change, then go to step 5.

5. Test the ground for the actuator. If the ground tests good, then replace the actuator.

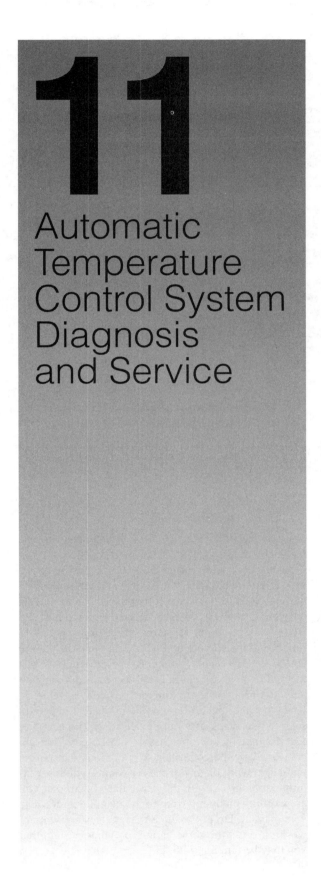

11

Automatic Temperature Control System Diagnosis and Service

Chapter 4 detailed the general procedure to diagnose, test, and service electrical circuits and components. This chapter covers diagnosis and testing of typical controls specific to automatic temperature control (ATC) systems. There are two basic types of systems in this category:

- Semiautomatic temperature control systems (SATC)
- Automatic temperature control systems (ATC)

The typical SATC system is a manual system that controls the temperature to a set temperature inside the vehicle. The driver controls all modes and the blower speed. Sensors monitor the ambient temperature and in-car temperature so the temperature door is in position to provide the desired air temperature inside.

AUTOMATIC TEMPERATURE CONTROLS

With automatic temperature control, the driver selects the desired temperature. All other settings, such as blower speed, mode, whether the air is recirculating or fresh outside air, and temperature of the air, is made automatically. An ATC system depends on a variety of different inputs sent to an HVAC controller, which in turn controls a variety of outputs, figure 11-1. A typical ATC system may consist of any or all of the following.

- *Controller.* Inputs for an ATC system may be sent to a Body Control Module (BCM), Powertrain Control Module (PCM), HVAC control head, HVAC programmer, or AC amplifier. All ATC systems have one controller designated as the decision maker that controls the functions of the ATC system. Based on the input signals, the controller will make decisions on blower speed, compressor operation, air delivery mode, and the position of the air temperature door.
- *Mode Door Actuators.* The temperature (blend) door and different mode and outlet doors are operated by either an electric actuator or vacuum actuators. They may also have feedback capability to show their position to the controller.

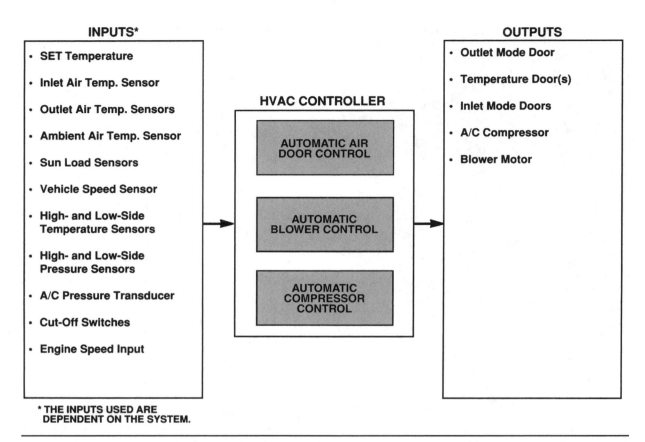

Figure 11-1. Inputs and outputs used in AUTO modes. (Reprinted with permission of General Motors Corporation.)

- *Sensors.* Thermistors may be used as ambient air temperature sensors, inlet and outlet temperature sensors, high- and low-side temperature sensors, and in-car temperature sensors. In addition, pressure switches or sensors may also be inputs to the controller. One or two sun load sensors may be used to help the controller determine sun load on the vehicle.
- *Compressor Protection Device.* Some systems may employ a compressor protection device such as an rpm sensor as an input to the controller.
- *Serial Data.* Many ATC systems communicate with and receive information from other modules utilizing a data circuit. This communication may occur with the PCM, BCM, or other modules such as trip computers that may display outside air temperature.
- *Evaporator Temperature Sensors.* Many ATC systems use an evaporator temperature sensor which sends evaporator temperature information to the controller.

For a review of how these sensors function and how to test them, refer to Chapter 7 of this manual.

There are a wide variety of ATC systems in use today. Every manufacturer has some version of an ATC system either as standard equipment or an option on some models. Each system is unique. You will find that some manufacturers' systems vary from model to model and model year to model year. Obviously there is no way that each system could be presented in this manual or that you could even become familiar with all the various systems offered on today's vehicles. Keep in mind that all these systems share similarities such as the types of input devices used, a controller that contains a microprocessor, and outputs that are controlled by the controller. It is obvious that before you begin work on any of these systems, you must familiarize yourself with the particular system that you are working on by referring to the manufacturer's service manual. Do not assume that the system you are working on is the same as any previous system that you may be familiar with.

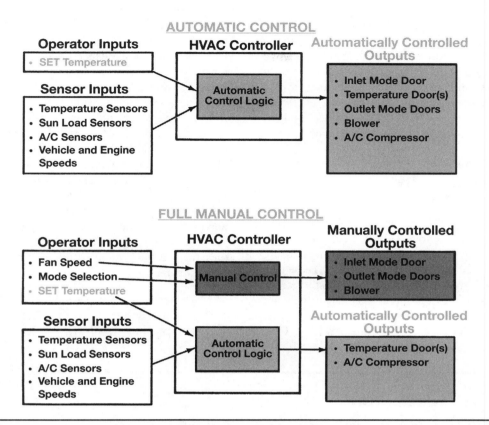

Figure 11-2. Full automatic mode versus full manual mode. (Reprinted with permission of General Motors Corporation.)

Automatic and Manual Modes

Most ATC systems are capable of operating in both an automatic mode and a manual mode of operation, figure 11-2. The AUTO mode may need to be selected by the driver, figure 11-3, or it may be the default operation whenever the system is turned on. In this mode of operation all the driver should have to select is the desired temperature setting on the control head. The ATC system when operating in the AUTO mode should control the air delivery mode, blower speed, and desired temperature. No further interaction from the driver is necessary. If the system is functioning correctly the in-car temperature should be maintained to within ± 2°F, and the blower speed should be at a low speed. The ATC system will respond to any change in the interior temperature to maintain the desired temperature.

Most ATC systems have the capability of manual operation. The driver may select this operation by a variety of means. On some systems, if the driver changes the blower speed or the delivery mode, the system will switch from automatic to a manual mode. In some other cases, the driver may have to enable manual

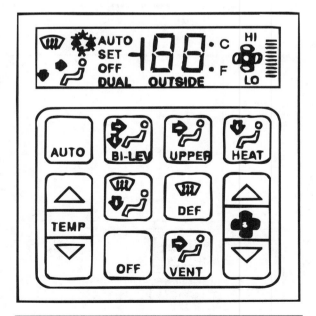

Figure 11-3. A 1992 General Motors heater and AC control assembly faceplate for an ATC system. (Reprinted with permission of General Motors Corporation.)

operation by pushing the AUTO button on the control head. Some systems will default to manual operation when the driver sets the temperature to either extreme, full cold or full hot. The system then will deliver full cold or heat with no regard to interior temperature. Once the driver reaches his or her comfort level, he or she will have to enable the AUTO mode again or change the temperature setting to the desired level.

DIAGNOSTIC CODES IN ATC SYSTEMS

Most late-model ATC systems have diagnostic capabilities. These codes may only be accessible with a scan tool or may be accessible by using onboard diagnostics provided through the control head. These trouble codes may be stored as current or history codes. Current codes represent failures that are currently present. History codes represent failures that have occurred but are not present at the time of testing. These

are usually the result of intermittent conditions. History codes are helpful in locating intermittent problems that may only occur under certain operating conditions. Diagnostic flowcharts are usually provided for each code; however, remember that most charts are written such that they will only be effective if the code is present at the time of testing. That is why it is necessary for you to determine which codes are current codes and which codes are history codes. Each manufacturer has different methods for accessing diagnostic trouble codes using the onboard diagnostics. Make sure that you refer to a manufacturer's service manual to determine the correct method for accessing and displaying codes for that particular vehicle being serviced. The following are some representative samples for accessing onboard diagnostics for different manufacturers.

1. Using the control panel shown in figure 11-4, simultaneously press the "OFF" and "WARMER" (temperature up) button to enable self-diagnostics.

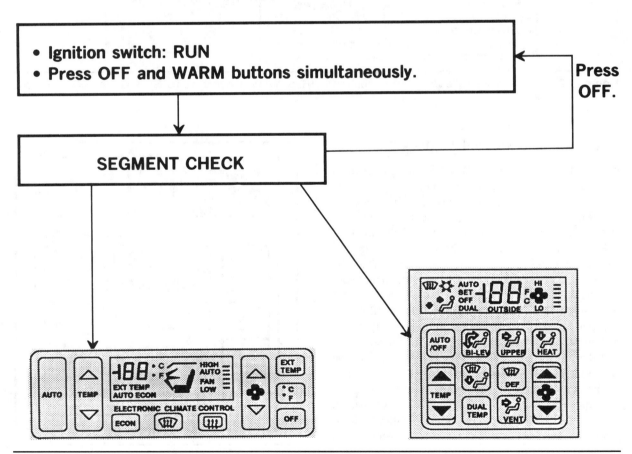

Figure 11-4. Press the three buttons simultaneously to enter the diagnostic test of this ATC system. (Courtesy of General Motors.)

2. After enabling diagnostics, the panel will display any codes that are stored. In addition, the status lights will indicate different modes of operation such as the air delivery or compressor clutch status.

3. Pressing the "LO" button, figure 11-5, progresses through three levels of diagnostics. Level one displays trouble codes and status lights, level two provides override functions that allow the technician to command different functions, and level three is used to clear trouble codes.

4. By using the "OFF," "LO," and "HI" buttons the technician can navigate up and down through the three levels of diagnostics, figure 11-6.

5. On some systems, codes can be cleared only by using the control panel. Disconnecting the battery will not clear codes. Be sure to consult the service information for the system that you are servicing.

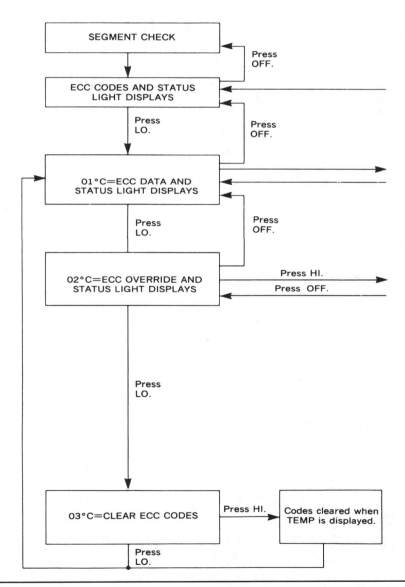

Figure 11-5. Use your test results to determine whether to begin repairs or perform further testing. (Courtesy of General Motors.)

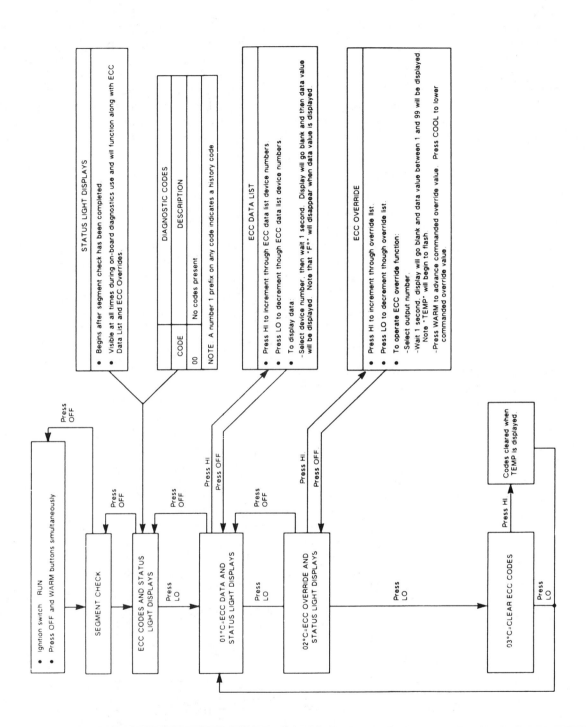

Figure 11-6. If any codes are present, diagnose and repair. If the repairs correct the condition, the code will change to a history code. (Courtesy of General Motors.)

Each vehicle has a unique method to enter diagnostics and obtain fault codes. There are too many different methods to list here. You must refer to a manufacturer's service manual to find the correct procedure and sequence of events. In addition, fault codes are unique for each manufacturer, unlike OBD II codes that are common between manufacturers.

ATC System Parameters

In addition to obtaining fault codes using onboard diagnostics, some ATC systems provide the technician with the ability to view input parameters of the various inputs to the controller. The technician may also be able to view output states of the system or even override outputs to help determine if they are working correctly. This can be a valuable tool in helping to diagnose faults in ATC systems. Being able to view input parameters such as temperature sensors and mode door positions aids the technician in diagnosing faults in the system. It also lets the technician avoid having to make direct measurements of various inputs to determine if they are working correctly. The following example shows the method of entering diagnostics and navigating through the menus on an ATC system on a Cadillac.

1. Enter diagnostics by simultaneously pressing the OFF and WARMER buttons on the control head, figure 11-7.
2. A segment check will occur and then diagnostic codes will be displayed if there are any stored in memory, figure 11-8.

3. After codes are displayed, menu choices are available for a variety of systems such as ECM (Engine Control Module), IPC (Instrument Panel Cluster), SIR (Supplemental Inflatable Restraint), and ACP (Air Conditioning Panel). Select the ACP by pressing the LO button until ACP is displayed and then press HI, figure 11-8.
4. The ACP menu consists of ACP Data, ACP Inputs, ACP Overrides, ACP Clear Codes, and ACP Snapshot, figure 11-9.
5. To view ACP Inputs, press the HI button when ACP Data is displayed. As can be seen in figure 11-8, there are a variety of input parameters that can be viewed, such as Commanded Blower Speed, In-Car Temperature, Actual Outside Temperature, and many others.
6. To view outputs and override output devices, press the HI button when ACP Overrides is displayed. This allows the technician to command certain outputs on or off to verify their operation, figure 11-9.
7. To clear codes press the HI button when ACP Clear Codes is displayed. This will clear all ATC codes that are stored in the system. This should always be performed after repairs have been completed.

Many ATC systems have similar capabilities as the one just illustrated. However, what is unique is the method of navigating through the menu system using the various controls. Once again it is essential that you have access to the manufacturer's service manual to perform any of these functions on an ATC system that has onboard diagnostics and parameter display capability.

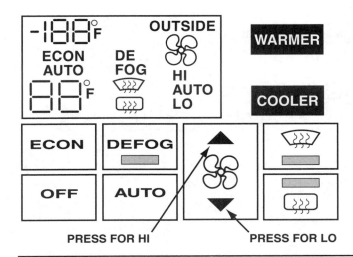

PRESS FOR HI   PRESS FOR LO

Figure 11-7. To enter the diagnostic test mode, press the OFF and WARMER buttons simultaneously until all displays are lit. (Reprinted with permission of General Motors.)

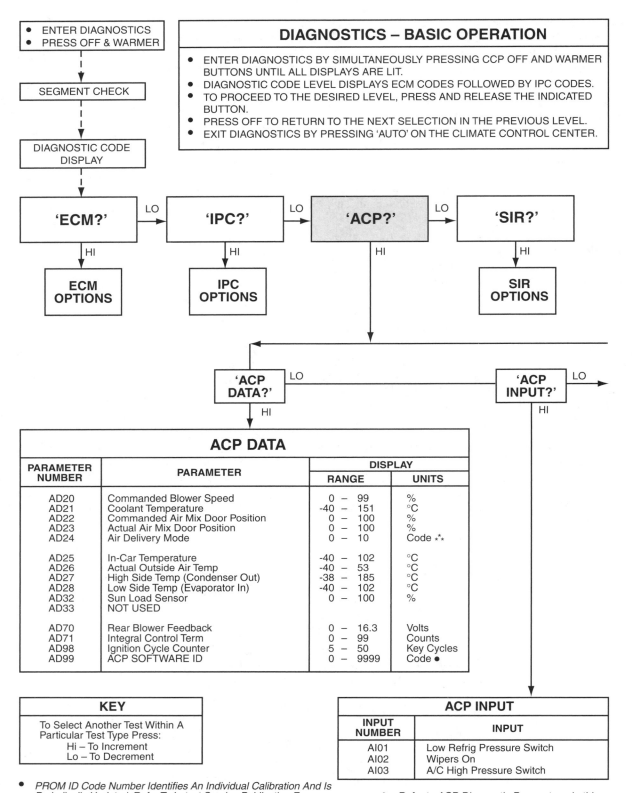

Figure 11-8. How to enter a Cadillac diagnostic mode. (Reprinted with permission of General Motors.)

ACP STATUS LIGHTS

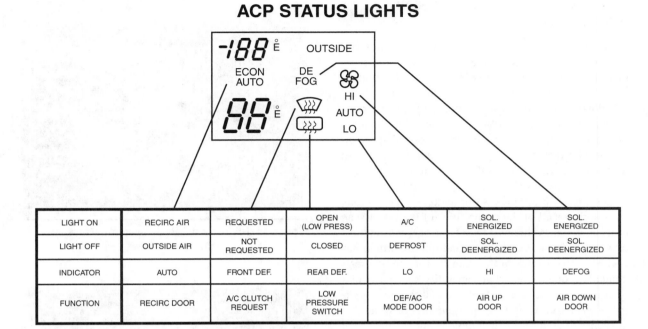

LIGHT ON	RECIRC AIR	REQUESTED	OPEN (LOW PRESS)	A/C	SOL. ENERGIZED	SOL. ENERGIZED
LIGHT OFF	OUTSIDE AIR	NOT REQUESTED	CLOSED	DEFROST	SOL. DEENERGIZED	SOL. DEENERGIZED
INDICATOR	AUTO	FRONT DEF.	REAR DEF.	LO	HI	DEFOG
FUNCTION	RECIRC DOOR	A/C CLUTCH REQUEST	LOW PRESSURE SWITCH	DEF/AC MODE DOOR	AIR UP DOOR	AIR DOWN DOOR

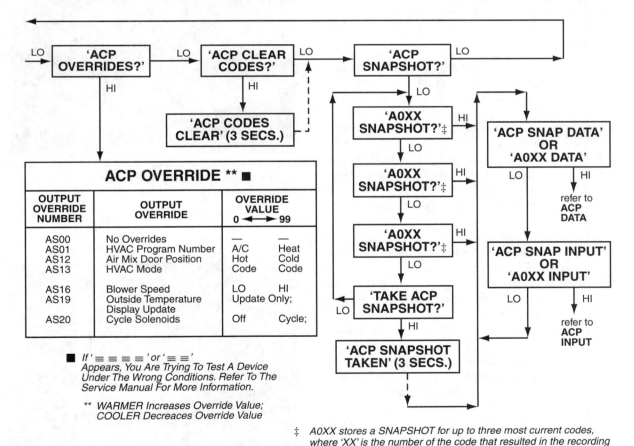

ACP OVERRIDE ** ■

OUTPUT OVERRIDE NUMBER	OUTPUT OVERRIDE	OVERRIDE VALUE 0 ◄──► 99	
AS00	No Overrides	—	—
AS01	HVAC Program Number	A/C	Heat
AS12	Air Mix Door Position	Hot	Cold
AS13	HVAC Mode	Code	Code
AS16	Blower Speed	LO	HI
AS19	Outside Temperature Display Update	Update Only;	
AS20	Cycle Solenoids	Off	Cycle;

■ *If '≡ ≡ ≡ ≡' or '≡ ≡'*
Appears, You Are Trying To Test A Device
Under The Wrong Conditions. Refer To The
Service Manual For More Information.

** *WARMER Increases Override Value;*
COOLER Decreaces Override Value

** *Refer to ACP Diagnostic Parameters, in this*
section for complete information.

‡ *A0XX stores a SNAPSHOT for up to three most current codes,*
where 'XX' is the number of the code that resulted in the recording
of the SNAPSHOT. After the last recorded SNAPSHOT the display
will skip to 'TAKE ACP SNAPSHOT?'

Figure 11-9. The ACP Status Lights indicate the condition of some of the components. (Reprinted with permission of General Motors Corporation.)

TESTING ATC SYSTEMS USING A SCAN TOOL

Most ATC systems that have onboard diagnostics also have scan tool access to their systems. In some cases this may be the only way to obtain DTCs. In addition to accessing trouble codes, if the scan tool is bidirectional it can be used to test actuators and other outputs. A datastream list may be available enabling the technician to monitor various input sensors to the controller. These scan tool capabilities vary between scan tool manufacturers. The OEM scan tool always has the most capabilities because it is specifically designed for those vehicles. Aftermarket scan tools may have some or all of the capabilities of the OEM scan tools on certain vehicles. Other aftermarket scan tools may have no access to air conditioning functions. Make sure you refer to the scan tool manufacturer's manual to determine what capability that particular scan tool provides for the vehicle that you are working on. The following is a representation of what type of scan tool features are available using a Tech 2 scan tool, which is a General Motors factory tool. It is also available to the aftermarket; however, it does not support foreign vehicles.

1. After entering the vehicle information, choose "Body Systems for Heating and Air Conditioning," figure 11-10. Usually if a scan tool supports Air Conditioning, it will be found in Body Systems or, in some cases, air conditioning codes may be found under ECM or PCM.
2. Choose "Heating and Air Conditioning" on the scan tool menu. There are now four submenus to choose from, figure 11-11.
   a. "F0: Diagnostic Trouble Codes" will retrieve stored trouble codes for the Heating and Air Conditioning system.
   b. "F1: Data Display" will allow you to view data parameters from the ATC system.
   c. "F2: Special Functions" will allow the scan tool to override certain outputs to determine if they are working.
   d. "F3: Snapshot" will allow the technician to record data from the ATC system, which can be useful in storing and analyzing data at a later time or locating intermittent conditions.
3. Choosing "Diagnostic Trouble Codes" will show two submenus, figure 11-12.
   a. "F0: DTC Information," which will allow the technician to retrieve stored DTCs.
   b. "F1: Clear DTC Information," which will allow the technician to clear any stored Heating and Air Conditioning trouble codes but not trouble codes stored in other systems.

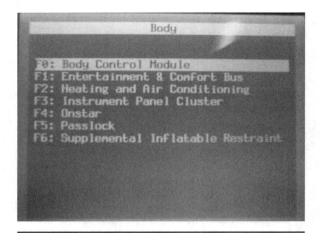

Figure 11-10. A Tech 2 Body Systems Menu.

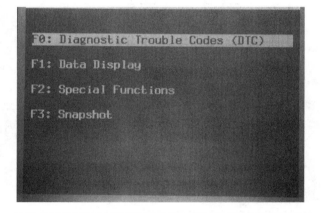

Figure 11-11. Choosing the "Heating and Air Conditioning" menu provides these options.

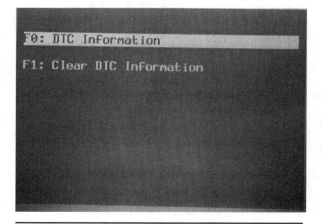

Figure 11-12. Choosing "DTCs" offers these two submenus.

4. Choosing DTC Information will show two sub-menus, figure 11-13.
   a. "F0: Current Diagnostic Trouble Code(s)" which will show any current fault codes that are set. This would indicate that the fault is present at this time.
   b. "F1: History Diagnostic Trouble Code(s)" which will show any fault codes that were set previously. These could have been set due to an intermittent condition or could be set due to a prior repair that was made and the technician did not clear the code(s).
5. If "F1: Data Display" was chosen from the main menu, the scan tool would display data from the various sensors and feedback devices that are used on the system, figure 11-14. Depending on the system being tested, the number of data parameters available for viewing will vary, figure 11-15.
6. If "F2: Special Functions" was chosen from the main menu, the scan tool would display "F0: Output Control," figure 11-16. This allows the technician to use the scan tool to command outputs to actuate, allowing the technician to determine if the actuator is working properly.
   a. "F0: Solenoid Test" will allow the technician to actuate each of the electric solenoids that control vacuum to the various actuators, figure 11-17. This would allow the technician to determine if the various blend or mode doors are functioning correctly or if the solenoids are functioning, figure 11-18.
   b. "F1: Miscellaneous Test" provides another submenu that allows the technician to control various other outputs of the ATC system, figure 11-19.
      i. "F0: Mix Motor" allows the technician to control the movement of the air temperature door to any position from full COLD to full HOT.
      ii. "F1: Blower Motor" allows the technician to control the blower motor speed to any position, enabling the technician to test the blower motor and blower control module.
      iii. "F2: AC LED" allows the technician to test the LED on the control panel that indicates that the air conditioning has been requested.
      iv. "F3: Rear Defogger" allows the technician to turn the rear defogger on and off with the scan tool.
      v. "F4: AC Request" allows the technician to use the scan tool to turn the air conditioning compressor on and off.

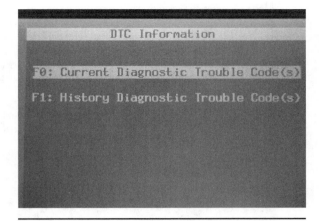

Figure 11-13. Choosing "DTC Information" allows you to choose between current or history codes.

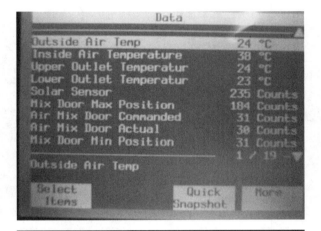

Figure 11-14. Choosing "Data Display" from the main menu provides a data list of parameters.

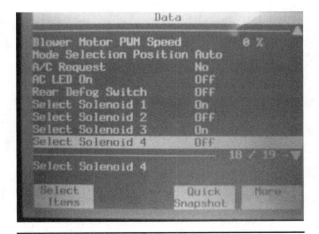

Figure 11-15. Additional data list items may be available by scrolling down the data list.

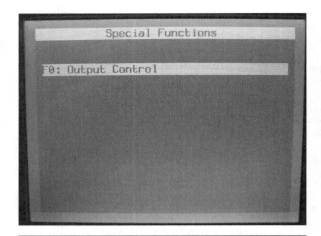

Figure 11-16. "Special Functions" provides output control of various output devices.

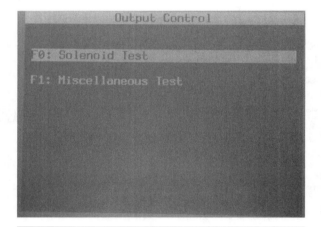

Figure 11-17. Choosing "Output Control," two sub-menus are provided.

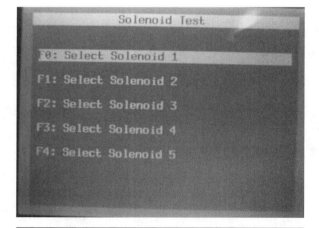

Figure 11-18. Choosing "Solenoid Test" lists the various solenoids that control vacuum to the actuators. Each can be energized separately.

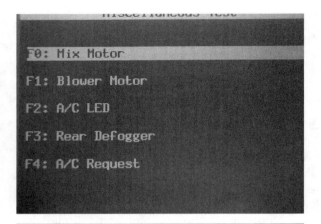

Figure 11-19. Choosing "Miscellaneous Test" provides a list of outputs that can be controlled with the scan tool.

As can be seen from the previous illustration, some ATC systems have a lot of scan tool support. While the system may support onboard diagnostics, the scan tool is much quicker and easier to use. Many of the functions that are available with the scan tool are not available through onboard diagnostics. Therefore, it is necessary for any repair facility performing air conditioning work to have available a scan tool to aid in the diagnosis and repair of ATC air conditioning systems.

DUAL ZONE AIR DISTRIBUTION SYSTEMS

Many vehicles are equipped with dual zone systems. These systems utilize ductwork that is split into two separate distribution systems that deliver air which is split between the right and left side of the vehicle or, in some cases, between the front and the rear of the vehicle, figure 11-20. In addition to ductwork that is separate from each other, these systems use separate air mix (blend) doors that are controlled by individual driver-side and passenger-side temperature controls.

Dual zone systems may be manual or automatic temperature control systems. If they are manual systems, each of the temperature controls is adjusted separately to provide the desired outlet temperature from the ducts. While the temperature of the outlet air can be modified, the outlet position of the air cannot be different from one side to the other. In other words, whatever the selected air delivery mode is, it will be the same on both sides of the vehicle. What can be controlled on these systems is the temperature of the outlet air. Many systems are capable of a 30°F (14°C) difference between the driver-side and the passenger-side outlets. This allows both the passenger and driver to select the desired

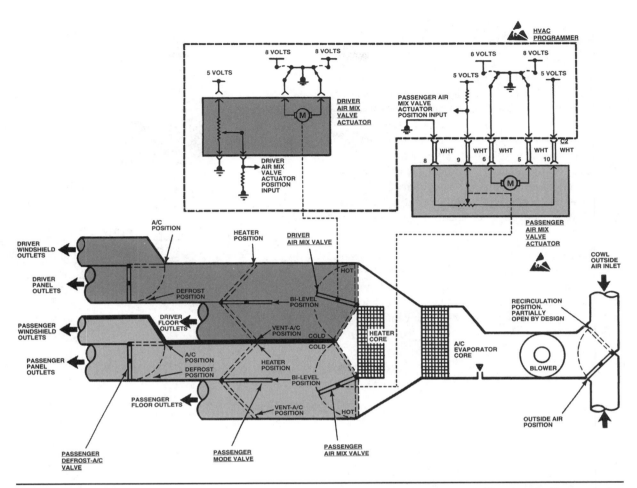

Figure 11-20. Dual zone air distribution system ductwork and temperature door control. (Reprinted with permission of General Motors Corporation.)

air outlet temperature that best suits their individual comfort levels. This may be especially useful when the sun load is affecting only one of the occupants.

Diagnosing dual zone systems is much like diagnosing other manual or ATC systems. Air delivery complaints should be tested the same as you would if the system is a single zone system. One important difference in your diagnostic approach should be to measure the outlet temperature with a thermometer on both sides of the system instead of just at the center duct as you would on a single zone system. If the outlet temperatures are basically the same between the left and right side of the system then the fault is not due to the dual zone system. Your diagnosis of the air delivery complaint should concentrate on the areas that are common to both sides of the system. If, however, there is a noticeable difference in outlet temperature between the left and right sides of the system, you should

suspect a fault in the components that are unique to the dual zone system. Test both the air mix (blend) doors, adjustment of these doors, operation of the air door actuators, and the signal from the temperature controls. A scan tool is very useful in testing these components on most dual zone systems. Be sure to consult the manufacturer's service manuals to diagnose dual zone systems. Much like ATC systems, there are many variations between different systems from the various manufacturers.

Electrostatic Discharge

One important factor to keep in mind every time you are working on or near an electronic system is electrostatic discharge (ESD). When handling any part or working on a circuit that has the ESD symbol, figure 11-21, follow the procedure to reduce an electrostatic buildup in your body, and the part itself. If in doubt, always treat solid-state devices as ESD sensitive.

1. Always touch a good ground before touching the part. This should be repeated intermittently while handling the part, especially after walking or sliding across the seat. Use a grounding wrist strap if you live in an area with very low humidity.
2. Do not touch any electrical terminals of the part unless specifically directed to in writing.
3. Connect the ground lead first when using a voltmeter or other electrical test equipment.
4. Open the package just before installing the part. If you open the package to inspect the part, ground the package.

Always be aware that ESD-sensitive parts can be damaged with static electricity. You can destroy a part without being aware of it. If you do, you just bought a part that cannot be used on the vehicle. You cannot return most electronic parts. Always use caution when working on these parts or circuits.

NOTICE

CONTENTS SENSITIVE
TO
STATIC ELECTRICITY

Figure 11-21. This ESD symbol is used to warn you that the part or circuit involved is sensitive to electrostatic discharge (ESD). (Reprinted with permission of General Motors Corporation.)

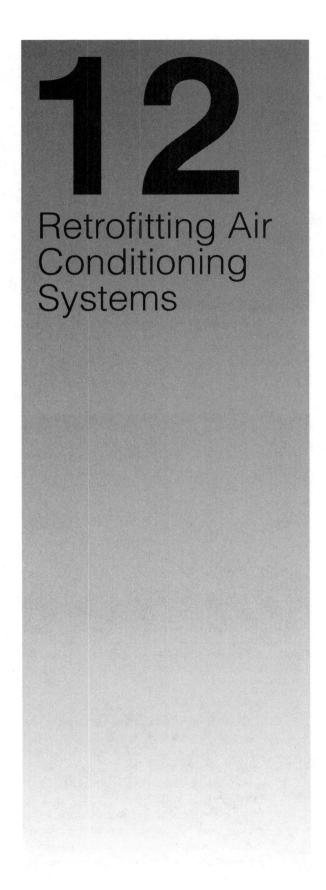

12

Retrofitting Air Conditioning Systems

This chapter deals with retrofitting air conditioning systems to R-134a refrigerant. While there are other refrigerant blends that are EPA approved for use in mobile air conditioning systems, they will not be covered in this chapter. No manufacturer recommends any refrigerant other than R-12 or R-134a. Therefore, if a retrofit is being performed, R-134a should be the choice in refrigerant. As the supply of R-12 diminishes, the need to perform retrofits is increasing. It was originally thought that the supply of R-12 would be more depleted than has happened. However, due to recovery and recycling efforts the R-12 supply has lasted longer than many people thought it would. While retrofit procedures have been developed for many vehicles, a large number of these vehicles have continued to be serviced with R-12. The decision to retrofit should be based on a number of criteria such as:

- Availability of R-12
- Cost of R-12
- Cost of the repair
- Compatibility of the vehicle to retrofitting

All these criteria need to be weighed before deciding to retrofit a vehicle. Obviously, if the availability of R-12 becomes an issue, then the decision to retrofit becomes much easier. Until such time that R-12 is no longer available, the decision to retrofit should be based on the previously listed criteria. Obviously, cost to the consumer must be a factor when making the decision to retrofit. Condition of the vehicle, condition of the air conditioning system, and the cost of the retrofit need to be factored into the equation before a decision should be made.

Some air conditioning service shops will no longer service R-12 systems, while other shops continue to maintain and service both R-12 and R-134a systems. While the majority of vehicles perform satisfactorily after retrofitting to R-134a, some vehicles located in extreme climates do not perform adequately. Through trial and error methods some shops will not retrofit certain vehicles because of performance issues that they have encountered on these vehicles in the past. At the same time, some of these vehicles perform adequately in cooler climates across the country. It is important to determine if the vehicle needs additional components installed during the retrofit procedure to ensure adequate air conditioning performance.

Another decision that has to be made when retrofitting a vehicle is whether to follow the manufacturer's retrofit procedure or to use the "least cost" retrofit procedure. Once again, the age and condition of the vehicle may play into this decision. In the majority of cases the manufacturer's retrofit procedure is more likely to deliver the best performance. However, given the age and condition of the vehicle, and the cost of the manufacturer's retrofit, this may not always be the best economic decision. In some cases the "least cost" retrofit might be the better choice even though the system may not perform as well as it would if the manufacturer's procedures were followed. Whichever retrofit procedure is being performed, it is important that you perform the retrofit properly and legally. To do otherwise exposes you and the shop to liability with the customer, the EPA, or the local authorities. For a review of the required retrofit procedures review Chapter 12 of the *Classroom Manual* before attempting a retrofit.

Once the decision to retrofit has been made, you and the customer must decide on what type of retrofit procedure to perform. It may be necessary to obtain the manufacturer's recommended retrofit procedure to help determine what the cost of the manufacturer's retrofit will be as opposed to the cost of the "least cost" retrofit. This will aid in determining which retrofit procedure should be performed. Also, the cost of the repair using R-12 as opposed to retrofitting to R-134a may influence the customer's decision. Remember to include the customer in this decision-making process as much as possible. You should explain the pros and cons to your customers so they can base their decision on all the information, not just on cost.

PERFORMING A MANUFACTURER'S RETROFIT

The following procedure is typical of many manufacturers' retrofit procedures. However, there are many variations to this method, both in the parts required and the recommended procedure. Make sure that you follow the manufacturer's published procedures to ensure the best performance from the system after the completion of the retrofit. Failure to follow all the recommended procedures for a particular model could result in a system that does not perform satisfactorily. In addition, failure to follow the recommended procedures could be illegal. Perform a manufacturer's retrofit as follows.

Step 1: Inspect the System

1. Obtain the manufacturer's bulletin, figure 12-1, to ensure that all the required parts are on hand before starting the retrofit. For a list of these bulletin numbers refer to Appendix E in the *Classroom Manual.*
2. Inspect the condition of the vehicle. Turn the air conditioning system on and ensure that it operates, then install gauges to determine the state of refrigerant charge, figure 12-2. With the gauges installed one of four conditions will exist.
   a. Refrigerant pressure is correct and the compressor operates. Proceed to step 2 (recovery).

Figure 12-1. Obtain a copy of the manufacturer's bulletin before starting the retrofit procedure. (Reprinted with permission of the International Mobile Air Conditioning Association.)

Figure 12-2. Install the R-12 gauges and check the pressure to determine if the system is full, partially charged, or empty.

   b. System is low in charge but compressor operates. Perform a leak test of the system before recovering the refrigerant. Note any leaks that need to be repaired before retrofitting, figure 12-3. Then proceed to step 2 (recovery).
   c. Refrigerant pressure is correct but the compressor does not operate. Perform diagnosis to determine and correct the lack of compressor operation. Determine if any components need replacement before retrofitting. Then proceed to step 2.

Figure 12-3. If the system is not full, leak test the system to determine where any leaks may be so that you can repair the leaks before retrofitting.

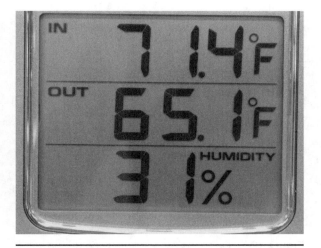

Figure 12-5. The temperature of the vehicle must be above 50°F (10°C) in order to perform the retrofit.

Figure 12-4. If the system is empty, partially charge the system with R-12, if available, to determine what is leaking.

Figure 12-6. Connect the R-12 recovery equipment to the high-side service port only.

d. System is empty, figure 12-4. Partially charge the system with R-12, and leak test to determine the source of the leak. Charge enough to operate the compressor to determine if the compressor works and all other parts of the system are satisfactory. Note needed repairs and proceed to step 2.

If the compressor is damaged and cannot be engaged, then leak testing of the system will have to be performed after evacuation of the system. This obviously is not a desirable way to perform the retrofit; however, it may be necessary due to a damaged compressor that must be changed first in order to engage the system.

Step 2: Recover the System

Notice: This recovery method differs from the normal recovery of an R-12 system. Normally R-12 system re-

covery occurs on both the low side and the high side with the system not operating. This method of recovery when retrofitting involves recovering the refrigerant on the high side with the compressor running.

1. Recover the refrigerant.
   a. Ensure that the vehicle is above 50°F (10°C); if not, allow the vehicle to warm up in the shop until it reaches this temperature, figure 12-5.
   b. Connect the recovery unit to the high-side service port on the vehicle's air conditioning system, figure 12-6.
   c. Start the vehicle, leave the hood open, open the windows, and turn the AC on to NORMAL mode, blower on HIGH, and temperature control to full COLD.
   d. Make sure that the compressor is engaged. Open the high-side service port to the recovery unit and start the recovery process, figure 12-7.

Figure 12-7. Open the high-side service gauge valve so the refrigerant can be recovered from the high side of the vehicle.

Figure 12-9. Continue to repeat the recovery process until the gauge stays below zero psi after a five-minute wait.

Figure 12-8. Monitor the gauge while the compressor is running and the recovery process is occurring. If the compressor does not turn off by the time the pressure reaches 15 psi then turn the AC OFF.

Figure 12-10. Install the appropriate low-side conversion fitting.

e. Monitor the high-side pressure on the gauge. The compressor should disengage by the time the pressure drops to 15 psi, figure 12-8. If the compressor does not disengage when the pressure reaches 15 psi, then turn the AC OFF using the control panel. Leave the engine running and the blower on HIGH.

f. Continue to recover until the recovery unit shuts off. Wait five minutes and observe the gauge. If the pressure rises above zero psi, then repeat the recovery process. Repeat this process until the pressure does not rise above zero psi, figure 12-9.

g. Remove the recovery unit and perform any needed repairs to the system that were detected during step 1.

Step 3: Install the Port Conversion Fittings

1. Install the appropriate low-side conversion fitting, figure 12-10. These are available in both straight and right-angle configurations, figure 12-11, depending on the clearance needed.

2. Install the high-side conversion fitting as required, figure 12-12. Some vehicles may use the high-side fitting as a gauge or switch port. If that is the case, then a special fitting called a saddle clamp, figure 12-13, is available to provide an additional R-134a high-side service port.

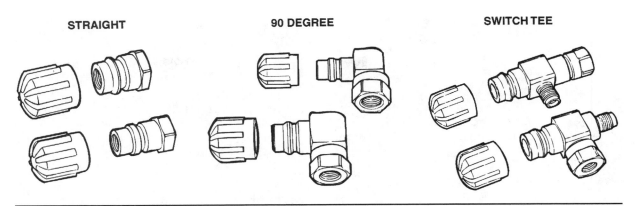

STRAIGHT   90 DEGREE   SWITCH TEE

Figure 12-11. R-134a service port adapters are available in straight and 90-degree angle configurations.

Figure 12-12. Install the high-side fitting.

Figure 12-14. Determine if the vehicle is equipped with a high-pressure cut-off switch. If not, one must be installed.

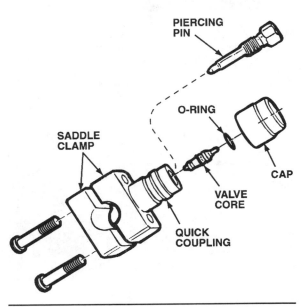

Figure 12-13. Saddle clamp adapters install on straight sections of rigid AC line to accommodate alternative refrigerant fittings.

Step 4: Install Any Additional Components

1. Determine if the vehicle is equipped with a high-pressure cut-off switch, figure 12-14. If not, one must be installed. These are available as part of the retrofit package or separately for some vehicles. Install the switch and the necessary wiring. **Important:** This step must be performed to be a legal retrofit. It will not affect the operation of the air conditioning system if not performed; however, there will be no safeguard to prevent the release of refrigerant into the atmosphere in case of a system malfunction.

2. Check the receiver/drier or accumulator/drier and determine if it needs to be changed, figure 12-15. If it is more than five years old it should be replaced. Replace the receiver/drier or accumulator/drier as required.

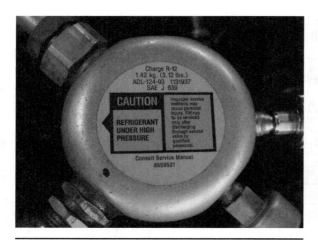

Figure 12-15. Determine if the accumulator/drier or receiver/drier needs to be replaced.

Figure 12-16. Connect the R-134a charging equipment to the system.

3. Replace any additional parts as required by the manufacturer. These may include auxiliary cooling fans, air dams or seals, thermostatic expansion valves, orifice tubes, or compressors.

Step 5: Evacuate the System

1. Connect the R-134a Recovery/Recycling/Recharging station, figure 12-16. Evacuate the system for a minimum of 30 minutes. You must be able to pull the vacuum down to 28 to 29 in-Hg at sea level. Reduce this figure by 1 in-Hg for every 1,000 feet above sea level.

2. Make sure that the system holds vacuum for at least five minutes after the vacuum pump is turned off, figure 12-17. If not, check and repair any leaks before proceeding with recharging.

Step 6: Add Oil to the System

1. Determine the amount of oil needed for the system by referring to the label on the compressor or vehicle, figure 12-18. If there is no label, refer to the manufacturer's service manual to determine the amount of oil needed.

2. Using the correct type of oil required by the manufacturer, inject the oil into the system, figure 12-19.

Step 7: Charge the System with R-134a

1. Determine the correct amount of refrigerant charge for the vehicle. This is based on the amount of R-12 the system originally contained, figure 12-20. Usually this amount is between 80 and 90 percent of the R-12 charge.

2. Enter this amount into your charging station, figure 12-21, or fill the charging chamber with this amount.

Figure 12-17. Evacuate the system for at least 30 minutes and make sure that the system holds vacuum for five minutes after the pump is shut off.

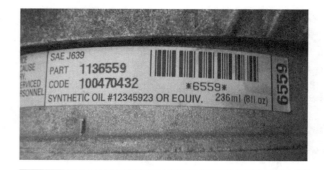

Figure 12-18. Check the label on the vehicle or a reference manual to determine the correct amount of oil charge.

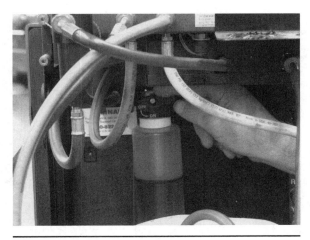

Figure 12-19. Add the correct amount and type of oil as recommended by the manufacturer.

$$(R\text{-}12\ \text{Charge lbs} \times .90) - .25\ \text{lbs} = R\text{-}134a\ \text{lbs}.$$

Figure 12-20. Follow the manufacturer's recommendation for calculating the correct R-134a charge.

Figure 12-21. After calculating the correct amount of refrigerant charge, enter this amount into the charging equipment.

3. Charge the system with R-134a following the instructions of your charging equipment.
4. Start the vehicle, turn the AC system on, and ensure that the compressor operates. Run the system for 10 minutes to stabilize the system. Check the gauge pressures and center duct temperature to ensure that the system is operating normally, figure 12-22.
5. Perform a leak test of the system, figure 12-23. Leak test all components and fittings to ensure that there are no leaks.

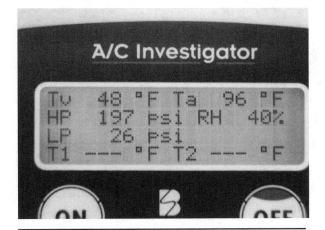

Figure 12-22. After charging, start the vehicle, turn the AC on, put the blower on HIGH, and set the temperature at MAX COLD. Allow the system to stabilize for 10 minutes, then record the pressures and temperature.

Figure 12-23. Leak test the system again to ensure that there are no leaks, especially around the conversion fittings.

Step 8: Install the Retrofit Label

1. Fill out the retrofit label with the required information, figure 12-24.
2. Install the retrofit label on the vehicle. If possible, install the label near the R-12 label that was originally on the vehicle. If this is not practical, place it in an easily visible location. Mark out the amount of R-12 charge on the old R-12 label with a marking pen or paint, figure 12-25. This avoids confusion at a later date.

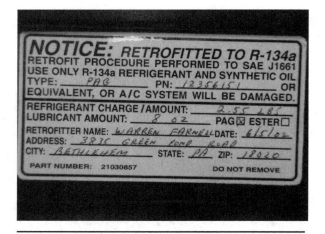

Figure 12-24. Fill out the retrofit label with the required information and install on the vehicle in a highly visible location.

Figure 12-25. Use a marker or paint to black out the R-12 charge amount on the original R-12 label. Do not remove the label.

PERFORMING A "LEAST COST" RETROFIT

A "least cost" retrofit may be appropriate for some vehicles. This may be dictated by the age of the vehicle, lack of availability of a manufacturer's retrofit procedure, or simply a customer decision based on price. While in many instances performing a "least cost" retrofit will provide satisfactory results, this is not always the case. Many factors can affect system performance after performing a "least cost" retrofit, such as the condition of the air conditioning system before retrofitting, the climate that the vehicle operates in, and the particular vehicle being retrofitted. All these factors will influence how well the system performs after the retrofit.

Many manufacturers of retrofit parts offer retrofit kits for particular models. These kits often include new O-rings, conversion fittings, Ester oil, orifice tube, and an R-134a label. Extra parts such as a high-pressure cut-off switch or saddle clamps may have to be purchased separately. Ester oil is often provided instead of PAG oil because the same oil can be used in all systems. However, if you are replacing the compressor as part of the retrofit, make sure that you consult the compressor manufacturer's recommendations on the type of oil that should be used. General guidelines to perform a "least cost" retrofit are as follows.

Step 1: Inspect the System

1. Inspect the system to determine what repairs may be needed before performing the retrofit.
2. Install gauges and determine if the system contains enough refrigerant to allow operation of the compressor.
   a. If the system is low, leak test the system to locate any leaks. Replace or repair these parts before performing the retrofit.
   b. If the system has sufficient refrigerant, operate the compressor to determine if the compressor is working correctly, the drive belt does not slip, and that the operating pressures are within the correct ranges. Note any problems that would require repair before retrofitting.
   c. If the system has sufficient refrigerant but the compressor does not operate, diagnose and repair the condition before starting the retrofit procedure.

Step 2: Recover the Refrigerant

1. Recover the refrigerant using approved recovery equipment. After the recovery unit shuts off, monitor the pressure. If the pressure rises above zero psi, recover the system again. Continue this process until the system pressure remains below zero psi for at least five minutes.

Step 3: Disconnect All Hoses and Lines

1. Disconnect all the hoses and refrigerant lines from the components.
2. Remove and discard all O-rings and seals.
3. Remove any parts that were found to be leaking.

Step 4: Flush the System

1. Flush the components that were not replaced. This will remove the mineral oil that is in the system.
2. Remove and drain the oil from the compressor.
3. Inspect the accumulator/drier or receiver/drier. If it is over five years old, or the system was contaminated, replace the accumulator/drier or receiver/drier. If the drier does not require replacement, drain as much oil from it as possible.

Step 5: Replace Parts

1. Replace the orifice tube as instructed by the provider of the retrofit kit if the old orifice tube is contaminated with debris.
2. Replace the pressure cycling switch if directed to by the retrofit kit provider.
3. Install or replace any other parts if directed to by the retrofit kit provider. Install a high-pressure cut-off switch if the vehicle is not equipped with one.
4. Install new O-rings and seals at all connections.

Step 6: Install Oil

1. Determine the system oil capacity by referring to the service information for the vehicle.
2. Install the correct amount of oil provided with the retrofit kit or recommended by the compressor manufacturer if a new compressor was installed.

Step 7: Install Conversion Fittings

1. Replace the low-side fitting with the appropriate fitting that will allow access with the charging equipment.
2. Install the high-side fitting with the appropriate fitting that will allow access with the charging equipment.

Step 8: Evacuate and Recharge the System

1. Install the R-134a equipment and evacuate the system for 30 minutes. After the pump shuts off, observe the vacuum for five minutes to ensure that the system does not leak. If the vacuum will not hold, check and repair any leaks.
2. Determine the correct amount of refrigerant charge. This amount may be found in the retrofit instruction manual or may be calculated from the R-12 charge amount. Remember that most systems only require between 80 to 90 percent R-134a. If the retrofit manual does not provide a recommended amount of R-134a charge, you may want to start with an 80 percent charge. Then perform a system performance test. If the outlet temperatures are not satisfactory, then gradually add more R-134a up to a 90 percent charge. Do not exceed a 90 percent charge amount of R-134a.

Step 9: Perform a Performance Test

1. Start the vehicle; turn the AC on MAX AC, set the blower on HIGH, and open windows. Operate the vehicle for 10 minutes to stabilize the system. Monitor the low-side and high-side pressures and center duct temperature. If the pressures are within the normal range and the duct temperature is acceptable, shut the vehicle off and remove the equipment.
2. If the pressures or duct temperatures are not normal and the initial charge amount was 80 percent, adjust the amount of R-134a charge slightly and retest. If satisfactory results are obtained, turn off the vehicle and remove the equipment.

Step 10: Install the Retrofit Label

1. Fill out the information on the retrofit label, including the final R-134a charge amount and the type of oil installed. Install the label in a visible location.
2. Use a marker pen and black out the R-12 charge amount and oil type on the old R-12 label on the vehicle. Do not remove the label.